THE FUTURE OF POLITICAL ISLAM

GRAHAM E. FULLER

palgrave
macmillan

THE FUTURE OF POLITICAL ISLAM
Copyright © Graham E. Fuller, 2003.
All rights reserved. No part of this book may be used or reproduced in any manner whatsoever without written permission except in the case of brief quotations embodied in critical articles or reviews.

First published in hardcover in 2004 by Palgrave Macmillan
First PALGRAVE MACMILLAN™ paperback edition: May 2004
175 Fifth Avenue, New York, N.Y. 10010 and
Houndmills, Basingstoke, Hampshire, England RG21 6XS.
Companies and representatives throughout the world.

PALGRAVE MACMILLAN is the global academic imprint of the Palgrave Macmillan division of St. Martin's Press, LLC and of Palgrave Macmillan Ltd. Macmillan® is a registered trademark in the United States, United Kingdom and other countries. Palgrave is a registered trademark in the European Union and other countries.

ISBN 1-4039-6556-0

Library of Congress Cataloging-in-Publication Data is available from the Library of Congress.

A catalogue record for this book is available from the British Library.

Design by Letra Libre.

First PALGRAVE MACMILLAN paperback edition: May 2004

10 9 8 7 6 5 4 3 2 1

Printed in the United States of America.

Dedication

I dedicate this book with my love to my wife Prue,
who has shared so many years
with me in the Muslim world,
raising our children Samantha, Melissa and Luke there,
partaking in Muslim culture and life
in the company of our many Muslim friends.

May the Muslim world find its way.

CONTENTS

PREFACE

THIS BOOK IS the product of long years of living in the Muslim world, watching and thinking about the phenomenon of political Islam. I have been influenced by countless people and writings over the years, a great deal of them entirely assimilated to the point where the original sources are no longer within recall. I have taken the liberty not to attach a bibliography since there are so many books that have profoundly influenced my thinking over the years that I would not know where to begin listing them or how to limit the size of that list.

Researching and writing the book has been an intellectual odyssey as well, since my views have been under constant evolution as they shift and take on new refinements and as the multiple aspects of political Islam continue to reveal themselves in more complex ways. Indeed, on a topic as complex as the place of political Islam in world politics, my thinking continues to evolve, but the book has to be completed, even though my own views will continue to evolve even after its publication.

I cannot begin to list all the people to whom I owe thanks and inspiration in granting me one or more interviews or for sharing their ideas, thoughts, and correctives with me over many years—a large number of whom I count as good friends as well. A partial list would include Imaduddin Ahmad, Qazi Hussain Ahmad, Mumtaz Ahmad, Akbar Ahmed, Fouad Ajami, Taha Jabir al-Alwani, Jon Anderson, Munawar Anees, Ali Aslan, Nik Aziz, Peter Bechtold, Akif Beki, Jonah Blank, Ali Bulac, Dick Bulliet, Francois Burgat, Rusen Cakir, Cengiz Candar, Louis Cantori, Ray Close, Juan Cole, Richard Dekmejian, Charles Dunbar, Michael Collins Dunn, Abdel Malik Eagle, Abdelwahhab al-Efendi, Dale Eickelman, John Entelis, John Esposito, Muhammad Fadlallah, Mamoun Fandy, Sa'd al-Faqih, Anisa Abd el-Fattah, Rend Rahim Francke, Greg Gause, Ashraf Ghani, Rashid al-Ghannushi, Nilüfer Göle, Fethullah Gülen, Fred Halliday, Mohamed Elhachmi Hamdi, Michael Hudson, Shirin Hunter, Rifaat Hussein, Hassan Ibrahim, Paul Jabber, Mansoor al-Jamri, Tarik Jan, George Joffe, Nadeem Kazmi, Musa Keilani, Geoff Kemp, Nat Kern, Muqtedar Khan, Yusif al-Khoei, Rami Khouri, Judith Kipper, Fehmi Koru, Martin Kramer, Charles Kurzman, Laith Kubba, Ian Lesser, Remy Leveau, Serif Mardin, Salam al-Mariati, Phebe Marr, Hisham Milhem, Roy Mottahedeh, Chandra Muzaffar, Basheer Nafi, Ghanim

Najjar, Emile Nakhle, Vali Nasr, Farish Noor, Dick Norton, Daniel Pipes, Yusif al-Qaradawi, Amien Rais, Ahmed Rashid, Bernard Reich, Alan Richards, Glenn Robinson, Eric Rouleau, Olivier Roy, Muwaffaq al-Rubaie, Barney Rubin, Bill Rugh, Hazem Saghieh, Jillian Schwedler, Saeed Shehabi, Tony Sullivan, Shibley Telhami, Hasan al-Turabi, Azzam Tamimi, Bassam Tibi, John Voll, Abdurrahman Wahid, Jenny White, Enders Wimbush, Robin Wright, Judy Yaphe, Hakan Yavuz, Ahmad Yusef, Imtiyaz Yusif, William Zartman, and Jim Zogby. There are many others whose names, through failing memory, I have inadvertently neglected to mention and who I hope will forgive me; their intellectual contributions have been important. Sadly, after the book has gone to the publisher I know I will think of many more names which I would like to have included.

The views in the book are, of course, strictly my own and should not be automatically attributed to any of the above individuals.

I would especially like to thank the following individuals who have helped me directly in taking the time to comment thoughtfully on the manuscript: Daniel Brumberg, Ibrahim Karawan, Mark Katz, Laith Kubba, Tamara Sonn, and my editor David Pervin.

Above all I must recognize the generous grant from the Smith Richardson Foundation without which it would have been impossible to write this book.

INTRODUCTION

WHAT IS POLITICAL ISLAM? How does it act in the world? What challenges does it pose to the world, and what challenges does it face? And finally, where is it headed? These are the fundamental questions addressed in this book.

These questions became a whole lot less academic with the 11 September 2001 attack on the World Trade Center and the Pentagon, which suddenly brought Middle East politics home to Americans with a vengeance. What is in many ways a struggle within the Middle East had burst out of its confines to affect everyone. The East and the West are now just beginning a long process of sorting out the repercussions that touch upon the nature of entrenched and ineffective Middle Eastern regimes, their Islamist oppositions, Western hostility, and the presence of terrorist groups feeding off all these problems.

Yet, even as the West demonstrates a new and heightened attention to Islam, a basic ongoing, long-term struggle for the soul of Islam within the Muslim world is also intensifying under the new pressures. Political Islam is growing, expanding, evolving, and diversifying. And it will be an inevitable if not a dominating feature of politics in the Muslim world for quite some time to come. Islamic terrorism itself may represent only a thin wedge of the overall Islamic political spectrum, but it has the power to set the broader agenda between "Islam and the West" as Usama bin Ladin and the resultant American War Against Terrorism have demonstrated.

Here we must immediately define terms. *Islam* is a religion. Use of this word applies, properly speaking, only to the religion itself. We cannot accurately say that "Islam is on the march" or that "Islam is anti-Western"; it is rather the practice and activities of *Muslims* that can be so described. Most of the time we are talking about how Muslims *choose to understand* what Islam says about a great variety of issues on the practical level.

I use the terms *political Islam* or *Islamism* synonymously and extensively throughout the book. Readers should be warned that I define these terms perhaps more broadly than some other analysts do, reflecting the reality of the phenomenon. In my view an Islamist is one who believes *that Islam as a body of faith has something important to say about how politics and society should be ordered in the contemporary Muslim World and who seeks to implement this idea in some fashion.* The term "political Islam" should be neutral in character, neither pejorative nor judgmental in itself; only upon further definition of the specific views, means, and goals of an Islamist movement in each case can we be critical of the process. I prefer this definition because it is broad enough to capture the full spectrum of Islamist expression that runs the gamut from radical to moderate, violent to peaceful, democratic to authoritarian, traditionalist to modernist.

I also employ the term *Islamic fundamentalism,* but only to refer to those Islamists who follow a literal and narrow reading of the Qur'an and the traditions of the Prophet, who believe they have a monopoly on the sole correct understanding of Islam and demonstrate intolerance toward those who differ. Many fundamentalists will insist on the absolute primacy of applying all Islamic laws as the sole touchstone of Islamic legitimacy. Fundamentalism is not the same as traditionalism at all; it can be radical in its departure from the status quo of traditional Islamic understanding and in fact seeks to implement change through a "back to basics" approach. All fundamentalists are Islamists, but not all Islamists are fundamentalist by any means, since Islamism includes those who interpret political Islam in a more modern or liberal sense as well.

THE LURE OF ISLAMIST POLITICS

There are important reasons for examining political Islam—quite apart from trying to understand Middle East terrorism. To the casual observer political Islam may be an exotic and remote world, seemingly locked in a time warp linked to seventh century values and struggles. The reality is rather different. Islamist politics could not be more central to modern political and social development: Islamists are struggling, like so much of the rest of the developing world, with the genuine dilemmas of modernization: rampant change of daily life and urbanization at all levels, social dislocation and crisis, the destruction of traditional values, the uncertain threats of globalization, the need for representative and competent governance, and the need to build just societies and to cope with formidable political, economic, and cultural challenges from the West. Most Islamists look forward and not backward in the quest to establish a better moral foundation for society in order to confront the demands of contemporary life and globalization. Their preoccupations reflect the ongoing concerns of much of the rest of the world, even if we are at different stages of managing them. It is a central thesis of this book *that political Islam is not an exotic and distant phenomenon, but one intimately linked to contemporary political, social, economic and moral issues of near universal concern.*

We in the West are often uncomfortable with the presence of religion, certainly in the public sphere. Yet a study of religion in society in general compels us to

grapple with many of the most complex, fascinating, revealing, and important issues of contemporary politics. Religion is intimately linked to human psychology
and culture. The history of the human quest to derive philosophical and spiritual
meaning out of life provides the raw material for much of the greatest literature,
thought, philosophy of history, architecture, art, and music. Religion encompasses
our values, aspirations, and vision of life, our quest to find meaning in our existence, our fears of our mortality, our concerns for what is right and wrong in this
world, our aspirations to bring moral values to bear on the construction of our political and societal existence, our quest for spiritual fulfillment on the often trying
paths of daily life, our sense of community and our relations with our fellow men
and women, and finally a sense of awe toward creation. All human beings are faced
with these issues and are compelled to provide some answers for themselves, including those who do not consider themselves religious. Political Islam is very
much at the heart of this quest in the Muslim world. And the superimposition of
contentious international geopolitics further complicates and intensifies the expression of political Islam at the local level.

Many in the contemporary post-industrial world have come to express a certain
antipathy to religion, especially organized religion, believing it to contain a measure of intolerance and the remnants of human superstitions not yet eliminated by
advances in natural science. Yet few can remain indifferent to the issues raised by
religion. That the disputation of religion is generally excluded from the Western
salon only underscores the reality of its continuing power as a sensitive and emotive force in human society.

When religion is linked with politics, two of the most vital elements of human
concern come together. This conjuncture can be for better or for worse: both religion and politics have consistently exploited each other across the web of history.
Indeed, how could politics ever remain indifferent to such a powerful motive force
as religion? And how could religion, with its vision of the place of human existence
in the grand scheme of things, remain uninterested in the form, expression, and
direction of human society and politics?

Americans in particular feel understandable ambivalence about the relationship
of religion to politics. The American secular tradition, ironically, is not due to an
American indifference to the role of religion in life. On the contrary, it emerged
from the concerns of those passionately committed to religion and the preservation of its diverse forms that brought its adherents early on to the American con-
tinent; their goal was precisely to preserve their faith and its expression from the
power of the state that had oppressed it back home. America today remains the
most religious country in the industrialized world while still broadly committed to

separating religion and the state as much as possible, for the protection of both. Yet the most emotional features of American politics are exactly those that entail religious concerns, even if they are not expressed in explicitly religious terms. The public goes to the barricades as soon as talk turns to abortion or the right to life, euthanasia and the right to die, the understanding and teaching of sexuality, the norms of sexual conduct and its alternative "lifestyles," the dilemma of cheating, the nature of divorce law, single-parent families, the nature and welfare of the family, and the search for the most desirable forms of social organization. These issues are profoundly religious (or moral) in content and character, even if we in the West do not always choose to formulate them in those terms. Islamic politics approach this linkage more directly, unabashedly, and explicitly.

To write about Islam in politics—and politics in Islam, then—is to examine the universal phenomenon of religion and politics as it happens to be expressed in the Muslim world. It sheds an indirect light on expression of these same universal issues in the West as well. And through examination of Islamic fundamentalism we also explore some of the most sensitive and central features of life in the Muslim world; we gain insights into the political, religious, social, and psychological aspects of Muslim society as a whole. Indeed, *the vehicle of political Islam might be one of the very best ways to understand the politics of Muslim world in general—far more revealing than to follow Marxist, socialist, nationalist, or even democratic politics of Muslim societies.* The reason is simple: Islam pervades the daily life of Islamic society and political culture more profoundly than any other single ideological or conceptual force.

The entire issue of relations between Islam and the West forces us to explore comparative civilizations, the reasons for their rise and fall, and the interactions among them. How do we explain a period of one thousand years when Islam was the preeminent world civilization, only to founder in the face of a newly ascendant West? To the West, history of course "ends" with the universal supremacy of the Western ideals. Yet any historian would be loath to make such an assumption, and indeed many Muslims today ponder the possibility of a time when the balance between the two civilizations will be restored—or even reversed.

ISLAMISM AT THE TURN OF THE CENTURY

One of the most striking features of Islamist politics today is the extraordinary pace and speed of its evolution. If this book had been written even a decade ago there would be numerous questions about the direction of its evolution—on issues such as democracy, civil society, parliaments, and political parties—that are now clearer, making it easier to sense their trajectory.

In fact, political Islam is probably the fastest moving force in politics in the Muslim world today. While the thinking of Western-educated Muslim elites may be quite sophisticated, such groups represent only a thin veneer of the broader political order and do not yet have serious mass impact. They speak a Westernized language that is not yet part of the normal flow of mass political discourse. Ironically it is often through an Islamist framework today that mass political thinking is advanced on questions of just government, representative, responsible and answerable government, and the techniques of mass mobilization for political ends. At the same time some of these movements can also be a force for intolerance, authoritarian impulses, and even great violence.

ABOUT THE BOOK

This book is ultimately about the future. *Does political Islam represent the last heroic stand of Muslim cultural resistance to galloping globalization with an American accent? Or does it represent the beginning of a new synthesis of Islam with contemporaneity, enabling Muslim society and culture to move into the new millennium more confident of its own cultural foundations?*

Throughout the book I emphasize the striking feature of the *youthfulness* of Islam in modern politics: we are talking about movements that have been important on the political scene for only a few decades (even if a few go back well into the last century) and that have been rapidly evolving over that period. Some of these movements may turn out to be as evanescent as a meteor in the night sky— arresting while visible but soon gone and forgotten. But half a century hence, what will we identify as having been the truly determinative elements in the history of political Islam? Indeed, will political Islam itself turn out to be only a transitional phenomenon in the Muslim world during a certain difficult phase of its development? Present difficulties have indeed contributed to its rise. Will it be viewed as having been a bad experiment, best forgotten? Or a seminal development leading to profound and necessary long-range change? Given the profusion of these movements, some will indeed be viewed as serious failures, others as evolving in useful new directions of benefit to society. The answers to these questions are not yet fully clear, but the impact of these movements are already evident, and so far few alternative parties have emerged to seriously rival the Islamists.

This book examines the broad phenomenon of Islamist movements across the Muslim world. I offer a number of hypotheses on the long-range future of Islamist movements, both within the Muslim world and in the larger global context of competing ideas. This book does not represent an exercise in formal academic comparative politics. It is precisely the *differing* specific characteristics that spring from a unique time, place, history, set of leaders and personalities, and the ultimate conjuncture of all these factors that lend the spark of life, character, behavior, and reality to each of these movements. Generalizations, to be of value, must not strip off too many of these aspects of uniqueness, for they are what determine the difference, yet regrettably, in a book of this scope, the case studies that informed my views cannot find space.

I focus on what I believe to be the most interesting, distinctive, important, and revealing aspects of this phenomenon, hoping to uncover some general trends or useful insights from a net deliberately cast wide. For a single author to seek to write about Islamist politics across the whole Muslim world in one sense may be a little presumptuous or foolhardy. No one can be an expert on the details of the political orders of all of these countries. Yet a single author representing a single vision can perhaps bring greater synthesis to the material than a multiauthored volume can. That is at once this book's greatest strength and weakness. A dozen or more books by single authors coping with the totality of this same problem would be of great value to all of us.

The book makes no pretense of "mastering the literature" on the topic—that would be nigh impossible—nor does it attempt to place itself within the corpus of academic writing on the topic. Such contributions are undoubtedly valuable, but that is not my contribution.

The book reflects not merely the examination of writings on Islam but a lot of personal experience living some fourteen years in five different countries in the Muslim world supplemented by visits to every single Muslim country (including the Muslim areas of the former Soviet Union and China), often repeatedly and for long periods. The one glaring lacuna in this book is the absence of treatment of sub-Saharan Africa, not due to any lack of interest but simply the result of limitations on time, energy, and finances. I know I am losing some critically important insights into alternative forms of Islamic practice as seen in Africa. Perhaps a later edition might rectify this serious omission.

I have also maintained a wealth of close personal friendships with Muslims almost all of my life as well as a great love of the languages, cultures, literature, foods, music, films and arts of the Muslim world. I believe culture is at least as revealing as is political science in understanding how societies function. As vice-chairman of the National Intelligence Council at the CIA in the 1980s I was responsible for long-range global forecasting, which sparked my interest in the challenge and analytic benefits of looking speculatively into the future. The effort of looking into alternative futures is essentially the function of the historian: it involves examining the past and trying to identify those trends and realities that might be projected into the future in some form. This book does not, of course, represent a clear-cut, single "prediction" about the future of the Muslim world at all, but it does offer a number of hypotheses about how to think about the problem.

MY "AGENDA"

I would like to offer a few words about what my "agenda" might be in writing this book, because from experience I know that others will attribute one to me in any case. My years as a CIA staff officer have predisposed many, especially in the developing world, to believe that "once an intelligence officer, always an intelligence officer," even though I abandoned government service some fifteen years ago. More to the point, many foreigners believe that my views somehow represent CIA or U.S. government views of the issues. I wish they did. I would be delighted if my views on these topics had more impact on the White House, the State Department, the Pentagon, or any others in a policy role anywhere, but I am under no illusion that the views expressed here are especially congenial to current policy circles.

As an American I naturally care strongly about the future and welfare of my own country. At the same time I believe that America's interests, conducted in an enlightened manner, need not differ radically from the interests of most Muslims. After many long years in the Muslim world I am also broadly concerned for the future and welfare of its peoples. This empathy should not render me uncritical of events, trends, or groups there. Nor is this book an apologia for the Muslim world, although a few may consider it so since it attempts to place Islamist politics in a rational light and suggests that not all Muslim grievances are groundless. Furthermore, there will be many Muslims who believe I am wrong in my understanding of their society or what constitutes their welfare. They may be right. But some element of empathy on the part of the analyst is essential if one is to understand the outlook and psychology of various forms of Islamists. Most Islamist views are far from crazy, marginalized, alien, or primitive at all, but quite rational within the context of local conditions and problems, even if these views are not always correct or successful.

I take most of the various missions of political Islam as worthy of serious consideration In aspiring to apply Muslim values to the new modern democratic order. I am willing to hear out the Islamists—at least initially—and to try to see the world through their eyes in line with their aspirations rather than impose some preconceived body of Western notions as the basis of judgment. I do not reject out of hand their experiment, even if I personally have some serious reservations about their chances of success. A willingness to listen to them sympathetically in no way excludes the right to criticize their record to date, to point out their failures and problems they face. Will these movements in fact be able to answer many of the major needs of Muslim societies of the future? I believe they should be afforded the opportunity to express their views, to articulate their programs, and to try to implement many of their ideas as long as they do not violate basic norms of contemporary international society. Indeed many have already violated several basic norms of international society, but in this they are joined by large numbers of other non-Muslim movements, parties, and regimes in the developing world. Some have already failed miserably and deserve outright condemnation, such as the Taleban in Afghanistan and indiscriminately violent groups like Islamic Jihad in Egypt, the GIA in Algeria, and above all the murderous al-Qa'ida—organizations that have made no political contribution other than to spill blood and polarize cultures.

Other Islamist movements are still evolving and deserve watching. Many of them can be excluded from the political process in the Muslim world only at high political cost since their roots are deep and linked to Islamic culture. They speak to problems and grievances that seek a vehicle of expression and that call for a program of action. They will not go away. Islamism happens to be the most current of those vehicles. The ultimate challenge is how to seek ways in which political integration of Islamism into the current political orders might be possible. Where movements are evolving, even out of unsuccessful or unwise early beginnings, they need to be given a chance to prove—or disprove—themselves until the world has a better sense about where they are going. I do not believe that the majority of Islamist movements by definition represent a dangerous and noxious ideology that must be repressed. A few by their actions do. But to stifle them all across the board today will only invite heightened confrontation and instability across the Muslim world.

THE STRUCTURE OF THE BOOK

The first chapter of the book discusses the "anguish" of Islamic history, nostalgia for what Muslims see as a glorious past of power and civilizational accomplishment, followed by a period of severe decline into backwardness and even marginalization. What went wrong, why, and what are the implications for future action? I also examine the trajectory of Islamic history through the last century to indicate its remarkable evolution and possible directions of change.

Chapter two is entitled "The Uses of Political Islam," suggesting the multiple roles that political Islam plays today across diverse societies. Not all of these roles are obvious to most Western observers. It is these multiple roles that also serve to guarantee political Islam a central role in Muslim world politics for some time to come.

Chapter three discusses "Islamic polarities"—how might we categorize Islamist movements in a few respects—particularly in terms of the two poles of radical/fundamentalist Islamism versus modernist or "liberal" Islamism.

Chapter four places Islam in the context of global politics. I contend that political Islam in no way represents an exotic aberration in world politics but rather bears close resemblance to most of the mainstream political movements and debates today across the developing world.

Chapter five discusses Islamism and terrorism and ways to think about the relationship between the two.

Chapter six looks at "Islamism in Power"—the cases of Iran, Sudan, and Afghanistan and a brief summary of their experiences to date. How does one assess their success or failure, who is the judge of this performance, and how is it affected by international politics?

Chapter seven focuses upon the behavior of Islamism as it operates in democratic and quasi-democratic orders. I argue that Islamist movements increasingly accept the "universality" of democracy, seek to become part of the democratic order, and believe that they will benefit from this kind of political order. As they become integrated into the system, they lose much of their ideological fervor and take on the characteristics of "normal" political parties. But this liberalizing trend is not universal, and there are some disturbing countertrends and genuine problems that these movements face in accommodating themselves to the philosophy of democratic governance.

Chapter eight looks at the problem of "Islam and the West"—a key determinant of the future of Islamist movements. Are we talking about a "clash of civilizations"? What are the concrete factors that drive this relationship? I suggest that Islam operates more as a vehicle of conflict rather than serving as the source of that conflict.

Chapter nine discusses the key determinative factors, domestic and international, that will influence the future of political Islam.

Chapter ten concludes with an examination of the future of Islamism, alternative paths of development for it, and the key problems these movements face.

THE ANGUISH
OF ISLAMIC HISTORY

THE ANGUISH OF HISTORY'S REVERSAL

The deepest underlying source of Muslim anguish and frustration today lies in the dramatic decline of the Muslim world, in over just a few centuries, from the leading civilization in the world for over one thousand years into a lagging, impotent, and marginalized region of the world. This stunning reversal of fortune obsessively shapes the impulses underlying much contemporary Islamist rhetoric. As Israeli scholar Martin Kramer tells us:

> "In the year 1000, the Middle East was the crucible of world civilization. One could not lay a claim to true learning if one did not know Arabic . . . An Islamic empire, established by conquest four centuries earlier, had spawned an Islamic civilization, maintained by the free will of the world's most creative and enterprising spirits. . . . [T]here could be no doubt that the dynasties of Islam represented the political, military, and economic superpowers of the day. . . . This supremely urbane civilization cultivated genius. Had there been Nobel prizes in 1000, they would have gone almost exclusively to Moslems."[1]

Yet, this very glory has now become no more than a fabled memory mocking present Muslim impotence. It is an especially bitter taste in the mouth when viewed against the overwhelming contemporary dominance of Western civilization that once had lagged so far behind the Islamic. Muslims today are understandably lacerated by self-doubt in contemplating what has gone wrong; indeed, for some it is tantamount to a fall from the grace of God.

The force of this perceived historical cataclysm and Muslims' subsequent impotence in the face of the West constitutes a key psychological reality of political Islam today. It provides vital impetus for Islamists who seek to recreate—so far without success—the edifice of past glory through drawing more deeply on the reservoirs of Islam to create a more powerful Islamic civilization. Indeed, for many Muslims, the present era of Muslim impotence, seen in the perspective of the long march of history, may be no more than an distressing historic interlude, after which the Muslim world may once again reassert its powerful place in the international order. But how do Muslims get there?

LEGACY OF A BRILLIANT PAST

The Muslim world has been more resistant to the inroads of a Western-dominated political and cultural order than any other civilization in the world, including China or India. Yet, viewed positively, this reality speaks for the strength and functionality of historical Islamic civilization over long periods. Indeed, no other culture in the history of the world can speak of a continuous high civilization for as long a period of time and covering as geographically diverse and vast a region of the world. This civilization formed the heart of the world order far longer than Western civilization has, and over a far broader region. How could Muslims not therefore think of themselves as perhaps the preeminent world civilization—even if temporarily lapsed?

But the negative aspect of this power of resistance of Islamic civilization is that Muslims were unprepared for a shift in the balance of power and creativity away from them starting sometime around the fifteenth century. Yet evidence of revolutionary change afoot in the Western world lay before Muslim eyes, requiring the urgent recognition that Muslim societies had somehow begun to founder. Indeed, it is one of the arrogances of any advanced and secure civilization, as Chinese, Indian, and Muslim history demonstrate, to be unable to believe that external barbarians can have anything serious to offer. (Should we note our contemporary Western certitude that the present Western order represents the final model of history and that there is has nothing left to learn from others?) Equally painful for Muslims, over the past several hundred years the West has continuously reinforced the message, both explicitly and implicitly, that it now offers a superior civilizational product. Indeed, the current backwardness of Muslim societies is a fact recognized by all, including Muslims.

Thus *many Muslims attribute the past achievements and durability of Islamic civilization to the very message and implementation of Islam itself. Logically then, any apparent straying from that faith might be perceived as a direct source of decline and failure.* This perception is one key generating principle behind most Islamist reformist movements of the past, including that of political Islam today.

The alternative model, imposed by Western colonialism, divided much of the Muslim world into so-called nation-states that were not in reality based on true "nations" at all as ethnically based European states were. The Arab world in particular was "artificially" divided into units that are perceived by Arabs as neither traditional, logical, useful, or successful. On the contrary, this Western principle of reorganization—based on divisive ethnicity rather than moral principles of Muslim unity—is perceived as a key source of contemporary Muslim weakness that only a move toward Islamic unity can overcome—even if creation of just one single pan-Islamic state is not realistic.

THE SOURCES OF ISLAMIC SUCCESS

To Muslims, it is self-evident that Islamic civilization created a system of belief, governance, and social order that withstood the tests of over a thousand years of history and across a vast variety of regions, cultures, and peoples. For many Muslims there is no need to speculate about Islam's success here; its strength lies in the very fact that it is the message of God as revealed to the last of God's prophets, Muhammad. To many Muslims for whom Islam supplies deep sustenance, support, and guidance, nothing more about Islam's demonstrative success needs to be explained. Even an agnostic cannot deny the power of this religious idea as evidenced in Islamic history.

Even from a Western perspective, the roots of any civilization must be grounded in a functional body of ethical and legal principles and practices that enjoy broad acceptance and legitimacy. Throughout most of human history religion has been a key source of those principles. The spiritual inspiration of Islam and its vision of society and the state obviously explains much about its permanent acceptance by such diverse cultures and peoples over so long an expanse of time. How else (in Muslim eyes) could one explain the success of a small, geographically isolated region of the Arabian Peninsula, heavily marked by tribal bedouin culture, in producing a religious and organizational idea capable of spreading quickly not only to the rest of the Semitic world but far beyond, crossing geographic, linguistic, and cultural barriers from Morocco to Indonesia?

Indeed, it is not just the conquest but its very durability that is also striking; it did not melt away in a generation or two, as did Mongol power. Vast numbers of adherents of different religious cultures—Christian Byzantium, Zoroastrian Persia, Buddhist Central Asia, large parts of the Hindu subcontinent, Hindu/Buddhist Java, and animist Africa—after the Muslim conquest ended up permanently accepting the spiritual, ethical, and legal principles of Islam. Traders and Sufi mystics were at least as important in laying the groundwork for the acceptance of the institutions of Islam as were armies. This body of ethical belief was neither so culture-bound to the Arabian Peninsula nor so complex and unique as to be unadaptable to the cultural conditions of African savannas, temperate forests, mountain peoples, riverine cultures, jungle regions, and high deserts—down to today. Rarely in history has any Muslim culture been supplanted, by whatever means, by some other religious culture. Indeed, as Ali Mazru'i points out, there has not been a single prophet since the Prophet Muhammad who has succeeded in establishing a divine or moral message that has taken over even one country.[2] Whatever Westerners may think about Islam, we cannot ignore the reality that in a political and social sense, Islam has in fact prevailed more widely, longer, and over more diverse cultures than any other religion. Surely this fact bespeaks a formidable cultural power, an ability to meet social, ethical, and moral needs of diverse societies for long periods of time under differing historical and regional conditions. The key question is whether Islam can continue to meet that challenge today especially as *all religious tradition* comes under assault in the face of evolutionary global forces.

WHAT WENT WRONG?

For Islamists the internal moral and spiritual decline of Muslim societies is the primary source of the problem. But even this argument raises further complex issues. What is it that Islam provided that has been lost? Precisely what element of a straying from Islam was most responsible for that subsequent decline? Lack of rightly guided—that is, good—leadership? Poor governance? Withering of just societies? Loss of moral values by the masses of the population? Weakness stemming from loss of direction? Even if these failures are acknowledged, specifically what mistakes were committed? Does it simply boil down to non-observance of the Shari'a (Islamic law)? Or a broader loss of faith (*Iman*)? Even less clear is how to address these things. Exactly what is it that Muslims must return to in order to once again achieve past levels of civilizational power? Surely more is involved than just application of Islamic law and establishment of selected Islamic governmental institutions. The Qur'an offers few clues about even what kind of specific governmental institutions are required. Indeed, we are now engaged here in *analysis of the qualities of good governance in general,* with or without reference to Islam. Here is where Islamists must decide how ultimately to determine the specific requirements for a demonstrable Islamic renaissance.

Of course even Islamists recognize that the decline of Islamic civilization cannot be attributed strictly to moral causation. Most Muslim and Western observers

alike would note at least a few other causal factors at work that need to be acknowledged if Islamic decline is to be righted.

CULTURAL AND INTELLECTUAL FACTORS

Islam brought massive intellectual change to the regions into which it spread, increasing communications and encouraging the study of the universe as a means of
understanding God and all his works. In a sense, Islam was proto-globalization. It
was the waning of this universalist tradition that led to localization and atrophy of
what was once an open and searching intellectual society.

The death of Islamic intellectual vigor and curiosity—an exhaustion of civilizational élan without dramatic new intellectual input—led to the decline of creative thinking in Islamic theology, philosophy, science, and technology. Ritual
replaced thought and inquiry in what passed for study of Islam. Analysis grew narrow and unchallenging. Thinking ossified over time, forbidding even the kind of
historical scrutiny of Islam's own texts and sources of authority that was possible
in earlier centuries. This atrophy of Muslim intellectual vigor was well demonstrated in the collapse of Muslim sciences and even a general passivity toward later
scientific and technological development in the West—until that same technology
overwhelmed the Muslim world. Even in the face of the West's challenge, most reformers looked at the West primarily as a warehouse of technological hardware,
without grasping the need for the all-important civilizational software or values
that made it all function.

GEOPOLITICAL FACTORS

External factors alike contributed to the decline of the Muslim world. The Mongol conquests destroyed a number of the great Muslim urban centers of the
world, along with their libraries and populations, which never quite recovered.
The emergence of a Shi'ite state in Iran at the start of the sixteenth century physically divided the Sunni Muslim world, erecting a barrier to communications
among Muslims across Eurasia. The shift of commerce from a Eurasian land-
based Silk Route to a seafaring one left much of the Muslim world in isolation.
Europe began to develop maritime trade into the Atlantic with the "discovery"
of the New World, opening a new chapter in global history that enriched the Europeans and largely marginalized the role of Muslim seafarers who had once
dominated Asian trade. And colonialism hobbled the development of Muslim
states across the globe, destroying traditional institutions and failing to provide

functional organic alternatives. Muslim societies today are still concerned with external domination, even if that domination no longer takes classic colonial shape.

CYCLICAL FACTORS

To some extent the Muslim decline has been absolute when measured against its own previous vigor and creativity. But Muslims also measure their own current dismal state against the meteoric rise of the West over the past few centuries. It is not only that the Muslim world declined but that the West itself developed a remarkable dynamism for complex historical reasons of its own, building on a solid foundation of preceding cultural attainments in the world, many of which were Muslim. Much of today's debate is about whether Islam can or should recreate for itself those key conditions that enabled the West to flower after the Renaissance, or whether those factors are unique to Western conditions and cannot simply be transplanted to the Muslim world.

ENVIRONMENTAL FACTORS

Finally, important environmental cycles can also be adduced that are linked to concepts of cyclical change. Jared Diamond has suggested that the Fertile Crescent, a cradle of civilization for a variety of environmental reasons, essentially began to fail as deforestation, desiccation, and subsequent diminution of natural and animal resources gradually caused the region to lose its cutting edge and cede its own civilizational power ultimately to Western Europe. He argues that as power gradually shifted West each successive civilization was able to build on the civilizational base of the previous one—scientific and technical, linguistic, artistic, artisanal, and agricultural, enabling the West to benefit from them all. Thus while Western Europe contributed little to world civilization until the late Middle Ages, its climate of fertile land and prolific flora and fauna coupled with new civilizational energy was the primary source for the eventual emergence of a new and powerful West European civilization, one built on the successes and knowledge of past societies whose environments were no longer as productive.[3]

Jeffrey Sachs at the Harvard University Center for International Development also points out the impact of climatic and ecological shifts: while Europe possessed a temperate climate, the Middle East was generally marked by growing aridity: "By 1900, at the final collapse of the Ottoman Empire, Europe had coal, hydropower, timber, and iron ore. The Islamic countries had few stocks of these nineteenth-century necessities for industrialization. The oil fields were discovered and exploited only after the Europeans had seized colonial control." In 800 A.D. the Middle East and Western Europe both had populations of around 30 million each. The Middle East had thirteen cities with populations over 50,000 while Europe had only one—Rome. But by 1600 the balance had shifted dramatically due to these conditions, as well as technological innovations stemming from new vitality.[4]

The Islamist task, then, is to correctly understand and to right this distressing trajectory of Islamic civilization. As Sachs points out, this must not be taken as a morality tale but as a problem in comparative development. Yet even comparative development must integrate intellectual, psychological, and cultural factors as well as economic and political issues. The great challenge for Muslims, then, is about how specifically to recover past achievements, establish a flourishing and advanced Islamic society, and redress the current imbalance of power between the Muslim world and the West. How much of this resurgence is dependent upon moral concepts and how much on the more complex and tedious elaboration through trial and error of the institutions of good governance? Most Islamists would agree that simply more personal religiosity is not a sufficient answer, but they would disagree on the means by which just and good governance is achieved.

THE TRAJECTORY OF ISLAMIC CHANGE IN THE TWENTIETH CENTURY

But Islamic history even during the past century has not been simply one of backwater isolation or stagnant languish. The reality is that the Muslim world has been on a breathtaking roller-coaster ride across a tumultuous century. This trajectory of political Islam offers signs—many of them contradictory—of genuine evolution in directions that include greater realism, political development, and an ability to learn from experience and reality. It also offers some negative indicators as well.

Political Islam in all its forms represents the uncertain beginnings of a vital process in which Islamic thinking comes to terms with multiple aspects of Western political thinking and institutions, expanding the range of its own outlook and activities—in both disturbing and heartening ways. The process in historical terms remains nascent, but it represents nothing less than the beginning of an intellectual reformation in Islamic thought.

The first series of body blows to the Muslim world in the nineteenth century was delivered by the West. The dawn of the twentieth century began with deep Muslim anxieties over the catastrophic weakness of the Muslim world, generating such thinkers as Jamal-al-Din al-Afghani, Muhammad 'Abdu, Rashid Ridha, and

Said Nursi Bediüzzaman, who sought ways to reverse this course of Muslim decline through examination of weaknesses in Islamic intellectual practice itself. A list of the dramatic and seminal events is imposing.

- The greatest Muslim Empire in history, the Ottoman Empire, underwent final collapse.
- Out of the ashes of the Ottoman Empire a series of new, nominally independent Muslim states were established by the Western imperial order across the Arab world, many of which were perceived as arbitrary and artificial.
- Western colonial powers asserted direct imperial control over virtually every one of these new Arab states except Saudi Arabia for a period that would last past mid-century.
- The central institution of Islam, the Caliphate, was abolished by Mustafa Kemal Atatürk, founder of the modern secular state of Turkey.
- Large segments of the Muslim world were dragged involuntarily into two world wars.
- Most of the Muslim world finally attained genuine independence, but only after World War II.
- The state of Israel was established within the Muslim world with incalculable regional impact that has not yet subsided.
- The Muslim world was broadly exposed to the extremes of European political ideology, which included socialism, Marxism, communism and fascism, all of which were implemented in one state or another. These ideologies brought new intellectual and ideological breadth and sophistication to debates between communists, secular nationalists, and Islamists that were unprecedented. It also brought strong fascist elements into the thinking of much of Arab nationalism from which it has not yet fully escaped.
- The Cold War dragged the Muslim world into highly divisive geopolitical equations, polarizing the Arab world. The West began to view the politics of the Muslim world nearly exclusively through the spectrum of its East-West implications. But the Muslim world also learned to play the West off against the Soviet Union, expanding its own room for maneuver and gaining benefits from each side. Muslim states grew accustomed to operating within a clear bipolar world.
- Despite all the forces for change, large parts of the Muslim world, to varying degrees, fell under the hand of autocracy and the police state, both in the form of monarchies and, even worse, in harsh post-monarchical "republican"

regimes ruled by presidents-for-life. The degree of state control over the daily lives of Muslims is unprecedented in Muslim history.

- The Western discovery of oil and demand for energy created unprecedented new wealth in some parts of the Muslim world. While oil has enriched a number of countries, it has also served to freeze the organic development of their economies and generally failed to create productive sectors independent of state collection of various kinds of "rents" and "unearned" income from oil.

- The Levant states of the Arab world—Lebanon, Syria, Jordan and Egypt— were defeated three times by Israel in major wars, and Lebanon and Syria were humbled in briefer invasions, occupations, or attacks as part of losing geopolitical skirmishes between them.

- The Muslim world has been attacked at least six times in the last forty-five years—sometimes with devastating results—by Western military forces, mostly American.

- The forces of globalization, especially since the end of the Cold War, have exerted major impact upon traditional Muslim culture and beliefs, lives, and interstate relations. The cultural impact of the West became overwhelming with the spread of information technology and the experience of millions of Muslims gaining advanced degrees in the West.

But the region has not remained strictly the passive object of modernization and revolutionary change. It has responded with new developments in the ideological and social arenas of the Muslim world itself, directly linked to political Islam and its future. Among them:

- Hasan al-Banna in the 1950s in Egypt established a political movement calling for the first time the concept of an "Islamic state."

- In 1948 Pakistan became the first modern state, carved out of India, to be created strictly on the grounds of the Muslim character of its population.

- Mawlana Abu'l A'la al-Mawdudi in Pakistan then established the first actual political party based on Islamism, marking the formal entry of Islamic thought into modern politics with the goal of establishing an Islamic state.

- The Muslim world was drawn into the broader politics of the Third World and joined a non-aligned movement that expanded its international alliances and shared concepts of Third World ideology on a global order.

- The Gulf oil states achieved a powerful global voice over international energy and economic issues as a result of a meteoric rise of the price of oil in the 1970s.

- Beginning in the 1970s Islamist movements proliferated across the entire Muslim world, in a range of forms of differing degrees of legal status within their respective political orders.
- The Iranian revolution in 1979 established the first Islamist state in history, a modern concept for which there is no precedent, raising an array of questions about what an Islamic state is actually supposed to be. Islamist states in Sudan and Afghanistan followed suit in subsequent years.
- The *jihad* (struggle, or holy war) against the Soviet Union in Afghanistan marked what many Islamists term the "first defeat of a superpower through armed Islamic struggle," an event that has had major impact upon the ideology, methods and cadres of political Islam in its struggle against perceived oppression, both foreign and domestic.
- Islam has come to provide much of the essential vocabulary for domestic struggle against tyranny in the Muslim world.
- Political Islam has readily embraced technology for the propagation of its ideas, including astonishingly wide participation on the Internet featuring provocative new debate on a global basis; an "electronic *umma*" (Muslim religious community) has created a deeper sense of international Islamic awareness and solidarity.
- Terrorism as a political tool used by certain radical Islamist groups achieved new global salience because of its effectiveness as an instrument by weak groups and states in resisting Western power. Powerful and effective use of terror has been applied against domestic or foreign enemies in such countries as Algeria, Egypt, Palestine, Lebanon, Pakistan, India, Iran, the Philippines, Saudi Arabia, Somalia, Yemen, Chechnya, and Uzbekistan. Terrorism against the United States engendered a global American War Against Terrorism with as yet unknown geopolitical repercussions.
- Terrorism in the name of Islam and the U.S. response has deepened popular acceptance of a "clash of civilizations."
- In Pakistan in 1999 the Muslim world gained its first nuclear weapon. At the same time other Muslim states (Iraq and Iran) began to develop strategic weapons programs that could seriously hinder Western military monopoly of power in the Middle East and perhaps change the regional calculus of power.
- Islamist movements, to the extent permitted, have moved into the democratic political arena in Morocco, Algeria, Egypt, Yemen, Jordan, Palestine, Turkey, Bosnia, Bangladesh, Pakistan, Malaysia, Indonesia, Sudan, Iran, Lebanon, and Kuwait. Islamists have fared well in elections in Turkey, Yemen, Jordan, Algeria, Kuwait, Malaysia, and Indonesia. Participation in the demo-

cratic order now includes several fundamentalist (back to quite literally defined basic principles) movements that earlier quite denied the validity of democracy in Islam but that have been unable to afford remaining outside the political game and its rules. Political Islam in Iran has undergone the broadest philosophical and conceptual debate and evolution of any Muslim state in the world.

- Large *da'wa* (reformist missionary) movements are underway in the form of the Nur movement in Turkey and the Tablighi Jama'at in South Asia and elsewhere that are affecting the tone of Islamic society, increasing awareness of the importance of Islam to individual as well as social life.

- The Western world has been forced to come to terms with the character of political Islam as a key reality.

- For the first time, an Islamist government was overthrown by an external force with the U.S. invasion of Afghanistan in 2001 that eliminated the Taleban.

- For the first time in Muslim history an Islamist party won a free national election in 2002 and took over the government—in Turkey.

- Islam has established itself in the West as a social and political force that is growing and beginning to exert powerful influence back in their homelands. The most advanced and unfettered thinking about Islam in the world is now taking place in the West.

- Politics in the Muslim world, including most Islamist movements and parties have essentially accepted the Western *vocabulary* of politics and its inherent values (democracy, human rights, pluralism, liberalization of the economy) even where sometimes those ideals are not really honored in practice by any parties in those political cultures. A handful of extremist fundamentalist movements continues to reject the entire Western framework of political values but in doing so it faces either marginalization or radicalization. The concept of human rights has taken on new salience in most Islamist movements because the concept so directly affects them.

- The spectrum and diversity of Islamist movements are increasing—even within one country—especially in the absence of other political movements.

It is hard to imagine a century that could contain more change of similar breadth, depth, and scope for the Muslim world since the initial spread of Islam across Asia and North Africa. These changes are probably more dramatic and comprehensive than at any time since the third century of Islam's existence. Some developments have been positive, others negative.

Martin Kramer, on the other hand, looking at the Muslim world across the twentieth century contends that "[W]hile the twentieth century has been the stage of numerous 'revolutions' in the name of the people or the nation or Islam, it could well be argued that Muslims have failed to resolve issues which appeared on their agenda [even] a century ago."[5] Kramer is quite right that the Muslim world has not resolved a whole set of key problems well known to any observer of the region. But where else, for that matter, has genuine "resolution" of key troubling issues actually occurred in most of the rest of the developing world, including China, India, Latin America, Africa, and Russia? Where have democracy, prosperity, genuine stability, good governance, literacy, and health triumphed in the globe except in the West and a handful of other countries mainly in East Asia? It is clearly incorrect to suggest that political Islam and the Muslim world have not gone anywhere in the last century beyond a lot of noise and heat. Indeed, the list of important changes I cite above represents a dramatic evolution—some of it admittedly negative—even if it does not necessarily involve "resolution" of problems. This evolution sets the indispensable groundwork for the possibility of greater movement toward "resolution" of political problems in this next century.

One encouraging indicator is the effect of time and generational change. We are already witnessing signs of an early shift toward greater openness, accessibility, and flexibility on the part of new leadership in several states—Jordan, Morocco, Qatar, Bahrain, Syria—and a great deal more change should come as multiple presidents-for-life and aged monarchs depart the scene, peacefully or violently. Even where the change is not dramatic, it is perceptible and newer rulers can't quite get away with what the old ones did. Generational change, of course, occurs not only among rulers but at the level of citizenry as well—new generations who have been socialized into both Islam and western democratic ideas, at least from afar, and many millions more educated in the West—all now regularly exposed to international media and the events of the world. They are increasingly seeking to reconcile, meld, and integrate into new forms of political discourse and practice.

It will not be business as usual in the Muslim world in the coming decades. But how do Islamists actually function in this world? Are Muslim concerns markedly different, bound to a unique cultural world? Or are Islamists actually participating in the broader issues of the developing world? We will examine that issue in the next chapter.

THE USES OF POLITICAL ISLAM

ISLAMISM IN ACTION

"ONLY WHEN RELIGION does something other than mediate between man and God does it retain a high place in people's attentions and in their politics," observes Steven Bruce—but in the context of Northern Ireland.[1]

But just exactly when *does* religion do something other than mediate between man and God? The moment religion finds some resonance among the public on political issues, it is sure sign that some need is not otherwise being met effectively by existing political means. Those needs can be multiple. This chapter looks at one of the key reasons for the vigor of political Islam: the immensely variegated roles it plays in the politics and society of the Muslim world.

A ROLE IN SEARCH OF AN ACTOR

In the early 1950s Gamal Abdel Nasser remarked that Egypt's vigorous activism in the Middle East was in response to "a role in search of an actor"—the existence of certain needs and aspirations in the region, a role not being filled. He won the adulation of the Arab masses in the process of attempting to fill this vacuum, and ultimately failed. The vacuum has reemerged. Indeed, the concept is a potent one: how does a leader or a movement successfully perceive a political vacuum and proceed to fill it? The question relates directly to the issue raised at the outset of the chapter: what needs, conditions, and circumstances invite religion to play a broader role in society than simply intermediating between Man and God?

Today Islamist movements meet a deeply perceived public need in the Muslim world, a need that continues to be felt after several decades of activism that have not yet reached their end. Otherwise how does one explain these movements' success and support? It is quite possible that the role of political Islam in politics will be sharply diminished at some point in this new century, but *one of two things must happen: either the conditions that helped impel Islamism into political life will have to weaken or disappear, or some other force or ideology will arise to meet the need more effectively.*

Obviously no political movement or ideology rides high forever; movements tend to be cyclical and responsive to specific needs at specific times. But neither do ideological movements completely die: having fulfilled a certain historical role and function, they simply recede in exhaustion and hibernate until new circumstances arise in which a fresh variation of their message might regain political and social relevance. That has been the history of intermittent Islamic resurgence since Islam began. But this time there is a brand new phenomenon here: this is the *first time that Islamic resurgence has played on the stage of modern politics in a democratizing and globalizing era.*

Islam itself, of course, is not a political ideology but a religion. Yet Islamism is different: while it has some aspects of political ideology, this ideology takes various forms. Islamism is a broad term embracing a body of quite variegated and even contradictory political, social, psychological, and economic—even class—functions. It is represented by differing types of movements that draw general inspiration from Islam. Islamist movements today are merely the latest wave among the many political and social movements in Islamic history that have developed out of the faith and culture under specific historical conditions. Islamism in some of its current guises will certainly run its course and recede in popularity and importance over time—indeed, that process is already observable in a few more fringe or extremist movements. But Islamism as a phenomenon will never fully disappear, because its message in one sense is timeless for Muslims: that Islam has something important to say about the political and social order. Political Islam will thus evolve and change, divide and unite, wax or wane in its popularity, but it will not disappear. We are talking here about multiple understandings and interpretations of Islam in politics and society; hence, it is more accurate to discuss "Islamisms."

In the end we are talking less about Islam than we are about *Muslims*—what can inspired Muslims bring to the political forum to help resolve current problems of the Muslim world? We are speaking not about what Islam is, but what Muslims want. Islamists have proven adept at offering striking critiques of today's realities, but so far considerably less ability to offer new *political* solutions from a position of power.

THE PARADE OF IDEOLOGIES

Muslims have been exposed to a variety of ideologies over the past century. The colonial period introduced certain Western values but did not truly provide Muslims with experience in genuine capitalist or liberal democratic governance. Liberalism was limited, and capitalism was primarily for the benefit of the colonial state. More important, *these ideologies never represented the independent and conscious choice of the population, nor were they widely internalized.* And they were thus quickly subverted by most of the postindependence rulers of the country who came to power and maintained it by non-democratic means while claiming to govern in the interests of the people.

Then, during the Cold War, communism billed itself in the Third World as an "alternative to capitalism." Due to the weight of the Soviet Union in international affairs, communism, or "socialism" was in fact able to present a plausible alternative movement with specific policies for solutions to Third World problems. But as we know, communism failed to deliver and with the demise of the Soviet Union nearly everywhere lost its cachet. Statism—socialism in many respects—failed spectacularly in the form of "Arab socialism" in the People's Democratic Republic of Yemen and Algeria and left an unimpressive and often ugly record in Egypt, Syria, and Iraq.

Arab nationalism as an ideology, after riding high in the Nasserist era from the 1950s to the 1970s, became linked with failure through its ineffective statist economics, its inability to meet social needs, its military failure against Israel, and its authoritarianism. Liberal democracy as practiced in the West is perhaps the ideology most likely to win out in the long run but is far from taking hold. Unfortunately few Muslim states show signs yet of serious embrace of this ideology; it cannot rally a crowd in Liberation Square in any capital city, and it remains primarily the preserve of a small Westernized elite, foreign to most of the traditions of the Third World. Liberal democracy unfortunately offers few successful models in the Third World, and it certainly has not yet been successfully adopted in the Muslim world due to both domestic and international reasons.

It is a key thesis of this book, then, that for many *reasons political Islam at the moment still remains the only realistic major alternative movement to most of today's authoritarian regimes.* This is so even though political Islam has generated its own failing authoritarian regimes as well, as we see in Iran, Sudan, and Afghanistan, where in each case it attained power by force, like most other Muslim regimes. But at this juncture Islamism is virtually the only movement that remains fresh and relatively untested in most Muslim countries. Its failures or shortcomings in Iran,

Sudan, and Taleban Afghanistan do not mean that other more democratic branches of the movement may not fare differently, or approach power differently, than these three states have done. Political Islam still claims an ability to meet key grievances of the Muslim world against other rivals. In the absence of any alternative ideology seen as both offering solutions and remaining true to the values of the Muslim world, *political Islam dominates the current field by default.*

We might further advance the hypothesis that *as advocates of political Islam, through their own increasingly perceived self-interest call for democratic process, they may well serve to assist in the evolution of liberal democracy and thus ironically serve as a key force in the process of adapting liberal democracy to the Muslim world.*

If in today's Muslim world there are roles in search of an actor, what are those roles? That issue will be the main substance of this chapter.

Whether talking about veils or ballot boxes, political Islam in multiple respects still represents a modernizing movement, the single largest, most vibrant, growing, widespread, and active movement in the Muslim world in seeking to strengthen democracy, human rights, civil society, and, generally, liberal economies. I hasten to point out that I refer to those movements that have *not* attained power, since those that have so far achieved power have done so by non-democratic means and have largely ignored these goals.

Let's examine the variety of forms and purposes to which political Islam is put today in three key areas: issues of identity and self-perception, internal political roles, and foreign policy.

ISLAM AS A FAITH

At the outset, it would be both mistaken and condescending to view Islam purely in instrumental terms, by ignoring its basic role as a *source of religious inspiration.* Islam obviously precedes political Islam and Islam will abide, whatever the fortunes of political Islam will be. Islam may inspire Muslims to formulate visions of political Islam, but Islam is the essence and remains independent of all political interpretations. Islam, as the faith of one-quarter of mankind, is a source of inspiration, explanation, guidance, solace, and fulfillment for life in this world and beyond. It offers a way toward understanding human existence and the moral principles that lend life both structure and meaning. It provides a community and a traditional way of life and outlook that is reassuring, familiar, and functional. Many Muslims are drawn to political Islam starting from the foundation of belief in Islam as a religion—as simply the best way to understand and order human moral existence. Therefore, whatever the appeals and role that political Islam may have for many Muslims, *it is imperative to remember that Islam's primary function for most Muslims is indeed religious and not political.*

I. ISSUES OF IDENTITY AND SELF-PERCEPTION

IDENTITY

By definition, Islam is the source of shared identity for the Muslim world. But over the centuries the *practice* of Islam in different regions by different peoples has generated a variety of forms and expressions. Political Islam seeks to create a single Islamic identity that takes precedence, at least in one's moral life, over even the national identity. *It is in fact quite striking how bold and broadly inclusive this concept of identity is at a time when the trend in most of the world is away from universalism and toward divisive ethnic and state identities or even local and clan identities.* In this sense Islamism as a political vision is clearly supra-national, even while it works on a practical basis within the confines of individual states. To most Islamists, Islam is the first and key identity but not the sole identity. But even as Islamists call for a single Islamic identity, the implications and results of giving that identity priority are unclear.

Now, whether or not an Islamist movement becomes truly radical hinges *on whether or not it rejects the very validity and legitimacy of the local state* and seeks universal revolution to undermine it in the name of an ideal *umma*. Most Islamists will accept the reality of working through national entities, however flawed. But the distinction between the two is far from clear.

And how should we understand identity? Every individual possesses multiple identities. The salience of any one element of identity over another is linked to its relevance to a given moment or process in daily life. One's ethnic group might matter mightily under conditions of persecution or conflict, such as a Jew in Germany or Eastern Europe in the 1930s, or an African-American in the American South in the 1920s. Religion also may matter vitally when one is either persecuted or highly privileged because of it. Class can matter in a struggle for better economic conditions, although class has never become the transcendent defining element of identity that Marx believed it would be.

Islamists did not invent Muslim identity, nor is it a contemporary idea. Indeed, the most traditional and powerful instrument of supranational identity-creation within Islam has been the *Hajj*, or pilgrimage to Mecca—one of the five pillars of obligations in Islam. Over centuries the accounts of *hajjis* stress the moving, galvanizing, and fulfilling role that the pilgrimage represents to them, in which millions of Muslims from Africa, Asia, the Middle East, Europe, and the Western Hemisphere meet in Mecca, rich and poor dressed alike in the same austere garments on a basis of total equality to profess their faith. The Hajj can inspire them to return to their native regions with a vivid new personal awareness of being part of a vast Muslim brotherhood and sisterhood with shared beliefs, despite differences in language, culture, skin color, ethnicity, or wealth. Specific events can likewise intensify common Muslim identity, especially in periods of major confrontations with non-Muslims, such as the Crusades, or during the colonial period when Muslims sought to throw off Western imperial control across the breadth of the Muslim world. All Muslims were dismayed at the abolition of the Caliphate by Mustafa Kemal Atatürk in Turkey in 1924, eliminating the position of nominal spiritual leader of the whole Sunni Muslim world. Muslims express strong support for the Palestinians in their struggle for statehood. And the U.S. War Against Terrorism also serves to evoke similar feelings of solidarity against the West.

Islam recognizes the reality and validity of other identities on a daily operational basis. But Islamic identity remains powerful, even at the national level, as a commitment to a specific course of political or social action, to place life on a sounder moral footing and to improve Muslim society. *In other words, to grant a certain priority to the Muslim identity is to make a statement about the character of the challenge that individuals and societies face and about the nature of the solution.*

AUTHENTICITY

The quest for "authenticity" proceeds directly out of the importance Islamists attribute to Islamic identity. To be "authentic" is to operate within "the tradition." But who defines the tradition? To successfully define tradition and authenticity is to gain political power. Thus tradition is what Islamists perceive it to be, with a clear political agenda in mind. The quest for authenticity is hardly unique to Islamists; nationalists also trade in the same coinage around the world. The claim to represent authenticity provides cultural and moral strength in a struggle against others who are perceived as less "authentic." As Islamists strive to create and shape identity, so too they seek a monopoly in defining the essence of the Islamic experience.[2]

The problem that Islamists face is how to determine what is "authentic" in the Islamic tradition. Indeed, the problem is similar to that of determining "whose Islam" is the "real Islam"—the heart of the political debate within the Muslim community. Authenticity is not about the past but about the future—the choice of which symbols will be selected to represent the essence of Islam in building some sort of intellectual construct for the future political order. This selection process can lend itself to authoritarian manipulation, stymying the creation of a pluralist society when some of its members can be marginalized as "unauthentic." Islamists furthermore suffer overall from a tendency to seek an idealized social unity, an idealized homogeneous national—or even *umma*—identity that discourages diversity and difference that is seen as fractious, divisive and harmful to the *umma*.[3]

UMMA VERSUS NATIONAL IDENTITY

Islam from the outset forwarded a bold and progressive idea: that tribalism and blood ties did not constitute a healthy basis for establishment of states, governance, or policy. Islam sought to transcend ethnicity in the name of a universal ideal of equality within a body of faith. Many would argue today that Islam is still fighting remnants of the tribal mentality that so hinder good governance in most of the Muslim world today. The *umma* is the vision.

Thus the *umma* as an ideal totally transcends the nation state: its spiritual unity is a constant goal, even if never to be fully attained in political form. The *umma* is blessed by God; the nation-state is not. This distinction does not necessarily eliminate loyalty to the nation-state as well, but such loyalty is on a different footing, especially when the state is run by repressive regimes. Thus there is a clear natural tension in the Islamist mind between the ideal of the *umma* and the reality of the nation-state. The tension is of particular interest in the Arab world where, by nearly universal acknowledgment, most Arabs observe that they have been divided up artificially by colonialist-imposed borders; and that even if some divisions within the Arab world are natural, historical, and geographic, the present number of states are excessive and often "non-organic" in character. This observation contains considerable truth, and one can interestingly speculate just what Arab borders might have been today if there had been no imperialism.

Ironically, the Islamists are actually pursuing a modernizing course here—the effort to *move away* from the parochial nation-state toward regionalization. Through the process of globalization, those artificial borders established everywhere by arbitrary historic accident can now evolve toward new organically based economic, political, and social regions that cut across and disestablish the old borders. It was the creation of a supranational European Union that gave license to the "breakup" of the UK into Scotland, Wales and England, that at last permitted Catalans and Basques to declare themselves virtual "countries" within Spain—all without upsetting much of anything. We may eventually see a redrawing of the borders of the Arab world in a process that may include separatism, mergers, and regionalization simultaneously. But to be successful, such a process can only come through democratic process and not as the fruit of arbitrary decisions by authoritarian regimes. The Islamists share in this supranational vision and progressive vision.

Similarly, at a time when the Muslim world is in some disarray, it is notably the Islamists who are most active in promoting the concept of *umma,* discussing its potential institutions, promoting certain common values, and working as apostles of coordination among Islamist movements. The Muslim Brotherhood in particular is the preeminent international Islamist organization, with branches around most of the Arab world and close sister relations with the South Asian network of Jama'at-i Islami. Islamists will generally favor any plans for common regional markets, defense agreements, or other coordinated policies among Muslim states—at least as an ideal. (One important exception is the security realm: coordination and planning among Arab ministers of interior and security chiefs is viewed by Islamists and others as nothing more than strengthening the repressive power of the authoritarian state to persecute dissidents.)

Today Islamists are carrying the word of the *umma* far and wide through their own transnational links and most importantly through a new electronic or "virtual *umma*" that brings the same issues to the entire Muslim world. The Internet now houses a staggering array of Islamic websites of every political hue. As a result Islam is becoming less Arab-centered as non-Arab parts of the Muslim world are no longer separated by distance; Pakistanis, Malaysians, Turks, and Indonesians, for example, all contribute to new thinking. Migration furthermore brings Muslims into contact with other Muslims and creates new awareness of general issues and views that transcend local ones. Indeed, Islamists create new ideological communities where they did not exist before, committed to concepts of a living *umma* with shared universal Islamic values.[4]

RESTORING MUSLIM POWER— NATIONAL AND INTERNATIONAL

Strong individual states nonetheless contribute to a strong *umma.* A powerful state is, after all, still the prime protector of the Muslim community and its culture. Over the past few centuries the key external challenge to the power of the Muslim state came not from other Muslim states but from Western powers that now dominate the international order. It is not culture but *imbalance of power* that fuels Islamist distrust and resentment of the West. While there is often an easy tendency to blame the West for much of what goes wrong in the Muslim world, there is concern today that the West will "never let" Muslims recover their greatness and power, a sense that the West fears and hates Islam and therefore seeks to keep it eternally subordinated. Islamists and other Muslims ask what Muslims can do to prevent the West from exercising overwhelming hegemony over Muslim sovereignty and interests.

The recovery of lost Muslim greatness is a basic theme of the Islamist litany and constitutes a religious obligation in moving to fulfill God's purpose on earth. The question is how to do it. Islamists today debate about what institutions are required for a recrudescence of Muslim power. Some stress moral revitalization through a return to the correct and sincere practice of Islam at the individual level, others stress Islamic institutions and just governance as being at least as important; still others emphasize the priority of challenging Western power that holds them back. Islamists are divided, for example, on whether an admittedly deeply flawed ruler like Saddam Hussein in Iraq is part of the *problem* of poor Islamic governance, or part of the *solution* in representing a net asset in the quest to stand up to the West. Most Islamists tend to see him as the problem but also as living proof of the reality that the West will block all aspirations to any independent-minded Muslim power that will not submit to the Western order.

NATIONALISM

If we think of Islamism as a nationalist movement, we will come close to capturing a great deal, but not all, of the spirit and function of political Islam as a movement on the international scene.

The several roles of Islamist movements discussed above—support for identity, authenticity, broader regionalism, revivalism, revitalization of the community—are not, of course, characteristics uniquely associated with religious revivalism. They are shared at least partially with other movements, especially nationalist. Even so, Islamism is in many important respects also quite different from nationalism. *In relation to the West,* say, it may be useful to think of its *functional behavior as resembling that of nationalism:* Witness its desire to strengthen the community and the state and a certain prickliness of style and suspicion of Western intentions and power. Such a stance does not at all rule out cooperation with the West, but political Islam will always be highly sensitive about its own dignity and requirements. Iran and China, for example, bear quite close resemblance to each other in this respect, despite the Islamist orientation of one and the Leninist orientation of the other. Both are proud ancient cultures who mourn lost greatness and are currently driven by powerful nationalist instincts, even if through an Islamist vehicle in Iran today.

A second example of Islam operating in a nationalist mode is its internal opposition to national leaders perceived as compromising the nation's integrity by doing the West's bidding: Sadat and Mubarak in Egypt, King Fahd in Saudi Arabia, and Ben 'Ali in Tunisia are just a few examples of leaders criticized by Islamists for doing the bidding of others. Islamists, too, often display economic nationalism in seeking to protect the Muslim state from powerful external economic forces potentially harmful to the welfare of local communities. In their occasional populist approaches to economic issues, Islamists demonstrate an unresolved contradiction with their overall abhorrence of socialism.

Islamists will reject comparison with nationalists, however, and do differ from nationalists in several important respects.

- Islamism has a strong moral component that is not a integral feature of nationalism.
- Islamism perceives its goals as far more lofty than nationalism and insists that, in the absence of transcendental and universal moral values, nationalist movements cannot be considered as having much to do with Islam.
- Nationalism is not inherently related to the concept of good governance but simply to power; Islamism in principle rejects the concept of power without moral purpose and good governance.
- Islamism condemns in principle the narrow and parochial vision of nationalists and believe that nationalism is actually a dangerous force within the *umma* because it serves to divide it. It is seen as a poison pill of colonial heritage. Here Islamism perceives nationalism as a retrogressive force—in the long run—although if it can strengthen a segment of the Islamic *umma* against non-Muslim power under certain circumstances, it is not an entirely negative force.

Bolstering National Liberation Movements

We should note that *Islamism functions almost purely in a nationalist mode when it is linked with national liberation movements against non-Muslim rule,* as in Palestine, Chechnya, Bosnia, Kashmir, Xinjiang, the Philippines, and other regions. This is an exceptionally potent combination when religion coincides with ethnicity against the external non-Muslim oppressor. In many of these cases (Palestine, Kashmir, Chechnya), the religious force is currently stronger than the secularist nationalist force in the national liberation movement. In all of these cases Islamists are dedicated to enlisting Islam as an essential component of the national character of the embattled community. We should expect to see Islamist movements increasingly active in supporting such moves by Muslim communities for greater autonomy or even independence from non-Muslim rule elsewhere in the world: the Balkans, Russia, Africa. Under these special circumstances of national liberation struggle, Islamism pays less attention to moral issues or other elements of reformism within society. Only after independence do Islamists predictably turn to issues of internal reform, morality, and good governance.

II. ISLAMISM'S DOMESTIC POLITICAL ROLES

Redefining the Meaning of Islam in Society

We witness throughout Islamic history periodic movements of Islamic revival or renewal (*tajdid*) in times of trouble, doubt, and crisis. Renewal did not necessarily suggest innovative new interpretations of traditional Islamic beliefs but rather an effort to purify, to get back to the essence—which can also be innovative.

Nearly all parts of the Muslim world witnessed efforts at renewal, especially in the late nineteenth and early twentieth centuries. The terms "old" and "new" thought are precisely those employed in almost every Muslim country in describing movements of intellectual, social, and political renewal in such diverse regions as Indonesia, Egypt, India, Malaysia, Central Asia, Turkey, and Sudan. The renewed faith represented a call for purification, but functionally the challenge often took on more formidable targets such as the backward, repressive state and the traditional clergy (*'ulama*).

Today Islamists everywhere are challenging the traditional basis of Muslim state power as bereft of morality, legitimacy, and even competency. These Islamist movements may often be led by clerics themselves. A few of the more dramatic cases include Indonesia's Muhammadiya and Nahdatul Ulama (NU) movements, and the ascension to the presidency in 1999 of Abdurrahman Wahid, leader of the NU. In Malaysia the rising power of the Islamist PAS party, which has strong *'ulama* elements in its leadership, is indicated by its capturing of two provincial governments in the 1999 elections in Malaysia.[5]

In Pakistan we witness the influence of the two key Islamist movements with strong *'ulama* presence: the Jama'at-i Islami, and the Jama'at-i 'ulama-i Islami. The role of Ayatollah Khomeini in the Iranian revolution and the continued dominance of clerics is familiar. Shaykh Rashid al-Ghannushi's leadership of Tunisia's banned al-Nahda movement, Shaykh Ahmad Yasin of Hamas, and the powerful influence of the Egyptian cleric Shaykh Yusif al-Qaradawi in Qatar are all examples of clerical leadership of Islamist movements. Most of these *ulama* have asserted a claim not only to moral power but to the political power based on it. They have also demonstrated an aversion for the ostentatiousness of state power and the privileged elite around it, and they have eschewed these trappings of power to live in humbler housing and lifestyle.

More commonly, however, it is not the *ulama* that is leading this rally for renewal. Rather it is self-trained "Islamic intellectuals" and perhaps a few dissident elements within the *ulama* who constitute the core of the new Islamists. Importantly, they not only challenge the state, but also *seek to radicalize the basic role of the traditional ulama itself,* which is perceived to be compromised and under state influence and control, or as having "sold out" to the state. These trends are strong in Saudi Arabia, Egypt, Algeria, Turkey, Jordan, Afghanistan, Pakistan, Chechnya, and Uzbekistan to name a few key cases. These two trends—either the renewalist *ulama* against the entrenched state, or new Islamist intellectuals against both the entrenched *ulama* and the state—express the two basic forms in which Islamism redefines the meaning of Islam in its political and social challenge to the state, thereby explicitly linking Islam to political change.

Challenging the Legitimacy of Existing Rule

Few regimes in the Muslim world today—or in the Third World more broadly—possess much legitimacy in terms of popular support, due in large part to their poor performance. Most are mired in long term authoritarianism; few leaders would win honest and open elections. In this unstable situation, Islamism, whether one likes it or not, *represents the single most important force for political change across the Muslim world.* Islamists present a broad critique of the current political order grounded in their interpretations of Islam and expressed in an Islamic political vocabulary close to the traditions of the mass of the population. The number of their supporters routinely exceeds that of most other political movements. (Pakistan has been a notable exception.)

In the Islamist view, the weakness and moral impoverishment of most of today's Muslim societies and states stem directly from the bad governance that characterizes their regimes. They are doubly illegitimate—both by Islamic standards through their failure to provide just and good governance, and by contemporary political standards as unelected and incompetent officials unwilling to face popular test.

PROVIDING THE VOCABULARY OF POLITICAL CRITIQUE

Islamists, not surprisingly, clothe their discourse on political issues in religious terms buttressed by regular quotations from the Qur'an. This practice is often taken by non-Muslims as suggesting that Muslims somehow live in a totally different political context suffused with religion and practices from the seventh century, bearing little relevance to Western political thinking. While the icons of Western political thinking are found in the Magna Carta and the American and French revolutions, for example, in Islamic society it is normal and appropriate that the Qur'an and the Traditions of the Prophet (*Hadith*) provide the legitimizing moral and legal arguments for political norms and justice; upon these foundations Muslim jurisprudence developed. These are quite simply the key sources of moral and even political argument and represent living and familiar texts and references to most Muslims.

But a traditional body of moral thought does not translate directly into modern political institutions. The contemporary implications and applications of this corpus of Muslim law and practice require reformulation when applied to modern public institutions, but the principles and philosophy of governance are there in general terms. The vocabulary of Islam will remain a critical point of reference for broader Muslim society, the coinage and vehicle of political discourse, and values—particularly at the popular level. Furthermore, the Islamic critique of the failures of contemporary Muslim society is quite pointed and relevant, and it exerts greater impact upon the public than do Western principles that are employed primarily by a small Westernized elite. The Islamists may therefore be the preeminent vehicle in the Muslim world today in introducing modern concepts of political reform, but in a vocabulary more consonant with Muslim tradition and culture.

These traditional categories of Islamic political thinking are not what they were hundreds of years ago. Western political ideas are indeed familiar to a large number of Islamists and have heavily influenced their thinking in terms of expectations of democracy, human rights, and civil society. But Islamists are in the process of translating these terms into familiar Islamic categories and investing the old Islamic concepts with new meaning reflecting Western practice.

MAKING THE CASE FOR REFORM, JUSTICE, AND SOCIAL CHANGE

Islamist movements today are a key vehicle for presenting programs of reform, social change, and social and economic justice. One could object that these are patently secular goals, that there is nothing uniquely Islamic about them and they could as readily be adopted by any secular movement or party. True, but in the absence of other political parties, Islamists dominate these issues by default and furthermore derive their position directly out of a contemporary Islamist political reading of Islam.

The same applies to the more elusive concept of "Islamic economics." Islamists have no clear or consistent vision of what economic policy should be except in terms of abstract thought—that economics must not be delinked, simply for the sake of efficiency and economic growth, from a moral vision that entails some degree of social and economic justice. Islam recognizes that inequalities of birth, endowment, and opportunities exist among all people and that differences in wealth are a reality of human society. What matters is the principle of some form of social justice—one not precisely defined.

At the same time, Islam does not favor, in principle, heavy state intervention in the marketplace or in the economic profile of society. On issues of market forces, Islamism respects them domestically but takes a protectionist, suspicious, and sometimes even xenophobic view of international market forces because they are seen to be dominated by the West and serving a Western agenda, and harmful to the population. Leftists share the identical view.

Yet, strangely, Islamists remain quite ambivalent about or even hostile to social revolution. In general, revolution has historically been perceived by Muslim scholars as an undesirable phenomenon because of its high cost in societal and governmental turmoil and the risk of anarchy. Such a position was also historically generated by 'ulama working at the beck and call of the ruler and hence it is quite convenient to the ruler's longevity in power. Pakistan presents an interesting case in which social injustice is rampant, extreme poverty exists, and a feudal political and social order are deeply rooted from eras preceding its founding. Yet almost no Islamist group in Pakistan preaches any kind of genuine social or economic revolution, except to urge, appropriately, that laws, including taxation, be universally applied. There is no mainstream Islamist organization (with the exception of Iran) with radical social views or a revolutionary approach to the social order apart from the imposition of legal justice.

Yet it would be a mistake to dismiss Islamists as supporters of the status quo or socially conservative in all respects. Certainly in more modern times Islamists interpret social justice in far more modern and egalitarian terms than in the past, consonant with contemporary world values, and even under the influence of socialist thought. Many Islamist movements speak out against ostentatiousness among the ruling classes, and attack the cozy relationship of the 'ulama and the state. Islamist leaders call for politicians to lead more modest lives and set an example for the avoidance of conspicuous consumption and for combating the feudal order in which ostentation always comes with power. Still, as Chandra Muzaffar points out, the Islamist performance has not always been adequate: "Islamic parties which have managed to acquire power in recent decades in different parts of the world have concentrated much more upon changing laws and policies rather than transforming the underlying political culture. And yet, in the ultimate analysis, it is the transformation of culture that endows a society or a civilization with a new character and a new ethos."[6]

CRITIQUING THE AUTHORITARIAN STATE AND CORRUPTION

Authoritarian states are, of course, more susceptible to corruption than states in which a more transparent political order and open press can uncover and expose corrupt practices. The Muslim world is no exception. Islamist movements typically take a direct bead on corruption as a key violation of their vision of "just governance"; secular movements often join them in this critique as well. Indeed, if there is any area in which Islamists in power can be said to have excelled, it is in the dramatic reduction of corruption in municipal or provincial governments in which Islamists have won local elections—Algeria, Turkey, and Malaysia, for example. This hardly means that Islamists are by nature above corruption—indeed, one of the lessons of the Iranian experience is how the clergy itself can become quite corrupted within government once it assumes unchecked power and full access to funds, fulfilling Lord Acton's dictum that absolute power corrupts absolutely. But since most Islamists are barred from power, they can readily adopt with clean hands the issue of corruption as central to their platform. Given the moral orientation of their program, their members are probably under greater pressure to avoid the temptations of power that encourage corruption. Once in power, however, the Islamists' reputation for honest government cannot remain indefinitely clean, given human nature.

ISLAMISM AS WELFARE NGOS: PROVIDING ALTERNATIVE SOCIAL SERVICES

A key source of the popularity of Islamist organizations has been their ability to move beyond mere rhetoric about social justice to implement a broad range of social services for the public, and especially the poor. They have succeeded to a large measure because the failing state has been unable to provide many of these services due to incompetence, inefficiency, or neglect. Islamist movements are well known for providing shelters, educational assistance, free or low cost medical clinics, housing assistance to students from out of town, student advisory groups, facilitation of inexpensive mass marriage ceremonies to avoid prohibitively costly dowry demands, legal assistance, sports facilities, and women's groups. The absence of similar state-provided services has been a key source of despair and popular anger against the regime, and the Islamists gain great political credibility as a result, most notably in Egypt, Algeria, Morocco, Turkey, Malaysia, and Indonesia. The success of these charitable operations is due to major private funding by pious wealthy donors, Islamic foundations, grassroots ties to local mosque organizations, a sense of commitment and dedication, and a desire to build a political basis for the Islamist movement.

As rapid, often overwhelming urbanization maintains its pace in the decades to come, state resources and competencies will be even further stretched and less likely to meet the social needs of the swelling urban masses. Islamist organizations in this new century are likely to figure ever more prominently as important nongovernmental organizations (NGOs), in an emerging civil society. Under conditions of civil disorder, anarchy, or high criminality, and social breakdown, Islamic organizations can help provide clear-cut terms of justice and a moral foundation for the policing of neighborhoods, more effectively than corrupt police organizations. In Chechnya, for example, a region struggling to reestablish order and authority after the massive destruction of two recent wars with Russian forces, the proclamation of Shari'a law is both a symbol of moral purpose and a traditional code of discipline broadly acceptable to the population in times of trouble. Even in American cities such as New York and Los Angeles, the Black Muslim organization has worked in the past to provide African-American neighborhoods with security and to drive out peddlers of narcotics.

Not only civil strife but natural disaster has also evoked widespread philanthropic and social action by Islamists to provide medical and burial services when the state was unable to meet these needs. In Egypt the Islamists gained great credit and the state lost support when Islamists bested the state in providing medical and social services immediately after a disastrous earthquake. In Turkey as well, after the terrible earthquake of 1998, the ultrasecularist military actually sought to ban participation of Islamist groups in providing social services even while the state was unable to do so itself, fearing the Islamists would make political capital from such activities. Islamist organizations are likely to place major emphasis on such social programs across the Muslim world in the future, and they have the resources to do so. The state, in turn, is seeking in many cases to weaken or undermine the financial resources of Islamist organizations under one pretext or another. The U.S. War Against Terrorism is being used as one pretext as the state attempts to tar all its Islamist opposition movements by accusing them of having "terrorist links."

CALLS FOR DEMOCRATIZATION AND HUMAN RIGHTS

The majority of Islamist movements have long since reached the conclusion that democratization is the best overall vehicle by which to present their agenda to the public and to gain political influence—and thereby eventually to come to power. The Islamist encounter with democracy is, of course, of relatively recent vintage; Islamist organizations could not participate in whatever little democratic processes the colonial period afforded; since independence, few Muslim regimes have provided Islamists or even any political party access to the political order either.

Islamists (out of power) are becoming prime advocates of concepts of democracy and human rights, *precisely because they are the primary victims of its absence.* Islamists, as the major opposition to entrenched regimes, languish in prisons in the Muslim world more than any other political group. It would not be excessive to state that today the Islamists are among the most insistent activists on behalf of introducing liberalization and democratic reform into the political order. Once they actually join parts of the political order, however, such as representation in the parliament, some of them still remain conservative about expansion of suffrage, such as Kuwaiti Islamists who—along with tribal conservatives—were opposed to extending suffrage to women; even male suffrage in Kuwait is itself of quite recent vintage.

Rhetoric, of course, comes easy. Skeptics doubt the Islamists' sincerity, and sometimes with good reason. Islamists in power in Iran took fifteen years to open up the political order to the electoral process. Islamists in Sudan who had once participated in periodic parliamentary elections blocked all political parties after coming to power by military coup and only ten years later are thinking of loosening the system. In Afghanistan there was never any real democratic process under any of the *mujahidin* (anti-Soviet Islamist guerrillas), including the Taleban. Islamists (in full power) thus have a poor record on democracy. Indeed, given the Muslim world's limited experience with democracy and alternation of power in general, *there are few political parties of any stripe in the developing world one can trust to come to power and still remain willing to be voted out of office in subsequent elections, if there are any.* Islamist parties—like most parties in most states—are untested in this respect, but as political liberalization gradually spreads, they are eagerly becoming socialized into the practice of democratic procedures. Since Islamists are confident of their ability to fare well at the ballot box, democratization offers nothing but benefits to them. Of course their support for democracy is self-serving—but what could be better? Would that politicians everywhere saw democracy as in their own interest.

The concept of human rights as espoused in the West has also gained currency among Islamists over the last several decades for the same reason. The original formulation of human rights *in legal terms* historically began in the West and for this reason is suspect to some in the Third World who remember how the call for "Christian values" spearheaded Western imperialism in the nineteenth century as a device of Western intervention in Muslim countries. But because Islamists are again the primary victims of the absence of human rights in their own countries, they have come to recognize the importance of the concept and therefore are beginning to call for its application. Islamists have formed a variety of Islamist human rights organizations—for example, the Mazlumder organization in Turkey, the Tunisian National Council for Liberties, the Islamic Human Rights Commission based in London, others in Cairo and Iran—or else work with secular human rights groups. Islam as a legal system has complex procedures relating to the rights of individuals, including non-Muslims, before the law. But Islamic law has yet to evolve a contemporary system of law appropriate for modern pluralistic and multireligious societies that would provide absolute equality before the law—although the principle of legal protection of minorities has always existed in premodern institutional form.[7]

Problems indeed do exist in making Shari'a law compatible with Western human rights law, including the equal status of women, but these problems are far from insoluble. Most Muslim states, including the Islamic Republic of Iran from the beginning, have adopted broad elements of Western law into their legal corpus, so such precedents have already moved well into the realm of acceptance. Iran, for example, has quietly put aside traditional Islamic divorce and inheritance law as it applies to women. While such law was progressive in its time, the Islamic Republic has recognized that it no longer addresses contemporary Iranian social needs.

However, two caveats need to be registered on Islamist openness to human rights law: first, Islamists' absolute acceptance of the principle is sometimes subject to the qualification that new legislation be "compatible with Islamic law." This qualification must be probed: the crux of the issue is indeed just how compatible these values are with *their particular understanding* of Islamic law. Second, Islamists in power so far—in Sudan, Iran, and Afghanistan—have hardly been scrupulous about human rights, to say the least (although Iran is recently showing some serious movement toward rule of law.) But again, groups coming to power by coups d'etat are never known for their adherence to democratic or human rights principles at the outset, and Islamists in these three cases are no exception. A truer test will be to track the record of Islamists who come to power through the ballot box—in which our first real test is in Turkey where the first Islamist party to win a national election came to power in 2002.

SUPPORT FOR POLITICAL PARTIES

Political Islam is now an active force—where permitted by the state—across most of the Muslim world in fielding political parties to contest the political process. (While *de jure* or *de facto* bans exist specifically on Islamist party activity in Egypt, Algeria, Turkey, and Tunisia, for example, these bans are unevenly applied.) An early Islamist debate on the appropriateness of creating political parties in the name of Islam is still underway—not on the grounds of the compatibility of Islam and democracy but out of concern that mixing politics with religion leads to compromise of religious principle. Given the course of political events in the Muslim world, not only are Islamist parties appearing in most Muslim countries, but there will likely be multiple Islamist parties within each country contesting the field, as there are already today in Algeria, Yemen, Kuwait, Pakistan, Indonesia, Iran, Malaysia, Turkey, and Lebanon, to name the most prominent.

CIVIL SOCIETY

Islamist movements are involved in the creation of institutions of civil society in the Muslim world today more than any other single party. Obviously Islamists work to establish civic organizations that are Islamist-oriented, but they serve to strengthen the overall power of civil society at the expense of the state. Indeed, many Islamists within the past several decades have emerged as articulate proponents of civil society across the Muslim world. Their support for the concept is both theoretical and practical. On the theoretical level, many prominent moderate Islamist thinkers such as Rashid Ghannushi (of Tunisia, in exile in London) and Hasan al-Turabi (of Sudan), state flatly that a powerful civil society is precisely the kind of society that an Islamic state instinctively favors.[8]

Neither in theory nor in practice has Islam ever stood for the all-pervasive centralizing state dominated by a single powerful ruler—even though Islamic history provides plentiful examples of rulers disregarding Islamic principles. The classical concept of a Muslim ruler is to rule within well-defined limits with the purpose of providing the optimum environment for Muslims to pursue a religious life in accordance with God's design.

Absolutism *in principle* is alien to Muslim political thought. Indeed, Muslim society has historically been marked by a high degree of what we would today might call civil society, in which rulers have focused upon limited interests such as revenues, military levees, hierarchies of political loyalty, provision of basic economic infrastructure, maintenance of political order, and defense against foreign enemies, most other endeavors belonged to civil society and were of limited interest to the ruler. Ironically these principles of limited governance were broken primarily in the twentieth century by new authoritarian regimes based on Western nation-building principles in which the Leviathan state assumed maximum control over all areas of life to build the all-powerful state. To be sure, civil society in Islam traditionally has lacked the full *legal* autonomy that it enjoyed in the period of state formation in the West, but it has a long tradition of de facto existence despite its lack of legal protection from closure by arbitrary state decision.[9]

A small minority of Islamists opposes encouragement of an autonomous civil society as a threat to the Islamizing state project—Islam from the top down. Iranian hard liners rightly perceive that the expansion of civil society threatens the unlimited power of the state—exactly as it is supposed to do. Their objection is based on an authoritarian vision of an Islamic state that grants no options in deciding whether or not to live the divinely ordered life, or how. This is as totalitarian as Islam can get—quite in contradiction to the Qur'anic precept that "there is no compulsion in religion." According to this authoritarian ideological position, because Islam is a way of life embracing all aspects of human life, all activities must be subject to the control of professionally trained Islamic jurisprudents in order to maintain the ideal Islamic state. Thus the determination of that divinely ordered life cannot be subject to popular will or expression but only to a single jurisprudent, or a body of jurisprudents, who will determine the law. This mode of thinking, however, is distinctly minoritarian and fading in the face of globally advancing concepts of contemporary democratic practice. Islamists, at least those out of power, are increasingly fascinated with the relationship of civil society to the ideal Islamic society.

Islamists are conducting an interesting debate over the concept of "sacred space" versus "secular space." This debate is less arcane than meets the eye since it grapples with the nature of civil society and the space for intellectual freedom in Islam. Indeed, it may mark the beginning of Islamist reconsideration of what genuine secularism (separation of church and state) might mean for *protection* of Islam from the authoritarian state—a key concern.

Furthermore, the idea of decentralization of power is implicit, sometimes even explicit, in the thinking of many modern Islamists, based on the belief that no human has a full understanding of God's purpose, much less a monopoly on it, and that it is only through diversity and pluralism that God's will and the preferred path for Muslims will be increasingly revealed. Here a few Islamists are working in quite modern conceptual categories of governance: pluralism is actually seen as an instrument to facilitate the discovery of eventual truth, superior to any state- or *ulama*-controlled theological thinking. Indeed, it is clear to many Islamists that the very subordination of the *ulama* to the needs of the state has been a key factor in the corruption and atrophy of Islamic thought and creativity over the past many centuries.

ISLAMIST SECULARIZATION OF SOCIETY

The net result of all this activity is that large numbers of Islamists are now *engaged in functionally privatizing and secularizing society* beyond the purview of the state. As both George Joffe and Olivier Roy point out, by promoting privatization of society, Islamists are thereby engaged in de facto "secularization" of society. I refer to "secularization" in its true sense: disassociation of religion and the state, rather than the rigid control or even negation of religious life by the state as radical secularists in the Middle East (especially Turkey) interpret it. As Islamists create civil institutions, whole new areas of private Muslim activity and Muslim areas of life become liberated from the control of the state. Islamists are in effect putting together a project based upon society and the public that is quite separate from the state and its instruments. They are creating a "Muslim space" within societies outside of and beyond government control that serves goals different from that of the state. Such space clearly represents a form of civil society that flourishes apart from state-controlled space. Here we have de facto separation of state and religion.[10] Most states in the developing world hate anything that lies outside the purview of their control. Islamist civil organizations are doubly hateful to the state since they are both independent and strengthen the Islamists at the grassroots level.

As the state squeezes the Islamists, they are able to retreat to the precincts of the neighborhood mosque, the natural center of Islamist organization. The state can close the nationalist or socialist party headquarters, but it cannot really close the mosques, which serve as operations centers for Islamist movements. It is here that they canvass neighborhoods in the course of providing social services, spread their political message, and campaign for votes where permitted to participate. In most Muslim countries today, Islamist grassroots organization is considered superior to that of nearly all other political parties. On a more disturbing note, this strong grassroots level of organization over the longer run could in the end operate as an instrument of civil surveillance and control by the authoritarian state, and has done so during much of the Iranian revolution and in Sudan as well. But as long as Islamists lack absolute power—dangerous in the hands of any party—they will likely remain tuned to public opinion and needs. Even in Iran where Islamism is now fully in power, local clerics are beginning to show an attunement to the limits of what the public will accept by way of religious austerity, and they are compelled to bend to these realities if they wish to avoid social upheaval.

VEHICLE FOR CLASS ASPIRATIONS

Political Islam, whether consciously or not, also tends to function as a vehicle for certain class aspirations. Now, Islamists strongly oppose Marxist interpretations of society, which they see as based on a purely material vision of life, divisive in its harshly drawn distinctions among warring classes, representative of the politics of hatred and envy, and unaccepting of inevitable differences among individuals in talent, wealth, status, and power. Nonetheless, when Islamist movements challenge the entrenched state, they tend to attract certain social elements, classes, or groups that feel excluded by the statist elite. Typically, Islamists have drawn their largest base of social support from the lower middle class, petty bourgeoisie, and the urban rather than rural population. They draw upon state bureaucrats, students, intellectuals, and some degree of professional support, although again mainly from the lower middle class. Where economic conditions are particularly bad, such as in Algeria, Egypt, Pakistan, and Iran, Islamists have garnered considerable following from lower classes and the unemployed (although often educated).

Support to the Islamists from certain classes is not to be interpreted only in economic terms but in cultural ones as well. Strata that are not highly Westernized or even much exposed to Western culture, clothing, music, languages, food, and life, tend to find the culture of the secular to be alien and out of reach; they therefore tend to associate Westernization with elite privilege. In Turkey, for example, much of the support base for Turkey's Islamist parties (Welfare/Virtue/Happiness/Justice) as well as for the Nur movement is comfortable with, and takes pride in, traditional Anatolian culture, music, food, and way of life. Islamist emphasis on cultural authenticity appeals to those who derive sustenance from the traditional, familiar, and comfortable vehicles of Islamic daily culture. Islamism also attracts rising new business elites whose roots are closer to provincial life, more traditional and "native" rather than foreign-oriented. An example is Turkey's new "Anatolian tigers," the powerful new emerging Islam-oriented business circles from traditional, not elite social classes. Indeed, Islamic culture represents the mainstream culture of the majority of the population across the Muslim world, however much it may be attracted to certain aspects of imported Western culture as well. Traditional Islamic culture works to create a newly self-conscious "Islamist counter-elite." As Nilüfer Göle, a keen observer of the Turkish Islamists, notes,

> In short, all three categories of the Islamist counter-elites (the engineers, the women, and the intellectuals) reveal a new profile of Islamist actors; all three are the product of secular education, urbanization and Islamization; all three are the result of the hybrid nature of modernism and Islamism; and all three are in conflict with the previous modern Westernized elites. The latter became elites when their members emancipated themselves from their religious beliefs and traditional ties, and acquired knowledge and education apart from, and in contradistinction to religion. Islamization, therefore, can be seen as a counter-attack against the principles of the Kemalist project of modernization and the vested interests of the Westernized elites. The concept of an Islamist elite is itself antithetical to secular elites who see it as anachronistic.[11]

Thus, the Islamist political program based on native culture—both Islamic and local—greatly strengthens its basis of support. This trend will continue as long as the small Westernized elite associates its values and interests with counterparts in the West—all the while hindering the entry into power of new Islamic-oriented elites more imbued with traditional culture and values.

Since the Westernized elite represents only a narrow part of the social spectrum, it is often ineffective in introducing social change into broader society. Many Westernized Muslim women, for example, who are working for female emancipation in their societies have actually chosen to work through Islamist organizations to achieve these goals—precisely because such organizations are closer to the cultural values of most women. Islamist organizations themselves become the central arena of social contestation. It is precisely in change wrought through this traditional and mass milieu—not through the much smaller organizations of the educated secular elite—that the greatest long-range impact will occur.

Thus Islamism can play a significant, if sometimes inadvertent, role in strengthening class consciousness, class aspirations, and values—both economic and cultural—within Muslim society. Islamism doesn't seek to be divisive, but it ends up empowering those traditional classes most sympathetic to traditional Islamic culture and values who then become the natural reservoir of support and the natural constituency for Islamist movements. Islamists therefore represent part of a broader revolution of rising new classes across the Muslim world with powerful potential for change in the future political and social order. It is instructive to compare this with the role of evangelical Protestantism in Latin America, where the movement is empowering a new bourgeoisie—serving as an ideology of individual assertion and commitment against older, often entrenched Catholic elites.

Political Islam may constitute only a way-station in the emergence of new elite actors, but its grounding in the native culture and traditions of Islamic civilization provides it with a powerful basis for maintaining popular support.

Feminism

The general position of women in the Muslim world is among the most disadvantaged in the developing world, with strongly undesirable and harmful effects upon the overall advancement of society. Even though this situation may result more from traditionalism than from Islam, the reality remains and the results are inexcusable. In areas of education, legal rights, social access, and protection against traditional customs that oppress women, the Muslim world ranks low. Even where this is contrary to the law or spirit of Islam, clerics usually have little to say about it because they don't want to challenge what is traditional, or they align themselves with male privilege. Only a new but small group of Islamists are beginning to champion the position of women as vital to the regeneration of Muslim society. Worse, long-standing social *custom* has often come to be taken as "Islamic" in the eyes of the population and is rarely challenged. Islamists are only slowly coming to an appreciation of the problem.

Interestingly, Islamist movements today are beginning to serve as conduits for the mobilization of women into politics. Islamist movements that seek to build political influence within an electoral system know that women's votes count as much as men's and that they must organize the female population as well for any victory at the ballot box. Traditional Muslim women in more democratic societies are becoming politicized, often for the first time, through Islamist movements that recruit them to get out the female vote. Once they are engaged in this public activity, it is but a short step to asking about why there are no women on the central committees of the parties. Indeed, women are now beginning to show up in the leadership circles of many of these Islamist parties such as in Turkey, Jordan, Egypt, Malaysia, and Indonesia.

Nonetheless, women's rights remains one of the most contentious areas of Islamist politics. First, the legacy of traditional culture all across Asia has not been kind to women in any of the great cultures of the world—China, India, and the

Muslim world—where women have been poorly treated: footbinding in China, the live immolation of widows with their dead husbands in India (*suttee*), and broad lack of functional rights. The litany is well known—women treated as an underclass, abused, treated as chattel, as the property of their husbands, enslaved to their mothers-in-law, honor killing, poor birth control awareness, and restrictive social activity. Islam at its foundation actually instituted a powerful, even revolutionary, legal agenda for women, and it was the first major religion to establish a clear independent legal identity for women—not derived from fathers or husbands—where none had existed before. Women were granted clear legal rights as distinct individuals before the law—even if not on a fully equal par with men. (Indeed, full female legal equality with men came very late even in the West—with female suffrage in the United States only in the second decade of the twentieth century, in Switzerland only after World War II.) Women retain their own names in Islam even after marriage, a custom only recently adopted by a handful in the West. Their rights of inheritance in Islam were legally explicit from the beginning, whereas women had no independent legal rights of inheritance in the West until the last century. In the seventh century a reforming Islam accepted the principle of up to four legal wives specifically in order to legalize relationships at a time of rampant concubinage—and stipulated that any additional wives must be guaranteed absolute equality of treatment in all respects. In practice, few Muslims maintain more than one wife, and exercise of the right to marry additional wives is increasingly viewed as an anachronism—but still existent. But few clerics have sought to address the issue on a legal basis, even as the practice has severely declined under the weight of modern life and contemporary international pressure. Islamist feminists wish to restore the pioneering role toward women's status that early Islam represented. But a predisposition toward patriarchy persists among clerics.

The essence of the problem for those concerned with women's rights is first to locate the source of a given restriction: is it clear religious stipulation, a debatable interpretation, or plain old custom? In Islam, educated women, including Islamists, have begun to assert themselves by demanding to know specifically what the Qur'an explicitly prescribes for women. Women are studying the Qur'an and Islamic law in order to see for themselves exactly what the texts say, and how they have been interpreted over time. Women also seek to understand how modern rights for women can be derived from Islam, recognizing that even in the West women's rights has been a gradually evolving phenomenon. An Islamist feminist movement has emerged in which women are now denouncing the fact that it is only men who have interpreted Islamic law over the centuries; they are demanding the right to read and interpret the religious texts for themselves before accepting "traditional" restrictions for women. Sisters in Islam in Malaysia is one such group actively engaged in Qur'anic interpretation and is educating women about what Islam genuinely does and does not teach, while encountering considerable social opposition in the process—as have all feminist advocates throughout history. Brave Saudi women, for example, have rejected the ban on driving cars as totally unsupported by Islamic law and based only on bedouin custom—but they have been punished for threatening the patriarchal order.

Islamist movements differ broadly in their understanding of the role of women. All Islamists stress the importance of women as the "source of light of the home," charged with the vital responsibility of the physical and moral upbringing of children. *Salafi* (fundamentalist) movements tend to be quite literal in their interpretation of the Qur'an and the Traditions (*Hadith*) and impose a highly conservative vision upon women—opposing all mixed sex schooling, mixed sexes working together in the workplace (or women working outside the home at all), imposition of extreme dress codes, opposition to women suffrage (and often opposition to the concept of voting at all). A great middle range of Islamist movements definitely stresses the rights of women to a place in public society but takes a cautious view of how this is to be implemented. But Islamic modernists have been quite clear in stating that any contemporary interpretation of the Qur'an leaves little doubt of the full equality between men and women on all levels, even if there may be some differentiation in social roles.[12]

ISLAMIST MANIPULATION OF BLASPHEMY LAWS

We have talked a great deal about Islamism as an agent of change. But of course there is a traditionalist and even opportunist face of Islamism as well, which has upheld traditionalist treatment of social and women's issues and blocked progress. Worst of all, the traditionalists have promoted and exploited blasphemy laws in Islam to intimidate freedom of speech and inquiry on Islam. The last thing the Muslim world needs today is further closing down of intellectual freedom and the right to debate varying interpretations of Islam.

What is traditional in Islamic society is not necessarily based on thoughtful examination of Islamic texts—this is the point made by many Islamist feminists. Yet many fundamentalists and other conservative Islamists often end up defending even traditional practice of Islam in social issues, particularly those involving the family and women. Saudi Arabia and Afghanistan are outstanding cases but hardly unique. In Egypt many Islamists have accepted, or at least not rejected, the practice of female circumcision, conflating it with "Islam," even though some senior clerics have explicitly stated that the practice is not sanctioned by Islam. The Muslim Brotherhood of Kuwait opposed the right of women to vote—after long internal debate. These practices say more about traditional social practice in the region than they do about Islam.

One of the most egregious and damaging roles played by some Islamists within relatively open political systems like Kuwait, Pakistan, and Egypt has been in the area of limiting intellectual freedom—perhaps some of the harshest measures taken in many centuries against intellectual inquiry within the faith, sometimes against avowed secularists but sometimes against well-qualified and distinguished modernist Islamic scholars. They have ruthlessly attacked and instituted legal proceedings against any writings on Islam they disagree with. Thus serious novelists as well as Islamic scholars have been persecuted in Egypt by Islamists who have also taken the lead in banning the publication of books and calling for punishment of authors who produce them. Egyptian Nobel Prize winner Naguib Mahfouz has been harassed and physically attacked; novelist Salahaddin Muhsin was sentenced to three years hard labor for writings that "offended Islam"; feminist novelist Nawal al-Sa'dawi has been repeatedly tried in court for anti-Islamic writing and her husband ordered to divorce her as a Muslim apostate, although the charges were ultimately struck down; Islamist lawyers also charged Islamic and Arabic literature professor Nasr Abu Zayd with apostasy for his writings on the background of the Qur'an, and his wife was ordered to divorce him. He left Egypt to avoid further harassment and potential attack; the case against him was ultimately overruled in an appeal. Thus the good news is that the Egyptian court system has in several cases overruled charges brought by zealous Islamists, but the bad news is that zealous Islamists have been engaged in such activities in various states, often with the intent of embarrassing the state by "out-Islaming" it. Many issues are reduced to vehicles of a simple struggle of the Islamists against the state. Hopefully their legal defeats will gradually undermine this effort at politicizing issues of freedom of speech. In Pakistan blasphemy laws against Islam have been badly abused and used as tools for persecution of liberals and Christians.

Thus political Islam has been employed in the interests of the most reactionary elements of society that stifle progress and the elevation of education and society. It has pandered to some of the worst tendencies of censorship and the closing down of the mind. Islamists have been opportunistic in adopting maximalist positions in order to gain political ground and to ensure that they are not outflanked on religious grounds and that they can maintain their position as "defenders of Islam." The lure of blanket condemnation on Islamic grounds is widespread among those Islamists who find it easier to ban than to think or to grapple with the hard work of modernizing within the framework of tradition.

ISLAMISM SERVING THE STATE

Political Islam largely functions as a movement from the bottom-up, challenging the state and the political status quo, but it can also play quite the opposite role in providing legitimacy to the state. Nearly all political leaders across the Muslim world use Islam in an effort to legitimize themselves. Muslims are not unusual in this respect: political leaders around the world—Catholic, Protestant, Jewish, Hindu, Buddhist, Shinto—seek to associate themselves with religious institutions and the power of spiritualism to enhance their own political standing. The Saudi royal family established its legitimacy of rule several hundred years ago as the sword of governance by propagating and defending the Wahhabi sect; it clings to that role even today. Even in officially secular Turkey, numerous political leaders ensure they are associated with public piety. Other leaders claim bloodline descent from the family of the Prophet, such as the Hashemites in Jordan, and the king of Morocco. Adopting laws that favor religion is also seen as an act of piety benefiting the leader, in republics as well as monarchies. Even Saddam Hussein reached for Islamic slogans to shore up his despotism in times of trouble.

III. FUNCTIONS OF POLITICAL ISLAM IN FOREIGN POLICY

ANTI-IMPERIALISM

Islamism has played a key role in the anti-colonial and anti-imperialist struggle across the Muslim world. It powerfully inspires national liberation movements, particularly when Muslims are pitted against non-Muslim rule or when foreign powers threaten Islamic independence and Muslim well-being, whether politically, economically, or culturally. The dominant imperialist threat traditionally came from the West, but today it comes predominantly from Russia, China, India, Serbia, Israel, and the Philippines; all are seen as colonial or imperialist forces involved in oppression or control of Muslim minorities. Even violations of civil rights of Muslims in the United States or Europe are closely followed, documented, and widely disseminated through Islamist channels in the press and on the Internet.

Islamist movements are likely to remain the foremost champions of oppressed Muslims around the world. Not surprisingly, their attention in these cases is single-mindedly focused on Muslims: they rarely show any interest in other Third World national liberation movements or oppression of minorities elsewhere if they do not involve Muslims. Islamists in power, however, demonstrate pragmatism in choosing which ideological concerns to highlight or let fade given the broader national interest—*raison d'etat.* Iran, for example, has been stunningly silent about Chechens in Russia, or Uyghur in China, simply because the Iranian state has important strategic ties with both China and Russia that need to be preserved in the state interest. Iran has astonishingly even supported Christian Armenia against Shi'ite Azerbaijan and has been careful not to lend too much support to Islamist Tajiks in Tajikistan, where the language is basically a dialect of Persian. Sudan, too, in its isolation is careful about not supporting Muslims in China or Russia at a time when it needs the support of these states. Islamist parties or movements not in power, however, lack these constraints. In this regard Islamists are no different than any other ideological parties in the world, demonstrating the duality of behavior between movements and governments. When Islamists are in power they demonstrate the same ideological dilemma as did the Soviets, for example, who frequently abandoned support to foreign communist parties when it served Soviet national interests to cooperate with the governments that were oppressing them.

PAN-ISLAMISM

Islamists in principle are dedicated to a clear pan-Islamist outlook and support for all Muslims. Arab states may show concern for some other Arab Muslims but this is based on ethnic—or geopolitical—interests rather than a religious basis. Even Islamists, however, cannot avoid the calculus of national state interests in looking at pan-Islamic issues. Iran and Saudi Arabia are the two globally active Muslim powers with a pan-Islamic vision, but the approaches of the two states on this issue differ sharply: Iran has been far more revolutionary in its policies, whereas Saudi Arabia has tended to support the status quo leadership in the Muslim world. On the other hand, the Kingdom has for decades sought to maintain a monopoly of support to Wahhabi-like radical Islamist groups, not all of which are violent, in the hopes of denying control to others and to prevent the radicals from attacking the Kingdom; the story of al-Qa'ida demonstrates how patently this policy has failed. The difference between Iranian and Saudi approaches is directly linked to the state interest rather than related to ideological differences between Shi'ite and Sunni Islam. The geopolitical interests of the two states are in direct competition, Islam or no Islam.

Other states competing more modestly in the pan-Islamist arena are Pakistan, Libya, and Sudan. To one degree or another, however, nearly every Islamist *movement* maintains ties with others, compares notes on tactics, and discusses ideological and strategic issues. And some movements, most notably the Muslim Brotherhood and the Jama'at-i Islami, function as an international organization with autonomous branch parties in a number of countries, all in close touch with each other. This should not be taken as a sinister relationship when movements are non-violent, any more than the Socialist International is a forum for world democratic socialist parties to compare notes and strategies.

IDEOLOGICAL ATTACK ON OTHER MUSLIM REGIMES

Political Islam in power also provides ideological foundation for verbal attacks on other Muslim states by targeting the Islamic legitimacy of neighboring regimes. Iran and Sudan in their early days both sharply criticized neighboring regimes as un-Islamic, or even illegitimate. Afghanistan's Taleban were far more restrained in this respect and less internationally oriented.

It is generally harder for Islamist movements out of power to undertake significant moves against neighboring regimes since they lack the resources of the state to back them up. The Muslim Brotherhood in Egypt expresses verbal support for its affiliated movements in other countries when they are in conflict with the local state. The Muslim Brotherhood organization has also been routinely accused of funding other Islamist movements in the Muslim world—not necessarily radical or violent ones. The Jama'at-i Islami in Pakistan has lent financial support to like-minded parties in Bangladesh, and to some *mujahidin* groups in Afghanistan. The FIS movement in Algeria, after being denied an election victory in 1991, has been critical of other states that repress their Islamist movements, such as Tunisia and Egypt.

Thus Islamist ideology, as any other ideology, can be used widely as an instrument in international relations to attack, delegitimize, or create unity of purpose. And as with all other ideologies and principles, it is often applied selectively in accordance with the immediate interests of the state or the movement.

CONCLUSION

We have examined the many and varied functions of political Islam that extend far beyond its appeal in a purely religious context. Yet it would be a mistake to think of political Islam as merely one end of a spectrum, the other end of which is "secularism." *In the real politics of the Muslim world these two concepts are not necessarily polarities at all, nor do they represent ultimate alternatives between which Muslims must choose.* Many of the functions of Islamism discussed above can and do appear as functions of other ideologies as well—nationalism, communism, and liberalism, for example. Political Islam appears in many forms and can be peaceful or violent, democratic or authoritarian, radical or moderate, traditional or modernist. *Secular movements can be equally radical, violent, racist, or authoritarian as well. Certainly most Muslims do not think of Islamist parties as the alternative to secular parties, but rather as one of many political alternatives, to be judged on the basis of their current program and effectiveness.*

The political culture of the Muslim world today places maximum emphasis upon certain key values: social justice, the need for a moral compass, preservation of Muslim culture, restoration of the power and dignity of the Muslim world, strength against external threatening powers, legitimacy of government, social welfare, economic justice, and clean and effective government. However, *at the mass level we do not see debate focusing upon the relative desirability of an Islamic state versus a secular state.* This is not the real issue. The real debate is about which system of government or which party will facilitate attainment of these key values and goals.

Thus competing ideologies may ultimately offer much the same programs, although achieved in part by different means and employing different language. The secular agenda speaks a largely Western vocabulary that is the property of a small Westernized elite. Even if its goals are similar to those of the Islamists, its rhetoric does not resonate among the mass public as Islam does. The larger public, however, will not choose among competing parties on the basis of Islam per se, but on a party's leadership, clean hands, or its ability to deliver. The public is accustomed to the Islamic vocabulary parties use in articulating these goals.

Nor are Islamists automatically viewed as the authentic bearer of Islamic values in all respects. They too have to prove themselves. There clearly is a pragmatic streak in much political thinking in the Muslim world. If an ideology has "already been tried" and failed, this will push people to try an alternative. For example, the defeat of leading Arab states in the 1967 Arab-Israeli war served as a catalyst to the perception that Arab nationalism had been "tried and found wanting" as a means of facing the Israeli challenge, strengthening the Arab world, bringing good governance, and raising living standards. This opened space for the Islamist alternative. In October 1999 in Pakistan the military takeover was in part supported by the popular perception that "democracy had been tried" and it "did not work." "Islamism" has now "been tried" in Iran, Sudan, and Afghanistan and has not succeeded (although Iran is still dramatically evolving) sparking the quest for an alternative approach in those countries at the popular level. Of course none of these ideologies has truly been tried and found wanting; only their interpretation and application under a specific set of leaders and conditions have been tested and seen to fail. Ideologies may or may not be flawed, but the leadership, application, and specifics are everything.

Thus political experience is a key determinant in affecting people's choice for the "next" ideology or the "next" party to vote for. Islamism in most states is viewed as untested and thus enjoys the additional advantage of no track record, hence no baggage. Furthermore, Islamism in each state is perceived as different because of the different natures of the parties, their leadership, and their political dynamics, all seen against the specific conditions of the country. Once political Islam has been "tried" in a given country, the chances are that it too will have delivered a mixed set of results that can then be debated and evaluated by others, and it will no longer have the freshness and attractive, untested quality that it does today. *But people will not be choosing the Islamists because they want an Islamic state so much as they want results that will achieve other goals they seek,* including issues of morality and religious tradition. But nothing can make Islamism seem unappealing faster than an unsuccessful stint in power.

In short, there are a number of important aspects of political Islam:

- When religion in politics clearly finds some resonance among the public, it is an indication that it meets some need that is otherwise not being effectively met by other political parties or ideologies.
- Islamism encompasses a broad spectrum, not necessarily coherent or consistent across movements, and is not at all monolithic; various movements are sometimes even in conflict with each other.
- Most of these movements tend to be functionally progressive—that is, whatever the ideology, they are functionally working for change rather than support of the status quo, and they introduce modern political ideas and practices even if in Islamic garb.
- Islamists disagree about the priorities to be attached to the competing goals of national liberation, democratization, community defense, change of regime, reform, defense of Islam, and other agendas.
- There are major contradictions between the ideology and practice of Islamism out of power and Islamism in power—reflecting the dilemma of any ideological program in power that must balance among the interests of the country, the interests of the state, and the interests of the ideological movement itself.
- Both radicals and moderates within the Islamist movement seek to exploit the same body of thinking and to rationalize their activities, even with quite different policies.

- The broad range of political and social activity makes it ever harder to say what exactly political Islam is. Each case will differ. Western governments should therefore lay less emphasis on whether a group is or is not Islamist, but rather focus on what it actually *does*.

Political Islam covers such a range of roles and positions that it frustrates summation in a single coherent whole. These are simply different Islamisms or different aspects of Islamism. When seen in this light, most popular Western attempts to characterize Islamism are inevitably simplistic and selective, often verging on caricature and worse, they are analytically unhelpful.

It is clearly *incorrect, then, to think of political Islam as a fixed ideology to be accepted or rejected as a whole*. It does not offer any predictable systematic or comprehensive set of programs, institutions, or style of leadership—except the regular, near obligatory call for "Islamic government" or an "Islamic state." What these terms mean precisely is not known since history has never seen a truly Islamic state to date. Different parties interpret the concept differently.

What the West objects to most about the handful of Islamist states today in any case is not truly the domestic policies related to Shari'a—which affect the West but little—but rather the implications for the international order, which do not stem directly from the principles of Islam but from geopolitical rivalry. In this respect the West, especially the United States, bears equal responsible for how the tone of initial bilateral relations are set with Islamist states in what is usually a minuet of the suspicious.

In the end there is little analytic accuracy or value in thinking of political Islam primarily in terms of a specific ideology as many claim. Islamism's embrace of such a broad spectrum of agendas suggests that we are dealing here with something far looser and vaguer than a specific ideology. Islamism is really a variety of political movements, principles, and philosophies that draw general inspiration from Islam but produce different agendas and programs at different times, often quite contradictory. Ideology is far too precise and coherent a term to apply to this variety of movements, although some of the more extreme ones do produce something akin to an ideology, however shallow. It is popular, for example, to contrast Islamism and liberal democracy. Yet they are not at all necessarily at opposite ends of a political spectrum. Islamism essentially proffers an Islamic cultural vehicle for the expression of a broad variety of social and political needs. The form of Islamist expression assumed locally reflects the local political culture and the needs and aspirations of that particular society under a specific leadership at a specific time. Islamists will be more nationalist and prickly toward the West almost for sure, but they will likely be pragmatic here as well if they do not feel they confront an existential challenge from the United States.

Islamism in its world-view, then, is capable of assuming a variety of political forms. None of these options is by definition included or excluded simply by reference to Islam itself. The positions most Islamist movements assume on a variety of political issues are not unique to Islamism. In the Muslim world these positions stem from the deeper impulses of the cultural experience of that Muslim country that can indeed include an anti-Western bias based on past experience.

A Muslim liberal democracy, for example, might be no less fervent in defense of Muslim interests, traditions, and values against foreign encroachment. (Observe how France and Japan fiercely defend their respective cultures.) Should not Muslim liberal democracy object equally to foreign economic policies that are seen as threatening to its own interests, just as the United States reacts harshly to certain Japanese or EU economic policies? Muslim liberals would share much of the Islamist domestic agenda on issues of reform, social and economic justice, civil society, answerable government, rights of political representation, and religious freedom from the state.

Thus as Islamist parties evolve they are in the process of absorbing many different programmatic elements; these may eventually come to include major elements of liberal democracy as their preferred political vehicle in constructing the architecture of the state. Some Islamists already argue this case. But some are moving in the opposite direction as their narrow vision and local pressures push them toward reaction, intolerance, radicalism, and even violence. The variety of Islamist expression is what is most striking and it is all in a process of evolution and change.

3

ISLAMIST POLARITIES

THE SPECTRUM OF ISLAMIST thought grows ever wider and more diverse—a positive development since it opens the door to greater internal debate, evolution, and consideration of the future path of Islamist politics.

I employ a broad definition of an Islamist to denote anyone who believes that Islam has something important to say about how political and social life should be constituted and who attempts to implement that interpretation in some way. Reflecting diverse interpretations, Islamists vary politically across a wide spectrum. Movements differ in their acceptance or rejection of violence, their choice to work openly or underground, the urgency with which they insist that change must come, the degree of political engagement they pursue within the system, the institutions they build and operate from, their preference for either an elite or a mass structure, their ideological or pragmatic nature, their degree of flexibility in attaining goals, and the degree of transparency and democracy in their internal proceedings. This is as true of secular political movements as it is of religiously based ones.

Most analyses of Islamist movements are naturally replete with references to various schools, trends, and branches. There are differing criteria representing many different positions along a spectrum. Many terms overlap or are imprecise, and they employ differing types of measurements in their classifications. As in Protestant Christianity, defining the differences among various sects is not easy or always clear-cut, and definitions can overlap. The main aim of this discussion is to suggest something of the range of schools and ideas involved, especially at the two ends of the spectrum—fundamentalist and liberal Islam.

The most familiar group within Islam are the *traditionalists* who basically accept Islam as it has evolved historically in each local culture. They are aware of accretions of pre-Islamic or local practice in the daily practice of faith, but they accept these as long as they are not openly anti-Islamic in character. The traditionalists cannot be considered to be Islamist since they have no specific agenda of political change, do not seek to shake up the system, and are generally accepting of existing political authority as a reality of life. The long tradition of Islam carries great weight in their thinking. As John Voll points out, the traditionalists (or conservatives) seek *to hold the lid down on too rapid change;* they represent a force of conservation and preservation, a critical factor of cultural and community coherence and continuity in times of turmoil. But this school will also adapt to new conditions when necessary to keep Islam alive.[1]

Fundamentalists, on the other hand, are not traditionalists, oppose the status quo, and represent the most conservative element among Islamists. They seek to correct contemporary (mis)understandings of Islam, and to return to basic texts (Qur'an and *Hadith*) to understand the faith as literally written for all time. They represent rigorous adherence to the rules of the faith.[2] This literalism represents a quest for purity in the practice of Islam. They usually seek to establish an Islamic state, although just what such a state should look like is not at all clear beyond acceptance of Islamic law. Most fundamentalists eschew violence, but some very radical ones employ it.

For fundamentalists the law is the most essential component of Islam, leading to an overwhelming emphasis upon jurisprudence, usually narrowly conceived. They pursue a high degree of social conservatism. On the other hand, fundamentalists, like other Islamists, are also selective in those features of Islam that they seek to emphasize today as part of their political agenda where they have one. They are closely associated with fundamentalism's strictest form, Wahhabism, sometimes also referred to as *salafiyya* (the faith of the founding fathers of the Islamic community). They tend to be highly intolerant toward branches of Islam that do not share their literalism and often even declare others un-Islamic (*kafir*). The fundamentalists, also sometimes referred to as *revivalists* place "emphasis on the Arabic language as the language of revelation, the illegitimacy of local political institutions (as usurpers of God's sovereignty), the authority of the revivalists as the sole qualified interpreters of Islam, sometimes drastic expression of personal piety, and the revival of practices from the early period of Islam."[3]

The fundamentalists stress precise and full compliance with the absolute totality of Islam in order to be a valid Muslim. Indeed, in radical Wahhabi thinking, acceptance of 99 percent of Islamic teachings but deliberate rejection of 1 percent constitutes unbelief. This fierceness of belief is indeed a stark interpretation, since Islam states quite categorically that one Muslim may not judge the validity of *private* belief of another Muslim; judgment remains the perquisite of God alone.

The term *reformism* can refer to two different time-honored Islamic concepts: renewal (*tajdid*) which does not mean introducing new elements at all, but refers to renewing the original and more correct understanding of Islam. A second term meaning *reform* (*Islah*) refers not so much to ideas but to reform of society and its mores in an Islamic context.

Islamists debate how far the purview of Islam should extend over life. Some conservatives proceed from the conviction that Islam is a total way of life, an all-embracing vision whereby the sacred transcends everything and figures in all aspects of human existence. The more conservative will even use the Arabic word *din* (religion) in English to denote this transcendent discipline, beyond traditional religion, in which the truly Muslim life is lived only when Islam infuses one's understanding of all of life and politics. Insistence that religion informs all aspects of life is a declaration that Islam dictates everything. Yet if all aspects of life are sacred, then in effect nothing can be singled out as truly sacred. Few Islamists in practice insist on this kind of sacralization of all of life.

Different scholars and Islamists debate these terms or use others to differentiate among various gradations and inclinations of belief including *neo-Islamist, radical Islamist, salafi Islamist,* and others. What is important is not that scholars should agree on labels, but that they should agree that these specific types of differing phenomena do exist, regardless of how one might choose to label them. It is important to remember, too, that all of these terms are ideological abstractions; few fit neatly into the total descriptive portrait of an individual, and an Islamist's behavior can differ significantly depending on the conditions under which he is placed. This phenomenon is no more esoteric than it is to use terms like *liberal* and *conservative, radical* and *moderate,* and to expect every Western politician to fit into a neat, fully definitive box. The real world trumps academic definitions. For practical purposes an awareness of this range of differences is what matters.

The same cautions apply to the *Modernist* side of the Islamist spectrum. In general, modernists place greatest emphasis on contemporary interpretation of the Qur'an and the Traditions. Contemporary interpretation particularly emphasizes the viewing of all language in these texts strictly in the *historical context of events of the period,* from which they try to derive basic underlying principles over and above the specific historical events and contexts, placing context over text. This examination of context should enable one to capture the true essence, universal and timeless, of the Islamic "message" that can then be interpreted and applied in the light of contemporary conditions. Important elements of this broad approach view the revelation of Islam, and particularly the Prophet's interpretation and application of it to communal life as a universal message but one inextricably linked to seventh-century Arabia, and dealing with the immediate problems of that time and place. Understanding the broader message and implications of those revelations for today requires thoughtful interpretation.

Cases in point: the Prophet's statement that wearing silk is undesirable. During his time silk was an ostentatious luxury in Arabia; in today's Indonesia, for example, silk clothing is commonplace and need no longer be treated as undesirable for Muslims. Similarly, some Muslims argue that the Prophet's ban on interest was really a ban on usury (as in Christianity), and that his ban on interest, taken literally by many Muslims, has little to do with modern banking interest or the price of money on the market.

Islamic *modernism* comes in diverse forms. A key early school of Islamic philosophical thought long ago abandoned is the *Mu'tazilite* rationalists. That school of thought is currently undergoing a rebirth and reinterpretation. The *rationalists,* as their name implies, today seek to restore intellect and rationality to the center of Islamic understanding. They are making a comeback, reopening the basic *Mu'tazilite* belief that God granted mankind reason and expects him to use it in understanding the message of Islam. The rationalists are willing to introduce a considerable degree of *ijtihad* (interpretation) into the contemporary understanding of Islam.

Many Islamists seek to creatively link the Muslim present to the Muslim past. One form of this is known in Arabic as *Usuliyya,* almost a literal translation of "fundamentalism." The *Usulis* too seek to return to the early roots or origins of Islam, but not through their literal application today. Instead, *Usulis* argue that contemporary Muslim life and practice should derive directly from the original principles and practice of Islam as it would be understood under contemporary conditions; they reject new borrowings from Western constructs or practice, but not interpretations of Islam accommodating modernity. Their chief problem has been that the body of recorded events from the days of the Prophet available to serve as precedents are too few in number and variety to serve as models or precedents to meet the vast range of contemporary demands of Muslim life. As a result, the *Usulis* have been forced to create their own interpretations of Islam on contemporary issues that simply could not be derived out of Islamic precedent, thereby diluting their philosophical approach.[4]

Muslim *liberals* represent another form of modernism and form a major school of thought, especially in modern times: "Liberal Islam, like revivalist Islam, defines itself in contrast to the customary tradition and calls upon the precedent of the early period of Islam in order to delegitimate present-day practices. Yet liberal Islam calls upon the past in the name of modernity, while revivalists might be said to call upon modernity (for example, electronic technologies) in the name of the past. . . . The liberal tradition argues that Islam, properly understood, is compatible with—or even a precursor to—Western liberalism."[5]

Many modernist Islamists object strongly to being referred to as *liberals* because they believe it carries connotations, at least in the Muslim world, of permissiveness, or casualness toward belief. They therefore prefer the term *modernist* or *moderate.* I respect their concerns, but believe that for Western readers the term *liberal* too has some descriptive value."

Islamic *mysticism* remains an ancient tradition in Islam, particularly at the folk level, usually referred to as *Sufism* (*tasawwuf*). Sufis may or may not be considered Islamists depending on the degree of political activism, but most focus on the faith of the inner being. Sufism has proven to be the most accessible form of Islam to many Westerners, particularly in the works of the poet Rumi, surprisingly the best-selling poet in the United States. Sufism emphasizes spiritual values, ecstatic and direct perception of God, and the heart of the believer and his or her love of God. Sufis often place higher priority upon inspiration and love than upon law. Many Sufi groups can be classed as modernist in their interest in dealing hands-on with social problems as they exist and in placing emphasis on gaining converts to Islam from among non-Muslims through this accessible form. Ironically, it is the Sufis today who are more concerned with gaining new converts to Islam than other Islamists, most of whom emphasize purification of the faith among *existing* Muslims. Sufi orders run a broad gamut of belief and practice. Despite a mystical orientation, they can often be conservative as well as liberal in their approach to social issues or be seriously involved in politics as some orders in Turkey, Egypt, Sudan, and elsewhere. Fundamentalists are usually quite hostile to Sufism, seeing it as an impure tradition, compromising Islam with local religious practice and tainted by an inclination to deemphasize the requirements of Islamic law and an engagement in saint worship, strongly offensive to fundamentalists.

Let's now examine more closely the two polarities of the Islamic ideological spectrum: Islamic radicals and Islamic liberals. The rationales of both groups are important to the future of political Islam.

ISLAMIC RADICALISM

All Islamist radicals are fundamentalist—that is, they accept narrow, literal, and intolerant interpretations of Islam, but most go an extra step in either promoting utopian visions of a pan-Islamic state or advocating violent action. Islamic radicalism actually occupies a small segment of the Islamist intellectual and political spectrum but derives great importance from its militancy and the sometimes violent actions that can include major acts of terrorism that a still smaller group of activists are willing to carry out. For this reason, radicals naturally attract disproportionate attention from the state and the international order.

The rationale and ideological foundation of radicalism is usually traced to the twentieth-century Egyptian Islamist Sayyid Qutb, whose views have been of profound importance in establishing the modern radical vision of Islam. Qutb, a member of the Muslim Brotherhood when it was still a radical and violent movement under the conditions of Egypt from the 1940s to the 1960s, borrowed a concept from the medieval Islamic scholar Ibn Taymiyya to categorize Muslim society as living in *jahiliyya* or "a state of ignorance" that is, bereft of true Islam. In Islamic writing the term "state of ignorance" originally referred strictly to pre-Islamic pagan society in Arabia. But first in Ibn Taymiyya's usage and then in Qutb's, the term "state of ignorance" is now, with shock effect, applied to *contemporary* Muslim society when it neglects the "true" message of Islam and in effect still lives "in ignorance." Contemporary Muslim society itself can thus be condemned as "infidel" (*kafir*), leading to a process of anathematization or excommunication (*takfir*) of society. When the state itself is perceived to be effectively in the hands of "unbelievers" (unrighteous, irreligious, corrupt, arrogant puppets of the West), then nearly all means are justified to overcome the state including armed struggle, which they refer to in this context as jihad.

Radical Islamist organizations operating from this basic philosophical context either declare jihad against the state itself, or condemn it as infidel (*takfir al-dawla*) and withdraw or "emigrate" (*hijra*) from impure society. We find some interesting parallels among radical Christian Protestant sects at the time of the Reformation who chose to reject the impurity of the established church and society and to live in isolated "communities of God" under laws derived strictly from the Bible. Some even practiced violence against the state.

A key ideological principle of the radicals is the concept of jihad as a "sixth pillar" of Islam, made popular in the 1950s by 'Abd-al-Salam Muhammad al-Faraj in his manuscript *Jihad: the Forgotten Obligation*. This thesis urges Muslims to undertake direct jihad (struggle, violent or non-violent) against its enemies in order to strive for creation of a unified *umma*. Those who reject Islamic law for Western law are apostates and enemies. Perpetual jihad against the infidel state—a state run by someone who claims to be Muslim but who is not true to Islam—is the highest obligation and the only solution for the creation of a Muslim society. Whether the struggle should be conducted directly against the impure Muslim state or against the source of its support and endurance, the United States, is a topic of ideological debate. Islamic Jihad in Egypt initially fought strictly against the Egyptian state whereas Usama bin Ladin saw the United States as the root source of the survival of the corrupt Saudi state. These radicals believe that failure to engage in jihad and to strengthen the Muslim world is the primary reason for Muslim weakness today.[6]

Radicals can also be divided between those with a transnational orientation and those who see local politics within their own country as the primary arena for action. Those whose driving goal is to build a pan-Islamist politically unified *umma* are usually quite diffuse, constituting movements and not parties, and therefore are not players in the official politics of individual states. They tend to be underground and not overt, in part because of state repression of their movements. While most Islamists would love to see a politically unified *umma,* this remains a distant and probably unattainable ideal and their behavior is accordingly local and practical, hence pragmatic and non-utopian. Most see the *umma's* emergence not as a single state but as a region of self-consciously shared culture engaging in broad interaction on a variety of levels.

Not all transnational movements are necessarily violent or radically pan-Islamic in their rejection of existing states. Some, like the Muslim Brotherhood and its South Asian sister organization, the Jama'at-i Islami, are linked in representation in multiple Muslim countries yet are mainstream among Islamists and do not practice violence. (An exception is Hamas in Palestine, an offshoot of the Muslim Brotherhood that is engaged in a national liberation struggle against foreign non-Muslim occupation, in which case violence is widely perceived by all Muslims to be justified.)

Radical and fundamentalist views in intellectual and practical terms fail to come to terms with contemporary thought and offer few solutions for the outstanding problems Muslims face. They will inevitably face marginalization among Muslim communities that seek genuine workable answers to their problems. But that does not mean that in the interim their ideas may not strike chords among embittered and frustrated Muslim communities and become the vehicle for their grievances and expression of political impotence, thus leading to potentially serious violence.

Some Islamist conservatives or hard-liners argue that their duty is to struggle against exactly those liberal formulations of Islam that reformists and many Westerners propose, insisting that Islam and the *umma* will prosper only through close adherence to the fundamentals of Islam and in opposition to the modernist, secularizing, and globalizing trends of the world that are designed to weaken Islam. They perceive "reform" of Christianity and its liberalization, for example, as having contributed directly to its social decline. They ask whether it is appropriate for religion to "conform with the realities" of contemporary societies if those societies are perceived to be morally degenerate or failing.

The age of radical Islam is far from over since contemporary political, social and economic conditions serve to create a radicalizing environment in the Muslim world that facilitates the recruitment of alienated individuals ready to carry out violent acts.

THE LIBERAL ISLAMIST RATIONALE

A liberal, modernist, and open mode of thinking about Islam is not yet the dominant trend among Islamists of the world. But the trend is growing with time, particularly as the need for a creative response to the realities and challenges facing the community grows ever more evident.

Islamist modernism represents an analytic approach, not a specific body of belief, and it can vary in results. As such, Islamic modernism lies at the opposite end of the spectrum from fundamentalism in terms of its willingness to maximize interpretation to derive new understandings of Islamic texts. Both fundamentalism and modernism are going back to roots in their insistence on change of understanding of Islam, but their methodology is vastly different, and they reach sharply differing conclusions and embrace markedly different practices.

A *modernist* and *pluralist* Islamist approach accepts the near-universal values of democracy, human rights, pluralism, and vibrant civil society as fully compatible with Islam and inherent in Islam's own original multiculturalism. Islamic liberals argue that these values simply could not emerge over the centuries when international values were different and when the theological and power structures of the Muslim world were in the hands of authoritarian regimes that interpreted Islamic law to their own benefit. Their primary goal is reinterpretation of the texts to create a modern understanding of Islam compatible with most contemporary political values.[7]

Advocates of a modernist approach to Islam may differ among themselves on their goals, but they agree on a call for intellectual freedom that would permit exploration of all aspects of the faith in order to better understand it and to improve Muslim society and its political order. Liberal or modernist Muslims ideally seek to generate new political ideas out of the Islamic framework itself. But they recognize too that Western experience is worthy of close examination since it already possesses a solid body of political thinking developed over the centuries that is complemented by an equally rich body of pragmatic experience in its institutional application. While Western models may be imperfect, this body of thought and experience addresses many of the very issues Muslims themselves are grappling with. Indeed, these ideas are not necessarily "Western" *per se* since they build on political thinking of several millennia, drawing on diverse heritages. They represent the intellectual evolution and universal patrimony of all mankind. But these ideas and institutions did happen to flower first in modern form in the West due to specific cultural and historical conditions. Islamist modernists can adopt many of these values as universal, but they are opposed by many conservative Muslims suspicious of the "Western" origin of these thoughts. There is no reason why Muslims cannot work to find Islamic pathways to the same goals that they admire in Western governance. Some Islamists mention that the U.S. Constitution comes the closest yet of any document to approaching what they think an ideal Islamic state should resemble.

As Islamist modernists seek to reopen atrophied channels of Islamic religious and political thought, they provide a clear rationale of how to justify it. The rough line of modernist Islamist argument is as follows:

- God bestowed upon mankind the power of intellect, rationality, and freedom of choice, which He clearly intended for humans to employ, even at the risk of erring periodically.
- Each individual must find his or her way to awareness of God and the message of Islam. No one can be compelled into belief. Nor can the state impose the religious message upon individuals (Qur'an: *La ikrah fi 'l-din*—there is no compulsion in religion). An understanding of God's message and a willingness to live in His way can only come through personal awareness, choice and conviction. To follow Islamic rituals under compulsion destroys most of the merit and value of those rituals for the individual because they were not freely and willingly chosen.
- Human understanding of God's message in the Qur'an has changed and grown over time, but is never perfect. Just as today's knowledge and understanding of God's creation and plan is richer today than it was in seventh-century Arabia, mankind will have a still better understanding of God's message in the future than today. It will also be understood in different ways in accordance with the needs, concerns, and circumstances of each generation and people.
- No one possesses a full understanding of God's message and purpose. Even though advances will be made, no one ever will attain perfect understanding. Therefore no one can claim to possess a monopoly on understanding God or

Islam; indeed, no one has the right to make such claims, which can only be self-serving.

- A democratic state offers maximum opportunities for freedom of study, discussion, and debate of religion—a process that best enables the individual and society to understand God's message and its relevance to constructing a just society.

The key instrument in achieving an understanding of Islam in the context of contemporary life is through the time-honored method of *ijtihad* or interpretation of the texts. Since the beginning of Islam, *ijtihad* by scholars has been a primary means of applying basic Islamic principles to new situations never addressed by Islam before, through extension or extrapolation of their primary meaning. In other words, if alcohol is seen as forbidden, then modern psychedelic drugs by extension fall into this category. But there is debate within Islam about just how far *ijtihad* can or should be extended to issues that have already been "resolved" by Muslim scholars in the past. How much is a "new" reading of old issues valid? How far can contemporary scholars reinterpret standing interpretations? Many modernist Islamists claim that past interpretations by Islamic scholars lack any inherent authority and are of interest and worthy of respect only as a reflection of the Muslim experience in the past. They are in no way binding or necessarily even relevant to contemporary needs.

UNDERSTANDING SHARI'A

An equally important debate surrounds the centrality of Shari'a in the building of an Islamic society or state, in which the very understanding of the word Shari'a is of crucial importance. In the Qur'an the word Shari'a means "way" or "path." It states that God bestowed upon every religion, teacher, and prophet a "shari'a" or path *toward* understanding of God. In the language of the Qur'an, "We [God] gave you one religion, but We gave every one of you his own Shari'a." (Sura 4:84). It was only later in Islamic history that legal scholars began to use the word Shari'a to apply to the body of Muslim jurisprudence, its various commentaries and interpretations. Yet, many modernists argue, jurisprudence is entirely man-made, written by Muslim scholars according to their various schools, based on their best understanding of how the Qur'an should be translated into codes of law.[8] Muhammad Sa'id al-'Ashmawi, a specialist in comparative and Islamic law at Cairo University, argues that "The term Shari'a, as used in the Qur'an, refers *not to legal rules* but rather to the path of Islam consisting of three streams: 1) worship, 2) ethical code, and 3) social intercourse [italics mine]."[9]

Thus al-'Ashmawi and many other modernists insist that the Shari'a is very different than Islamic jurisprudence (*fiqh*) and that *fiqh* must be reinterpreted anew by scholars in every age in accordance with their understanding that this man-made compendium reflects a variety of understandings appropriate only to its own time. Many modernists thus insist that blanket acceptance of the existing body of Islamic jurisprudence is highly debatable, has been subject to a great variety of opinions over time on some quite basic issues (equality of men and women, punishments, and women's dress) and must be subject to constant interpretation. Many would argue that there is no specific Shari'a, only derivations of the concept as practiced in Saudi Arabia or Iran, for example. There is no one Shari'a but rather many different, even contesting ways to build a legal structure in accordance with God's vision for mankind. A single Shari'a doesn't exist. It is not a book that one can purchase.[10] It is formed, shaped, and interpreted by humans' differing understanding of what the Qur'an and the Prophet's life and experience means.

Sudanese cleric 'Abdallahi Ahmad an-Na'im argues that implementing the *spirit* and overall intent of the Qur'an as understood today must take precedence over selective, historically conditioned rulings by clerics under past conditions no longer pertinent to today. He insists that thoroughgoing reconsideration of the intent of the Qur'an is essential. In speaking of the traditional death penalty for apostasy in Islam, an-Na'im states: "[T]oleration of unorthodoxy and dissent is vital for the spiritual and intellectual benefit of Islam itself. The shari'a law of apostasy can easily be abused and has been abused in the past to suppress political opposition and inhibit spiritual an intellectual growth. This aspect of *shari'a* is fundamentally inconsistent with the numerous provisions of the Qur'an and *sunna* which enjoin freedom of religion and expression."[11]

Egyptian cleric Shaykh Yusif al-Qaradawi has commented that "one of most serious problems is failure of some religious people to observe that the *ahkam* [judgments] of al-Shariah are not equally important or permanent and therefore, different interpretations can be permitted."[12] In Turkey, the Islamist Ak party has many members who speak of Shari'a as a *metaphor for a moral society.* While many Muslims might not agree with such a broad interpretation, these thoughts indicate the kind of thinking underway that seeks to break Islamic interpretation free of the dominance of narrow legalists. Islam is obviously a great deal more than law, and its spirit far transcends the jurisprudence of earlier centuries with which it is no longer in tune.

THE DILEMMA OF 'ULAMA VERSUS MODERN ISLAMIC INTELLECTUALS

Throughout most of Muslim history the 'ulama were the primary if not sole interpreters of Islamic texts and jurisprudence in Islam—this is what they were trained for in a period of limited literacy. But with the bolder emergence of Islamism in the latter half of the twentieth century a new class of "Islamic intellectuals" appeared on the scene many of whom were not trained as clerics at all but possessed advanced degrees in Western disciplines such as engineering and medicine—frequently from Western universities. Their knowledge of Islam is based on their own readings and study of the Qur'an and the Hadith—reminiscent of the Protestant Reformation when Christians were encouraged—indeed, required—to go back to the texts and understand them for themselves. These Islamist intellectuals seek to derive practical and relevant meaning from the Qur'an and the Hadith applicable to current political and social issues. Islamist feminists emerge from this school as well, intent upon liberating true understanding of the Qur'an and Hadith from hoary patriarchal traditions and interpretations that have so long held sway. All these Islamic intellectuals and philosophers today play a major role in the reinterpretation of Islamic thinking. Some of it is modernist, creative, and wise; some of it is primitive, ignorant, and even destructive.

Most Islamist intellectuals challenge the monopoly clerics have over the interpretation of Islam. A liberal, Farooq al-Mawdudi, son of the renowned Abu al-A'la al-Mawdudi, the Pakistani founder of Jama'at-i Islami, takes on the 'ulama quite sharply:

> The Ulama have become the disease of Muslim society. They are the ones who stand in the way of the Muslim scholars and intellectuals who want to revive the intellectual tradition within Islam. Whenever a Muslim scholar raises a new controversial issue, the Ulama are the first ones to accuse him or her of attacking Islam itself. Any attempt to question the dominance of the Ulama is re-interpreted as an attack on Islam. Any attempt to question the outdated fiqh [jurisprudence] of the Ulama is seen as an attack on Islam. How can we Muslims ever develop if we have to face such opposition on a regular basis? Instead of intellectual development and original ideas, the Ulama have merely emphasized the ritualistic aspect of Islam.
>
> [What we need is] a class of revolutionary thinkers, scholars and lay Muslim experts who have broken from the mold of the Ulama of the past. Rather than acting as the watchdogs of the Muslim community, these Muslim intellectuals need to be brave enough to be able to re-think some of our most basic suppositions and adapt them to the needs of today. We cannot go on reproducing the same old legal codes from one thousand years ago.[13]

Few Muslims, Sunni or Shi'a, support the concept of rule by clerics. The problems of clerical rule are manifest and multiple. Issues of statecraft and policy involve far different and broader disciplines than that of textual interpretation and religious jurisprudence. The Malaysian scholar Dr. Farish Noor argues:

[W]hile it is true that the Ulama have performed a great service to Muslim society, culture and civilization, we need to remember that they remain a class of religious savants and functionaries. The Ulama, whose main field of interest and work lies in religious discourse and law, have always been engaged in conservative hermeneutics: theirs is a science of minute and deliberate codification, interpretation and legal reasoning. While this is fine (indeed normal) for the field that they work in, we must also remember what the Ulama are NOT.

The Ulama are not human rights activists. Nor are they necessarily democrats. They do not speak the discourse of rights, but rather the language of religious obligations and moral duties. The educational network that produced them and the institutions that they inhabit are constructed upon hierarchical structures. Furthermore theirs is a science predicated on the terms of a theological-metaphysical discourse that attempts to avoid contamination by Realpolitik and secular, profane concerns. We should therefore not feel ourselves cheated if the Ulama do not talk about matters related to present day concerns.[14]

Nor, as Noor points out, can the *'ulama* claim to "rise above politics" when discussing real political issues, simply because no such realm exists. Similarly, they cannot claim immunity to political attack when they themselves are trading in the coinage of politics. They must play by the rules of the game of democratic politics.

Thus the presence of *'ulama* in politics, *acting as 'ulama,* is clearly unworkable unless they operate as private individuals in accordance with the workings of these state institutions. The proposal to legislate in accordance with Shari'a cannot be declared beyond criticism *when it applies to specific legislation.* All legislation in effect represents some kind of interpretation of *concepts* of Islamic law; any proposed law should naturally therefore be subject to debate by Muslims—a reality linked to the interests of political and social harmony of the community. Debate over this issue ranks high among Islamists.

The *'ulama* thus come under attack on several grounds: (1) their historically close association and complicity with rulers and regimes whose political needs they had to meet—in what in today's parlance might be called a "dial-a-fatwa" response to political exigency; (2) the *'ulama's* frequent ignorance of secular knowledge and the world; (3) their often narrow understanding of Islam based on adherence to dated jurisprudence, ignoring the spirit of Islam. It would be inaccurate and unjust to suggest that most clerics are guilty of all of these failings. Indeed, there are many clerics who rank among the modernists themselves. But clerics are coming in for greater criticism and intellectual scrutiny than ever before.

This is where modern Islamic intellectuals emerge who are not formally trained in theological schools but who have educated themselves about Islam. Reflecting the various trends in political Islam, these intellectuals too run the gamut from radical to conservative. But the new Islamic intellectuals pose a dilemma: they are the product of secular education, often in the West, and offer new understandings and approaches to Islam through their own studies. And this carries the risk, as in the Protestant Reformation, that when every man is his own theologian, erroneous and distorted understandings of Islam can emerge that can serve to justify violence or even terror. Usama bin Ladin is one kind of self-declared "Islamic intellectual" with pretenses to Islamic knowledge.

Properly trained *'ulama* will point out the dangers of citing the Qur'an for extreme political ends by those with little or no training in Islamic theology and who often cite verses out of context or regard for the specific events and conditions that elicited the Qur'anic verses in the first place. Other Islamist intellectuals make vital contributions to the understanding of Islam under contemporary conditions.

SECULARISM

A smaller group of Islamist liberals argue that it is the *genuinely* secular state—in which the state grants religion autonomous space and does not interfere in the functioning of religion in society—that actually provides the optimum freedom and protection to religion from the state, its autocrats, or the enemies of religion. An Islamic state, however constructed, would be less likely to grant that same freedom of inquiry, even to Muslims, because the state itself is then a player in the interpretation of Islam.

By now there is a large body of thought and writing on by Muslims on the subject of liberal Islam.[15] I cite below from various sources some key thoughts by a number of liberal Islamists who offer some sense of the interesting range of their thinking, particularly as it relates to democracy and freedom of thought, demonstrating how Islam indeed can be compatible with contemporary international values.

One of the great modernist Islamic thinkers, the Pakistani Fazlur Rahman, longtime professor at the University of Chicago, takes a holistic view of Islamic legislation that insists upon viewing the Islamic message in its entirety before specific legislation possesses sense or efficacy. He declares that "a doctrine or an institution is genuinely Islamic to the extent that it flows from the *total teaching* of the Qur'an and the Sunna" designed to meet a specific problem or task.[16]

According to Shaykh Rashid al-Ghannushi, the founder of the Tunisian Islamist movement al-Nahda (Renaissance) now in exile in London, "The negative attitude of Islamic movements toward democracy is holding it back. We have no modern experience in Islamic activity that can replace democracy. The Islamization of democracy is the closest thing to implementing [the Islamic concept of] *shura* (consultation). Those who reject this thought have not produced anything different than the one-party system of rule."[17]

According to Dr. Muhammad Shahrur, a leading Syrian Islamic intellectual, "democracy, as a mechanism, is the best achievement of humanity for practicing consultation (*Shura*)." Similarly, he observes, "democracy is the best relative mechanism for organizing opposition." He sees the concept of opposition as a means by which to attain the Qur'anic precept of "urging the good and forbidding the evil." He states that these principles bring the Muslim to belief in the values of "political pluralism, freedom of expression, and freedom of opposition through peaceful means . . . Opposition and political pluralism is the basis for the Islamic civil society."

Shahroor points out that "democracy, as a form for governing and as a framework for organizing human relations, has negative as well as positive characteristics. Whatever the negative side is, there is no justification for abolishing democracy and replacing it with the absolute rule of one person, one party or one elite."[18]

Sadek J. Sulaiman, former Omani Ambassador to the United States and thinker on issues of Islamic governance, states that "As a concept and as a principle, *shura* in Islam does not differ from democracy. Both *shura* and democracy arise from the central consideration that collective deliberation is more likely to lead to a fair and sound result for the social good than individual preference. . . . The more any system constitutionally, institutionally, and practically fulfills the principle of *shura*— or, for that matter, the democratic principle—the more Islamic that system becomes."[19]

M. S. Zafar, a Pakistani and former director of the now defunct Muslim League organization, states that "accountability, interpretation of Islam (*ijtihad*), and democracy are Islam's true foundation, by means of which Islam establishes a just and equitable society. And as long as the human intellect cannot create any institution better than parliament, there should be no problem in adopting this institution."[20]

Laith Kubba, an Iraqi Islamic intellectual in exile in the West, writes that "democracy is not to complement or replace Islam, but it is necessary to improve the management of the Muslim world. Democratic societies may or may not be Islamic but I can hardly envisage an Islamic society in the 21st century without it being democratic and respectful to basic human rights. . . . It is true that democracy has many faults; it is not perfect; it is open to abuse. But so is every other system that is man-made or man-derived. This observation *includes systems derived from the values of Islam, and including the systems that governed the Muslims in the past 1400 years . . .*"[21]

Kubba observes "No one can have sovereignty over you except God. But God is not present except inside one, he is present in a set of values. States may exercise social control, perhaps with consent of governed. But for the state to be sovereign over me is against my faith."[22]

Once we understand the political and social context within which the Prophet spoke and made rulings, the *underlying principles* of these rulings become clear, making possible an extrapolation of what those same values and rulings would mean under contemporary conditions. For example, interest in money-lending is banned in Islam, but many modernists point out that the Prophet was speaking of the predatory practice of *usury* at the time (which was also banned by Christianity) as something quite distant from the modern concept of the *price of money* on the market, which in principle should not be banned by Islam. But because Islamist scholars have not arrived at a consensus on this issue, they have become largely irrelevant as most of the Muslim world has gone on to accept interest as the de facto basis of the world economic order.

Islamist modernists ultimately perceive in Islam the quest for justice, one of the essential foundations of the faith that leads Dr. Asghar Ali Engineer, a modernist (Shi'ite) Islamist thinker, to seek equality of men and women: "The Qur'anic notion of justice is quite comprehensive. . . . It is necessary to understand that it is justice which has to be rigorously applied to all the issues in framing laws. We must rethink the issues in Shari'ah laws based on the notion of centrality of justice, particularly in the sphere of family laws."[23]

Many modernists use as the point of departure the well-established Islamic concept of *maslaha* (the public interest or common good.). For those schools that place priority on the role of *maslaha* in Islamic thinking, Islam *by definition* serves the common good; therefore, if a given policy or position demonstrably does not serve the public interest it simply is "not Islam." This formulation is used by the huge Muhammadiya movement in Indonesia, among others. The pioneering Egyptian Islamic thinker Muhammad 'Abdu spoke in similar terms when he criticized Muslim neglect of the concept of "common good" and rulers' emphasis on obedience above justice.[24]

Clearly the concept of the common good must be applied with caution since in the end almost any legislation could be justified simply on the terms of some perceived common good, without any regard to Islam. But according to Fazlur Rahman, because Islamic jurisprudents were unwilling to undertake the necessary rethinking of the dilemmas and contradictions that had developed in the human evolution of Islamic law, the 'ulama simply took refuge in "minimal Islam"—reducing its tenets to the "five pillars" (statement of faith, prayer, fasting, zakat tax and pilgrimage)—or clung to "negative or punitive Islam" which focuses on certain physical punishment for crimes such as theft, consumption of alcohol, or adultery.[25] Modernists thus seek a holistic and especially contextual understanding of Islamic law in order to make it relevant to today's conditions.

In the view of modernist Shi'ite Islamist thinker Laith Kubba, the Islamic past today may no longer be of relevance in the contemporary context of constructing a modern society in accordance with the values and precepts of Islam—except as a valuable record of historical experience. The historical practice need not be binding. There was only one perfect Shari'a or way that was right for the time, and that was the Prophet's. But this exact practice was not necessarily relevant to new circumstances later on. As Muhammad Shahrur has commented, Muslims need to think about what the Prophet would do if he had come to today's West and not to sixth-century Arabia. The basic message of Islam would not change, but its contemporary understanding and application certainly would. In short, the modernist view suggest that the experience of Islamic scholars and their thought in the past may offer some insights, but they do not constitute a reliable guide to Muslim action today.

LEVEL OF AUTHORITATIVE *IJTIHAD*

Debate exists about the level at which "authoritative" *ijtihad* can take place. In Iran the clergy has sought to maintain a rigid monopoly on interpretation and application of religious law. At the opposite extreme, many Sunni fundamentalists claim that every individual is responsible for his or her *ijtihad* and thereby has an obligation to study and understand the texts. Shi'a have the option of choosing a *marja'* or personally selected religious authority among various ayatollahs whose views and philosophy of interpretation they find most congenial.

Many clerics with serious reputations have individually set up their own *fatwa* centers and offer authoritative readings through websites (such as Islamonline.com) to all who submit questions that deal with either problems of understanding or even guidance on how Islamic teaching relates to their immediate personal circumstances and problems. Yet state-appointed 'ulama insist on the legitimacy and monopoly of their readings of the law, while many independent Islamist intellectuals in the last decades have established serious rivalry in their readings and alternative interpretations. This issue represents in itself a form of democratization within political Islam, with unforeseen consequences that can strengthen radicals or moderates, fundamentalists or modernists, depending on how local and international conditions evolve.

THE PROBLEM OF RELIGION AND FREEDOM

Philosophers have struggled for centuries in many different religious traditions trying to reconcile religion with freedom. Do religious imperatives, established by revelation, contradict principles of freedom? If one must fulfill the dictates of God, is one free?

The liberal Islamist view is that a society that is not free introduces elements of compulsion into religious observations; such compulsions deprive the observant of the credit for following God's order through personal volition. Only free acts of piety and worship have merit in God's eyes. Society is able to impose rules only when society itself agrees, by free choice, on a social covenant it wishes to establish for its members. Additional religious precepts and prohibitions may exist, but they are the responsibility of the believer to observe, or, through social consensus, to become community law for as long as society wishes—that is, votes—to make it law.

Freedom is not the end in itself, for there is nothing inherently religious about the concept of freedom. But it becomes the essential vehicle, the enabling medium by which the individual can choose a way of life in conformity with his or her understanding of God, God's will, and the individual's role on this earth. Thus a democratic social order, more than any other order, empowers individuals to attain God as each sees fit.

This view will be challenged by many Islamists, especially fundamentalists, who view God's plan for mankind as fully established in detail, leaving no room for doubts or options about what is right and wrong, and that only by fulfilling God's desire and instructions to the letter can the individual avoid God's wrath. In this view, it is the obligation of authority and society to compel people to adhere to this path established by God. Freedom for them, then, is only another word for license to ignore or violate God's will and pursue one's willful way. This fundamentalist view, as well as the contradictory liberal view, can both be amply backed by quotations from the Qur'an and the Hadith—often taken out of context. Liberals would insist that the precise conditions and circumstances under which revelations were received are critical to an understanding of their nature and true intent.

CONCLUSION

The fundamentalist-modernist struggle in Islam is just warming up, producing infinite gradations of positions along the spectrum. The fundamentalist position is not new but is bolstered by uncritical tradition even if it is not traditional itself. Negative pressures, both domestic and international, on Muslim communities tend to strengthen a back-to-basics cultural reaction, meaning that fundamentalist Islam will still find fruitful soil within the harsh conditions of the Muslim world.

Liberalism in Islam emerges from contemporary conditions and reflects other global trends and movements. Both are likely to coexist for some time, but time over the longer run would seem to be on the side of the liberals if the history of the development of other world religions is any indicator. Yet other religions as well—Judaism, Christianity, and Buddhism—show not only a gradual evolution *toward* modernism and liberalization, but betray the same sharp dialectic between fundamentalist and modern views, a search for change versus a zeal to preserve the basics.

ISLAMISM AND GLOBAL GEOPOLITICS

THE DRAMATIC MANIFESTATION of political Islam on the Middle Eastern scene over the past several decades has captured greater world attention than the activities of any other religious, nationalist, or ideological movement since communism. The insatiably commercial eye of the world media has brought theatricality to the process that was never present in coverage of the drab proceedings of global communist politburos. Numerous dramatic incidents of revolution, wars, coups, terrorism, angry anti-Western mobs, suicide missions, bearded men in robes, and veiled women have all been combined to produce an image of strange and seemingly incomprehensible fanaticism, suggesting a group of peoples determined to willfully turn backward into history rather than forward. Yet we will never grasp the essence of this phenomenon until we realize that *political Islam stands not so much for conservation of the present or past, but as modernizing movements that look for change.*

It is also quite powerful. The simple fact is that political Islam currently reigns as the most powerful ideological force across the Muslim world today. Nor is political Islam operating in grand theatrical isolation but rather in striking parallel to other globalizing forces in the world and especially the developing world. Indeed, Islam as a globalizing force in its own right once created a new, clearly identifiable common cultural continuum across Eurasia. The various forms of contemporary political Islam share a great many concerns similar to those of other developing countries relating to power, culture, authenticity, values, religion, reform, political weakness, democratization, and the dilemmas of modernization and globalization. This is not surprising since common problems and their ideological responses all represent efforts to cope with modern challenges across religions, cultures, and continents. In this perspective political Islam is an integral part of a broader developing world.

THE CHALLENGES OF MODERNIZATION

In recent centuries the forces of modernization unleashed first by Europe and then the United States have spread over most of the world, stimulating dramatic social, political, economic, technological, and institutional change. It was European imperialism that brought many of these changes to the developing world, thereby creating an early local ambivalence toward the changes themselves. Today there is scarcely a place left on the planet untouched by the impact of modernization with its rapid sprawling urbanization and marketization. And the velocity of change is increasing under the stimulus of recent dramatic breakthroughs in information technology.

The benefits of modernization themselves are not an issue, but the associated ills of rapid development and change are. Already more of the developing world lives in vast new urban conglomerations rather than rural areas—a process quite destructive of all traditional order. Traditional values associated with rural and village life, the extended family and its support structure, social ties, and the comfort of traditional ways of life are often shattered upon entry into the city, creating psychological stress and the search for some continuing familiar framework of values. "Honor killings" of young women by their families in the new urban environment is just one harsh reflection of the traditional value of protection of virginity that stretches and snaps under the new values of freer social behavior in the city.

Yet however harsh the new living conditions may be, urban centers still attract millions of peasants who see urban impoverishment as preferable to the traditional hardships of poor rural life that offers few opportunities to earn significant wages, purchase manufactured commodities, and enhance lives through education, medical treatment, self-advancement, and other urban amenities and recreations. Frustrations also rise as billions of people become aware through modern media of what a better life could be, yet are often trapped in desperation, knowing that such improvements may not come in their own lifetime, or even that of their children. Two-thirds of this growing population is under the age of twenty-one, producing a dissatisfied volatile floating youth increasingly exposed to a drug culture.

These problems blanket the Third World, and the Muslim World is no exception. Massive urban conglomerations in Cairo, Istanbul, Tehran, Karachi, Dacca, and Jakarta each have well over 12 million citizens. Islamic movements are highly attuned to precisely these stresses of urban life and seek to alleviate their pressures while providing some kind of moral framework of familiar values designed to maintain social coherence and discipline in the face of the centrifugal forces of the city.

The blessings and curses of modernization are furthermore distributed un-evenly across the world, permitting the fault lines between rich and poor *within* these countries to widen. A thin strata of elites in most Third World countries now have more in common horizontally with elites in other parts of the world than vertically with the poorer and less educated elements of their own society. As disparities in wealth, privilege, and power grow, tensions arise within societies and take political form, especially when the political order is relatively authori-tarian. Elites, fearful of the potentially harsh consequences of social change, are generally on the defensive in the desire to maintain the status quo and above all to maintain "order"—thereby negating the possibility of change. They have be-come adept at developing empty forms of quasi-democratic governance, basi-cally institutional shells that continue to deny political power to all but the elite. Yet, mass emotions and frustrations inevitably seek expression. In the Muslim world Islamist movements directly address these very issues in speaking of the goal of a just society within a traditional framework of known values and the need to create private social support structures. To the extent that the current elitist power arrangements become identified with, or are openly supported by the United States or the West, opposition movements readily adopt anti-West-ern positions.

THE "FAILURE" OF SECULAR NATIONALISM

After gaining independence, most Third World states adopted a Western ideology: secular nationalism in the Western mold, usually with a socialist tinge, characterized virtually every new regime to come to power in the Third World immediately after independence, including the Muslim world. Colonial regimes had encouraged secu-lar values in general, and in the Muslim world they specifically sought to weaken the institutional and financial power of Islam because it was perceived as a powerful cen-ter of resistance to colonial authority. The first generation of independent leaders often tactically cooperated with religious forces during the national liberation strug-gle but were themselves usually schooled in the colonial metropole and steeped in its secular ideology. The Western model of state building dominated their vision. Un-fortunately, independence in most cases failed to solve many of the key national problems, creating new ones instead. Once the euphoria of independence wore off, the authoritarianism, incompetence, corruption, and internal strife of the new regimes led to reaction against them. The Islamists accused the policies of this first generation of leadership not only for failing to meet national needs but also for being untrue to Islam and lacking "authenticity."

As the new native elites began to build the first postindependence regimes based on secular nationalism they invariably looked to the transformative and even coercive power of the state for fulfillment of their agenda. The state, in effect, became the "nation," requiring veneration of the abstract all-powerful European state model as the engine of national power. Under this rationale the state itself—not the people—becomes the symbol and representative of the nation. This has important implications: opposition to the state—that is, to its narrow ruling elite—becomes treasonous.[1]

The equation of the state with the nation, all in protection of a ruling elite often supported by the military, led governments to resist change and to stifle debate and dissent. We see this same clash of interests across much of the developing world, to the detriment of the broader population and by a growing civil society. Islamists (out of power) so far strongly identify with the broader masses of the population against the ruling elite and thus become a major vehicle of latent anti-state (and anti-elite) hostility. Although a form of class friction is in evidence here, Islamists are loath to think in class terms at all, and they are rarely revolutionary in a social sense. Nor is the phenomenon unique to the Muslim world: in India, the following of the Hindu revivalist party has been drawn not from the traditional postindependence elite but from an aspiring lower middle class challenging the existing order.

Any challenge to Westernized-entrenched ruling elites from forces claiming to represent "authenticity" and tradition not surprisingly finds a powerful vehicle in *religiously oriented nationalism* that emerged as a strong element in the politics of the whole Third World starting in the 70s—as indicated by resurgent Hinduism in India, ultra-Orthodox Judaism in Israel, militant Buddhism in Sri Lanka, resurgent Sikh nationalism in the Punjab, "liberation theology" of Catholicism in Latin America, and, of course, Islamism in the Muslim world. In the 1990s we see religious politics linked with the Orthodox Church in Russia and the Serbian Orthodox Church in Serbia, and even as a strong factor in Greek nationalism.[2] And religiously based nationalism frequently overlaps with secular nationalism. In fact, we might say that nationalism actually reaches its pinnacle of effectiveness when religion coincides with ethnic identity in nationalist conflicts.

THE CONSEQUENCES OF RESURGENT ETHNICITY

Resurgent ethnicity on a global scale is a key feature of the last half of the twentieth century and has intensified with the end of the international discipline imposed by the Cold War. Today most traditional multiethnic state structures are in peril, challenged by rising ethnic separatism. Minorities dissatisfied with the regimes and borders within which they have been arbitrarily assigned by history increasingly struggle for greater rights, autonomy, or even independence. New international focus on democratization and human rights only strengthens the incentives for minorities to demand new rights and equitable treatment. The onus then falls on governments to provide good governance, or else risk losing their minorities. Regimes can of course turn to violence and repression to keep their minorities under control, but in so doing run the risk of becoming international pariahs, shunned by the international community, investors, and tourists alike.

Muslim states and peoples are in no way immune to this process. Muslim minorities in non-Muslim states are among the most vocal about their dissatisfactions and oppression under bad non-Muslim governance. They almost invariably express their cause in Islamist as well as nationalist terms as we have seen in Palestine, Chechnya, Kashmir, Bosnia, the Philippines, and elsewhere. While Muslim minorities will take advantage of this to pursue their own autonomy or independence, Muslim states that impose bad rule over non-Muslim minorities or even Muslim minorities, face similar threats—Berbers in Algeria and Morocco; non-Muslim peoples in southern Sudan; Kurds in Iraq, Turkey, and Iran, Azeris in Iran, Baluch or Sindhis in Pakistan—all make similar demands on Muslim states. The argument for autonomy cuts both ways. But Islamists tend to defend the rights of separatist Muslim minorities while being less forthcoming about minorities in Muslim lands. They will need to face this dilemma.

THE CHALLENGE OF PLURALISM

When any group or society chooses to utilize its religious, ethnic or regional in the political arena, tradeoffs are involved. Every open society possesses its own "identity politics," including the United States to a high degree. The politics of identity can work in two ways: it can provide a valuable social glue, helping strengthen and unite a society under a common identity. But more frequently it can act divisively, particularly in multiethnic states traditionally held together primarily by authoritarian regimes, where economic and social fault lines intersect with ethnic and religious ones. Growing ethnic diversity is a reality—in the long run, multicultural societies are ineluctably the wave of the future, whether we like it or not. Populations are on the move more than ever before in history, across the Third World and into the developed world. Societies have never before in history been so ethnically mixed; where permitted, ethnic identity is no longer timidly concealed but often openly paraded and celebrated, especially in the West. But it is only the *voluntarily formed* multicultural societies that will succeed; states that are prisons for unhappy minorities are destined to suffer wrenching disorder. The Muslim identity figures prominently when oppressors are non-Muslim.

European nation-states are now deeply unsettled with the arrival of large numbers of immigrants, newcomers who look and speak differently, bring unfamiliar customs and traditions, and often try to preserve many of their cultural traditions and norms in their new environment. Frequently they are not readily absorbed into their new milieu, partly because they may not be very welcome—Arabs in France, Turks in Germany, or Albanians in Italy—or may be ill-equipped for entry into modern societies, or may themselves cling to traditional identities in enclaves. Islamists are among those working actively among immigrant communities in the West to provide community aid and protect the Islamic values, identities, and structure of these distinctive communities. Islamism may strengthen community cohesion and self-discipline, but it also perpetuates differences with the host culture. Where Muslims constitute willing immigrants to Western societies, Islamists need to seriously consider the meaning and appropriate extent of preserving Muslim identity in multicultural Western societies.

Just as Western societies face the challenges of adjusting to new immigrants, many Muslim countries face the opposite problem of multiculturalism in their own societies, as established unassimilated minorities, especially non-Muslim communities, are now less willing to hide their own identity or apologize for it and are demanding full legal and social rights. Resurgent and assertive minority ethnicity in traditional Third World societies is creating major new crises that in most cases are not being handled wisely or successfully through integration and accommodation. The Muslim world shares this global problem, and Islamists are one of the key political groups to champion Muslim community rights, interests, and identities within their own societies against resurgent non-Muslim minorities. Islamists are often in a difficult position since Islamic law is very clear in prohibiting ethnic distinction among Muslims and calling for minority religious communities to be protected by law. Yet the political reality is often otherwise. While only a few Islamists (primarily Wahhabis) would advocate suppression of their non-Muslim minorities, the fact is that Islamists in practice have primarily focused on strengthening Islam and Muslim community rights. In Indonesia, Malaysia, and Egypt, for example, Islamists are not so much against minorities as they are primarily interested in the welfare of the Muslim community and the stability of the Muslim state. In sum, Islamists are deeply involved in issues of interpretation of multiculturalism across the Muslim world and do not present a unified view on the topic.

THE ILLS OF GLOBALIZATION

Globalization is not, of course, a new phenomenon. It has been taking place for a long time across history, dating back to early "universal" empires such as the Persian, the Greek, the Roman, Mongol, Chinese, and others that unleashed new modes of thinking and technology across broad areas under some form of political unification. The Islamic world always represented a high form of globalization in an earlier era. But today, just as with modernization, much of the Third World today sees globalization as representing a new and essentially *Western project* containing its own ideology and agenda, whose challenge generates new threats, dangers, discontents, and reactions. Globalization to many is simply a new form of Western or American hegemony in a massive economic, political, and cultural package of questionable benefit. Furthermore, the losers in the globalization process may seek alternative "ideologies" to resist such an American-led globalization, such as some kind of alliance of "antihegemonic" states fighting "neoliberalism" (the Latin American ideological term for globalization as an American project.)[3]

Nor are these views unique to the Third World. The disruptive rioting in Seattle in December 1999 or Milan in 2001 helped scuttle the negotiations of the World Trade Organization, uniting an unlikely group of quite disparate forces—American trade unions, Third World representatives, ecological crusaders, and economic and cultural nationalists—all agreed on one thing: fear of the unknown consequences of a treaty sanctifying higher levels of globalization, and distrust of the United States' role in it.[4] The Muslim world, representative of the regions of the Third World *par excellence,* and with its strong focus on "social justice," betrays deep ambivalence toward contemporary globalization that is often perceived as a deliberate Western cultural juggernaut. Islam need not be anti-Western or anti-global by definition, but it functions as guardian and repository of cultural tradition that emerges from Islamic faith, culture, and tradition.

The voices raised against the negative impact that globalization and its assumptions may inflict are not only Muslim. The questions raised are general: What kind of a project is globalization, and who are its primary beneficiaries? Is it a "natural" process flowing out of modern technology, or does it represent the pet project of advanced states, promoted only by the massive support of an institutional infrastructure that only the United States is capable of providing? And are the virtues of a "free market" readily demonstrable to all, or do they rather represent a new "theology," the "IMF [International Monetary Fund] consensus" pushed by the United States, which sees itself as the universal model for the future?[5] These selfsame issues are debated broadly in the West itself, especially in Europe.

Many Islamists, along with other nationalists in the Muslim world and beyond, speak out against the dangers of globalization. Their objections are based on concerns for the preservation of local culture and values against the massive exportation of American media, for the sovereignty of the state, and above all against the potentially negative economic impact on states and large segments of their populations. We hear these same concerns expressed across Asia, Latin America, and even France. Islamists sometimes talk about "Islamic economics," by which they refer not to some arcane laws of economics operating only in the Muslim world but rather to their concerns for the ideological assumptions and values underlying global marketization. Basic to that objection is the focus on market efficiency at the expense of the human and social impact of globalization. This is not unique to Islamists. What John Gray attributes to East Asian societies equally well applies to Islamists: "In Asian cultures market institutions are viewed instrumentally, as means to wealth-creation and social cohesion, not theologically, as ends in themselves. One of the appeals of 'Asian values' is that by adopting a thoroughly instrumental view of economic life they avoid the Western obsessions that make economic policy an arena of doctrinal conflict. 'Asian' freedom from economic theology allows market institutions to be judged, and reformed, by reference to how their workings affect the values and stability of society."[6]

Major Asian economies—such as China, Japan, Korea, Taiwan, and India—are pursuing independent trajectories in the development of their economies, none of which is based on the classic Western model, and nearly all of which are concerned at least as much with social stability (or regime stability) as they are with avowed economic efficiency. "They reflect differences not only in the family structures but also in the religious life of the cultures in which these diverse capitalisms are rooted."[7] None of these states cited by Gray happens to be Muslim. All of them are likely to resist to one degree or another the risks they perceive in acquiescing to the theology of globalization. Gray argues that we are entering an age in which the "identification of the West with modernity is being severed."[8] Islamist thinking on economic and globalization issues reflect these very same ideas (although Muslim states have problems in bringing about even their own version of modernization, under any ideology, compared with much of East Asia's greater success story.)

Finally, Islamists share with much of the rest of the world concerns for the fate of social and economic justice in what they see as a more Darwinian social order of Western capitalism. They share too a traditional comfort with certain traditional communal values that are strong in the developing world but that have been eroded by modernization and the enhanced role of individualism in society, especially in the United States.

THE RISE OF LOCALISM
WITHIN GLOBALIZATION

While globalization reduces isolation and particularism and stimulates homogenization on the economic, cultural, and political level, it paradoxically also engenders its own counterreaction in the form of localism and appeal to authenticity. We cannot all be simply "global citizens"; cultural homogenization does not furnish warm and fuzzy feelings of belonging. The more our identities are exposed to powerful international influences, the more we seek comfort and meaning in our local culture, mother tongue, customs, food, clothing, and identity as well. When globalization is seen as foreign and threatening (witness popular early American derision at the idea of Japanese car imports) local identities quickly rise to the defense. Islam is one such identity. Islam particularly strengthens identity when arrayed against non-Muslim power. But the protection of local identity is not a worry confined to lagging Third World nations. A profile of Felix Rohatyn, longtime distinguished American international banker and U.S. Ambassador to France in 1999, noted:

"Understanding how Europeans feel about America has become a tricky business these days, with France leading the muttering chorus of anxiety about the absence of any real counterweight to U.S. economic, technological and military power. . . . [A]s his last year as President Clinton's envoy begins, Rohatyn believes the gap between Americans and Europeans is widening. "Now I sense a feeling that the very existence of the United States, and our enormous weight in the world, are causing a threat to the [Europeans'] identity, making it absolutely necessary from their point of view to counter what they see as a menace to their culture and their society," he said. . . .

"You find everywhere—on the left, the right, in business, in labor—a very strong feeling of cultural vulnerability, especially in language, and thus in movies and in television programs," Rohatyn said. "I think what Seattle [rioting at the location of the World Trade Organization talks in December 1999] represents to them is globalization with an American face . . ."[9]

Our new century is likely to witness increasing tension between the forces of globalization and regionalism, giving political Islam new range of play.

THE PEOPLE VERSUS THE STATE

The state has been sacrosanct and central in the development phase of most countries. But do the people serve the state or does the state serve the people? In the West the evidence appears to have shifted in favor of the latter. But in most of the

Third World the state continues to play a central role in politics and the economy. As a result, there is still a struggle underway to capture the prize of the state and thus control its resources, even as the state itself becomes increasingly perceived as part of the problem. The Turkish state, for example, is the most militantly anti-Islamist in the Muslim world. As one of the more advanced democracies in the Muslim world, the concept of the supremacy of the state in Turkey has only recently come under scrutiny at the popular level. (The preamble to the Turkish constitution begins with the Orwellian words, "The Turkish state is eternal.") Islamists have been drawn into this argument, mainly because the existing state has been a key obstacle to their participation in the political order. As long as the Islamists are not in power—and they are not in most of the Muslim world—they will champion "the people" against the dominant state.

As the state's sovereignty is weakened, it comes under assault across much of the Third World: from above by globalization, international organizations, the spread of new global norms, global interdependency, ease of transportation reducing isolation, loss of control over internal communications due to satellite communications and the Internet; and from below by rising regionalism, ethnicity, criminal organizations, and the breakdown of state control and authority at local levels. These breakdowns of authority are particularly pronounced in Africa, but they also appear in Colombia, Mexico, Sudan, the Congo, Nigeria, parts of Central America, Russia, and potentially in China, among others. In the Muslim world the threat of state breakdown is vividly present today in Indonesia, Pakistan, Afghanistan, Central Asia, the Caucasus, Sudan, Iraq, and Algeria, to name just a few.

In fact, this phenomenon is closely linked to the problem of the "failed state," in which the breakdown of authority, legal norms, and the institutions of central control, result in rising anarchy, lawlessness, criminality, and even a vision of a "Mad Max" world, best summed up in Robert Kaplan's article "The Coming Anarchy."[10] In this kind of deteriorating environment, reassertion of central authority becomes paramount, and with it the requirement for some kind of clear *moral authority*. Chechnya, under siege and domestic breakdown in its wars against Russia in the 1990s, for example, adopted Shari'a law in order to restore order through the only moral code that still enjoyed authority and respect, a reversion to basics. As the specter of social breakdown advances, the search for moral foundation for society becomes more compelling—about which Islam has much to say. But whether Islam can provide the necessary "social glue" or moral force that will help prevent political collapse and preserve social values and social coherence in failing (Muslim) states depends greatly on how Islamists apply it. As such, Islam probably has as good a chance of working as any other ideology when the challenges are so great. Indeed, Kaplan sees Islam in Africa as particularly vital in providing social cohesion in a sea of collapsing states.[11]

THE AUTHORITARIAN STATE AND CHANGE

If the failed and collapsing state is one specter, the oppressive state is the other. Everywhere across Asia, Latin America, and Africa, we witness popular movements against entrenched autocrats and new efforts to lay the foundations for more democratic and representative government. The end of the Cold War in particular brought a new wave of change and democratization, some of it quite transient, as we have seen in the reversion of most of the newly emerged Central Asian states of the former Soviet Union to dictatorship. The Muslim world has lagged behind other regions of the world in developing democratic structures. Today Islamists play a key role in challenging the authoritarian state in the name of democracy.

RELIGION AND SOCIAL CONSCIENCE

Religious institutions in all states and at all times are torn between two poles: they preach a message of idealism, justice, and morality, but in the real world they must acquiesce to the de facto power of the ruler and the state, however disreputable. Religious leaders of all faiths have generally found it safer and more convenient to work *with* the state rather than brandish the values of religion against the state. The Catholic Church historically lent strong support in countless European wars to those states that supported it; it was a key ally in the conquest of Latin American by the Spanish. It was only a small minority within the Catholic Church, for instance, that ever concerned itself with issues of welfare and moral justice for the conquered and brutalized indigenous peoples of North or South America. But the appeal of idealism reemerged in the mid-twentieth century when formal doctrines of "liberation theology," reflecting a more left-of-center vision of the just struggle against oppressive conditions, won adherents. Today the Catholic Church still houses an active wing that champions the rights of the dispossessed poor and oppressed indigenous peoples in Latin America and has come close to supporting rebellion against state authorities in the name of human dignity and equality—such as in the Zapatista rebellion of 1994 in Chiapas, Mexico, with the strong support of the local Catholic archbishop Samuel Ruiz.

This call for social justice and a moral compass emerges even in the most authoritarian of states, as with the mass demonstrations of the Falun Gong movement in China beginning in 1999. Note that the analysts of the Falun Gong point out impulses strikingly similar to those of the Islamists: "Falun Gong reflects a deep-seated opposition among many of China's dispossessed who, over the last few years, have not benefited from economic reforms. 'It represents their alienation from society,' [one analyst] said. . . . 'Many people, especially older cadres, are bothered by the moral vacuum in China today,' said a senior Western diplomat. 'With its Chinese roots and its emphasis on clean living, Falun Gong has provided a convenient way to express opposition to the direction the party is taking—toward patronage, corruption and sleaze.'[12]

Islamist politics fit precisely into this mold, which combines religious values with political implications. In short, the struggle for social justice based on moral principles is likely to intensify in this new century. Political Islam, like other religions, will likely remain closely linked to these ideals.

INCREASING GLOBAL RELIGION IN POLITICS

The combination of the disruptive effects of globalization and the desire to establish moral foundations for authority have contributed to the increasing role of religion in politics. Islam is just one of many religions to engage in political and social involvement. Comparable is the role of the Catholic Church in Latin America and Asia in its increasingly activist role in respect to social programs for the poor—Pope John Paul II went so far as to offer a direct criticism of capitalism as a force with a dangerously deficient social conscience. Religion has been central to the conflict in Northern Ireland. Judaism has produced its own militant "nationalist" terrorists. The Eastern Orthodox Church supports various national causes against the non-Orthodox. Buddhists demonstrate a militant and violent side in their politics in Sri Lanka against Hindu Tamils. American fundamentalists are directly active on the American political scene, fielding candidates for Congress and even the presidency. A handful of American religious activists have engaged in violence and murder on the abortion issue. And mainstream Protestant churches protested the war in Vietnam and demonstrated for the rights of indigenous peoples around the world, as well as the cause of the homeless and underprivileged in the United States. So Islam is not alone in taking an active interest in politics today on the issues of social justice.

LOSS OF MORAL COMPASS

Muslims are not unique in their concern about their possible loss of moral compass; it is not unfamiliar in the West. What is the proper source of moral values in the face of the decline of religion? Should the West become the main provider of contemporary values to the rest of the world? For many Muslims the problem in the West is not Christianity but its abandonment; it is the replacement of religious values with secular humanist values—a theme we hear from Christian fundamentalists in the West as well—that upsets Muslims in what they see not as new values but the practical disappearance of community values. The adulation of the individual is seen to lead to hedonism. ("If you feel it, go and do it," as an old TV commercial proclaimed.)

Indeed, not only Muslims but many Christians and Jews question whether in the West the dominant contemporary ethical code of humanism has produced a sufficiently rigorous value system to sustain Western society over the long run. Muslims question the strength and efficacy of Western humanistic legal and ethical codes that in the end produced the most vast and immoral killing machines of all history, fascism and communism, not to mention the two deadly Western-generated global wars. No non-European states or rulers, however bestial, can begin to match the quantity of deaths inflicted, and certainly not in Islamic history, from which no holocaust emerged and where there is no record of violence exceeding the norms of comparable world standards of past millennia. Is the carnage of the twentieth century a reflection upon those humanistic Western values themselves, or is it merely a reflection of the unprecedented power of the modern state coupled with radical ideology, unimpeded by moral codes? To many, including some Muslims, this is a distinction without a difference; the inhumanity provides vindication that the West is losing its moral compass and is headed for eventual cultural decline. Muslims are not alone in this vision which is also reflected in the moral concerns of much of the Western church as well.

Many observers of the problem of global values and ethics legitimately raise these questions, regardless of faith. With the relativization of moral values and the atomization of society characteristic of the postmodern Western world, how can any coherent body of spiritually based moral belief prevail and inform society? Are secular humanist ethics strong enough to inspire their acceptance as a source of values when they are shorn of the emotive and inspirational power of religion, ritual, ceremony, and culture? Perhaps no divinely based religion will ultimately survive the inexorable logic of postmodern humanism—and that is precisely what bothers many Muslims as well as Christians and Jews. Secular ethical humanism may indeed represent the long-range future of morality and ethics in a postmodern world; it may be that the West is simply the first to have (partially) attained this stage of development, for better or for worse. The whole question of the source of values remains open to debate and is followed by Muslims with interest.

Radical secularists, agnostics, and atheists tend to view the force of religion in general, and in politics in particular, as a likely potential source of intolerance, obscurantism, superstition, and fanaticism. Certainly history periodically reveals that particular face of religion across times and cultures. Yet few in any society would actually believe that society would be better off if religion were to disappear altogether as a social and moral force. Objectively viewed, radical secular ideology in its fascist and Marxist-Leninist incarnations, the twentieth century has proven far more lethal in terms of numbers killed, than any religion in history. Despite many attempts in the United States to forge some kind of secular moral values to replace traditional religious values, it is interesting that many communities are now beginning to recognize that the *understanding of religion* might well have a place in schools—not in the form of proselytization or initiation into a faith, but as an effort to familiarize students with the teachings and values of all world religions and their search for common moral values. Religion, in short, is not about to go away, anywhere. But the political ends to which it is put will matter very much. Religion is capable of productively transforming human lives and ways of living. Abused, it is also capable of justifying and facilitating the worst of latent human impulses, motivations, and actions.

POLITICAL ISLAM: A PROGRESSIVE OR CONSERVATIVE FORCE?

Islamist movements can be viewed simultaneously as both conservative and progressive. Even purveyors of a conservative vision are forced to recognize the need for the free political environment if they wish to prosper and flourish. In fact, the terms "progressive" and "conservative" may not be analytically very helpful here. Movements may be "conservative" to the extent that they are interested in religion and questions of values and pursue a conservative social agenda. But they function "progressively" within the political order in their focus upon the need for change, democratization, greater openness, human rights, and an expansion of the political arena.

Consider Evangelical Pentacostalism that is not a movement of political or social protest but that nonetheless has major implications for these areas. Its impact in Latin America is to encourage pluralism, market economy, and democracy—given its roots.[13] Above all it demonstrates that the force of religion as a source of political and social change is alive and well in places outside the Middle East where Islamists today also speak out against traditional hierarchies, stress family relationships and a disciplined and frugal life, and push for democratization.

Ironically, in the contemporary Middle East it is the *secular authoritarians* who most represent the forces of reaction today as they exercise power nominally in the name of modernization and Westernization, but in reality they are not politically progressive but repressive in seeking to preserve at all costs their entrenched political power and the non-democratic status quo. It is they who preside over the emasculation and withering of civil society and stifle personal initiative in the political order. Unfortunately many Western policy-makers are often beguiled by this authoritarian pretense to "modernism" and pseudo-Westernization as contrasted with the threat of "reactionary" Islamism.

CONCLUSION

Political Islam is remarkably in tune with many major trends evolving elsewhere in the world in response to contemporary global challenges. In our Western self-confidence and West-centric outlook, we tend to be ignorant of ideological trends developing in the Third World except when they infringe spectacularly on our own technologically advanced and rarified world and its gated mentality. But even a casual examination of these world forces demonstrates how unexceptional political Islam is in its focus in the context of developing world concerns and frustrations. Will Islamism continue to parallel and reflect developments in the rest of the world, or will it diverge in some unique direction? Is political Islam growing more congruent with many trends in the developing world, or is it moving toward isolation? I argue that it is largely congruent in many respects when viewed on a world basis, even if some of its elements are moving toward reactionism. But to see political Islam as distinct from these global trends is to miss what it is all about.

ISLAM AND TERRORISM

AL-QA'IDA AND THE IMPLICATIONS
OF THE 11 SEPTEMBER ATTACKS

Academic discussion of the problem of terrorism became a whole lot more real after the devastating terrorist attacks of 11 September 2001. The magnitude of such an event may make analytical discussions about the broader nature of political Islam seem irrelevant when terrorism becomes the riveting issue. Yet a focus solely on terrorism would be a mistake, ignoring the overwhelming majority of Islamists who have nothing to do with terror and making them virtually irrelevant and stigmatized in Western political discourse. Indeed, Usama bin Ladin's catalyzing attack upon the World Trade Center made a bid to decisively determine the nature of the Muslim world's relations with the West. To ignore the complexity of political Islam and tar all Islamists with the same brush of terrorism guarrantees Bin Ladin's success. The implications of both the attack and the subsequent U.S. War Against Terrorism began a chain of events whose long-term consequences are still far from evident.

The attack had immediate and sweeping consequences for Muslims. President George W. Bush's response immediately moved to overthrow the Taleban regime in Afghanistan, to hunt down and destroy as much as possible of the al-Qa'ida infrastructure inside of Afghanistan, and to find its links in other states as well. Bush declared the War Against Terrorism to be open-ended and without borders in an effort to eliminate the scourge entirely. Although the military aspect of the campaign largely concluded with a victory in Afghanistan, the war continued along broad dimensions with the marshalling of extraordinary resources—diplomatic, intelligence, immigration and police personnel, special forces, and financial investigations—in order to uncover, block, and neutralize terrorist forces wherever they may be and to persuade, pressure, or compel all states to share in the action.

The shock effect of such a spectacular act galvanized many other states, especially in the West, to examine more deeply the nature of the threat from Islamic terrorism. Muslim immigrants in the United States and in Europe were widely detained for the slightest infringement of immigration irregularities and the entire Muslim community was asked to cooperate with law enforcement officials in discussing potential radicals within the community. New United States visa regulations were issued that placed special requirements on Muslim males from eighteen to forty years of age. Muslim "racial profiling" became standard procedure for all security and law enforcement officials.

Muslims around the world responded in different ways. Nearly all Muslims shared the universal horror at the images and the enormity of the attack and loss of innocent human life, reportedly including several hundred Muslims among the over 3,000 dead. Nearly all Muslims, including a broad range of Islamist leaders, immediately condemned the attack as a crime and against the tenets of Islam. But this widespread Muslim condemnation was generally followed by the observation that as terrible as the attack was, perhaps the United States had brought it upon itself through its long history of bad policies. Many hoped that, at least the attack might serve as a "wake-up call" to the United States to reconsider its disastrous policies in the Middle East, in which the chief grievances focused upon unqualified U.S. support for Israel, terrible suffering of Iraqi civilians and children as a result of the U.S. sanctions against Iraq, and U.S. lack of interest in democratic reform in the Muslim world. Some saw it as punishment of the United States for its "arrogant" ways.

But many in the Muslim world remained in denial, expressing doubts that Muslims had anything to do with the attack, pointing to the Oklahoma City bombings in which Muslims were originally suspected until it was revealed that Caucasian Americans were behind it. Widespread conspiracy rumors claimed that Israel had foreknowledge of the attack and had warned 4,000 Jews in New York not to go to work in the World Trade Center that day, or that Israeli Intelligence (Mossad) might have actually been behind the operation to discredit Muslims. Some astonishingly claimed that the operation was "so sophisticated that Muslims could not have carried it out." Large numbers claimed to withhold all judgment until the United States produced convincing evidence that Bin Ladin was responsible—whatever "convincing" means. Whether or not they believed Bin Ladin was responsible, nearly all Muslims condemned the resulting U.S. military operations against Afghanistan that caused thousands of civilian Afghan deaths. Anger sprung up at images of U.S. warplanes once again killing Muslims. Muslims denounced U.S. arrogance at treating the deaths in New York as some unique crime when thousands of Muslims themselves have been dying unnoticed under constant military attack in Palestine, Chechnya, Bosnia, and Kashmir. The legacy of years of Muslim perception of wrongful, unjust, and neglectful U.S. policies seemingly came to a head.

At the popular level, many Muslims perceive the War Against Terrorism to be in reality a war against Islam, despite repeated statements by Bush to the contrary. Since Muslims were held responsible for the attacks on 11 September, Muslims became in fact nearly the exclusive targets, both in the Muslim world and within the United States and Western Europe as objects of investigation.

More thoughtful Muslims, however, also recognized that the attack had brought the Muslim world to a moment of truth. While all Muslims point out that Islam is basically a religion of peace, the violence of a tiny handful of extreme radicals was able to dominate the perception of Islam by others in much of the world. The event spoke for itself and brought forth drastic consequences for Muslims everywhere, particularly the risk that Muslims will inadvertently cede to Bin Ladin the power to negatively affect their future and damage the perception of Islam among non-Muslims. Whatever Muslim grievances may be, do Muslims want a Bin Ladin to provide the "solution"? The attack may now place primary responsibility upon Muslims themselves to monitor and control radical elements within their societies and to intellectually discredit their arguments.

Muslims were affected by the event even more widely afield. Key leaders—in Russia, India, Israel, the Philippines, and China—took advantage of the U.S. policy to declare their own War Against Terrorism locally and to put down with ever greater force and justification their own Muslim minorities—Chechens, Kashmiris, Palestinians, Moros, and Uyghurs. Israeli Prime Minister Sharon declared that Yasir 'Arafat is "Israel's Bin Ladin." Other regimes also took advantage of the incident to crack down with greater violence on their own Islamist groups as in Uzbekistan, Egypt, the Philippines, Malaysia and Algeria.

Prosecution of the War Against Terrorism should in principle contain three levels of action. The first is punitive and defensive: the elimination of terrorists and the infrastructure that was responsible for the 11 September attack and for earlier attacks by al-Qa'ida in Saudi Arabia, Somalia, Yemen, Kenya, and Tanzania; it was necessary also to eliminate the Taleban regime, which had hosted al-Qa'ida and *mujahidin* from other countries. A second goal involves deterrence: intensified intelligence and police work both in the United States and abroad to identify and block other terrorist groups and their actions. But the third and most important level is of a more positive and constructive nature and involves the need for change and reform in the Muslim world, attending to deeper sources of grievance that constitute the soil for terrorism. Why are such attacks taking place, and how can they be stopped?

Analysis of the failings and ills of the Muslim world—political, social, and economic—clearly represent a key part of the necessary examination of longer-term problems and their solutions. At the same time, serious examination of dangerous overseas levels of grievances cannot avoid considering whether U.S. policies themselves might also have contributed in part to the problem. Bush suggested early on in the campaign that these attacks were the result of "people who hate our values," but this analysis was simplistic and self-serving. Most Muslims including most Islamists admire U.S. political values, even when uncomfortable with many U.S. social values (or the absence thereof.) They too want a democratic order, respect for human rights and the ability to get rid of hated regimes. A constructive U.S. policy should begin to address these sources of Muslim political grievance, especially the need for major political liberalization and reform in a host of Muslim states that are harshly autocratic. But successful prosecution of the War Against Terrorism on the punitive and investigative level required, at least initially, the support of existing authoritarian regimes in the Muslim world and elsewhere, support gained in exchange for overlooking violations of human rights and repression generally. Bush could not simultaneously seriously criticize their own domestic policies. Yet a failure to levy criticisms results in a war that serves to exacerbate those very sources of anger that originally spawned terrorists and created the publics that cheered them on as Robin Hood–style heroes.

The nature of the War Against Terrorism and subsequent U.S. policies in the Middle East also dispelled the considerable Muslim sympathies generated at the human level for the American public after 11 September. The killing of innocent Muslims in Afghanistan disturbed many. Longer-term perceptions of the suffering and deaths among the Iraqi population under United States sanctions were augmented by determined rhetoric in Washington that Iraq would shortly be the target of a new and far-reaching military campaign. And finally, Sharon's harsh invasion of the West Bank in the spring of 2002 in response to Palestinian suicide bombings in Israel was widely broadcast across the Arab world creating great anger. Washington was seen as taking a largely hands-off approach toward Sharon, bringing the level of Muslim dissatisfaction with the United States to one of the highest levels in decades. Muslims began to view themselves once again as primarily victims of global events, crowding out any initial feelings of guilt for the Muslim perpetrators of 11 September.

A constructive War Against Terrorism involving political liberalization in the Muslim world could inaugurate a new chapter in international relations. But if these issues of political reform are left unattended, the War Against Terrorism will aggravate the tensions within the existing international order that help produce these radical movements. Repression stifles change and reform in most of the Muslim world. The psychological mood of the region is worse than ever before, and the reservoir of a vague anti-American ideology is deepening. In the end it is not the terrorists alone who are frightening, but more the atmosphere of popular admiration for anti-American actions that cheers on Robin Hood actions and facilitates the emergence of new Bin Ladin recruits.

Applause for Bin Ladin is of course more an emotional outburst than a serious desire to see terrorism spread. But the War Against Terrorism has also brought greater sobriety to Muslim views. It burst a bubble of Islamist radical euphoria and the sense of invincibility stemming from the anti-Soviet jihad in Afghanistan in the 1980s when Muslim *mujahidin,* with much external logistical support, drove the Soviet Union out of Afghanistan and proclaimed that "Islam has overcome a superpower." Any expectation that the same *mujahidin* movement could now bring the United States to its knees has been shattered with the fall of the Taleban and the scattering of al-Qa'ida. In Pakistan, many citizens whose sons volunteered to defend the Taleban came to blame the zealousness of mullahs in sending their children to their deaths in a feckless campaign. Punishment upon the powerful West may on occasion be gratifying, but few would advocate punishment as a way to deal with the West with its far greater capacity to cause damage.

Whether 11 September was a final gasp or the opening salvo of a more violent confrontation with Islamic radicalism depends in part upon how effectively international intelligence and police operations can break up terrorist infrastructures. It also depends on whether the atmosphere of Muslim anger with the United States can be changed, leading to a diminution of the pervasive ambivalence with which many Muslims (and many non-Muslims around the world) view attacks on the United States—recognition of the criminality of action that causes innocent suffering at the human level, yet modulated by the feeling that Washington "had it coming." The burden of change lies primarily in the Muslim world itself, but the United States is not exempt from considering what kind of policy changes it might take to help bring about that change. It would be disingenuous for the world's sole superpower to pretend that its policies have no consequences.

Yet there are some very radical Islamic views and some very violent Muslim individuals out there, including some who live in the West. A few appear to be totally dedicated to the "defeat of America" as a presence or influence in the world, while others focus on the elimination of Israel. It would be naïve to believe that if the United States had been less supportive of Israeli policies Bin Ladin would never have struck (although more importantly, the reception of his act in the Muslim world might have been different.) To some radicals, the bombing of the World Trade Center was a "success," showing that a small handful of activists can deal a grievous blow to a superpower, regardless of the cost. Yet other Muslim radicals, perhaps nonviolent, possess utopian views that perceive the creation of an "Islamic state" as the solution to all problems, or as a way to empower the Muslim world and restore the power of Muslim civilization. Many such individuals view the world in Manichaean terms of good versus evil, sometimes reaffirmed in their minds by mirror-image pronouncements of President Bush in which one is either "with America or with the terrorists." Surely life offers a few more options than that.

ISLAM AND TERROR

Islam, like other world religions, seeks to attain a world of peace and justice. But just as Christianity, Judaism, Hinduism, Shintoism, and other religions have been used by radicals to justify violent and ugly actions, so too has Islam. Monotheistic faiths in particular offer a few scriptural passages, drawn out of ancient and specific historical context, that call for graphic and terrible acts in God's name against the enemies of the true faith.

Today Islam is invoked by a tiny proportion of the Muslim population to justify acts of guerrilla warfare, assassination, kidnapping, bombing, and skyjacking, usually against their own rulers or foreign oppressors, however defined. Sometimes it is even done in the name of profit, as with the Abu Sayyaf guerrilla group in the Philippines that kidnapped foreigners for publicity and money. Sometimes violent actions are carried out by groups whose very name invokes Islam, such as Hizballah (Party of God), Jundallah (The Soldiers of God), Mujahidin (Strugglers for Jihad), Islamic Jihad, and the Armed Islamic Group in Algeria (GIA). Other groups use names drawn directly from Qur'anic concepts such as al-Takfir wa'l Hijra (Anathematization and Flight), and Sepah-e-Sahaba (Legion of the Comrades of the Prophet). A proportionally miniscule group of radicals thus dominate the media and the attention of policymakers, imposing a violent image of Islam for the non-Muslim world.

"TERRORISTS OR FREEDOM FIGHTERS?"

This facile question captures the broad recognition that the use of term "terrorism" has become subjective and politicized. It also indicates the intensely political nature of terrorism and the variety of political interests that are affected by it. "Terrorism" can be applied to actions by national liberation movements like the Chechens in their 250-year struggle for independence from Moscow, or for the near psychotic fringe movements like Aum Shinrikyo in Japan or Baader Meinhoff in Germany, or criminal groups who engage in terrorism for profit such as the Abu Sayyaf group in the Philippines, or other leftist and rightist movements, secular, or religious movements. Different violent groups have different targets: presidents, police, security officials, government officials, political rivals, "traitors," businessmen, foreign ethnic groups, foreign states, polluters, abortionists, tourists, unveiled women, innocent bystanders. The distinction between guerrilla warfare and terrorism lies in part in the eyes of the beholder when officials and not innocent civilians are assassinated.

Governments don't like to get into the definition game because it deprives them the option of selectively and subjectively using the term "terrorism" in pursuit of their own interests. The United States suffers particular problems in employing double standards: first because of the American penchant to moralize, and secondly because of American involvement in a wider range of international relations than any other state. Washington's selective application of the term "terrorism" is therefore more apparent and vivid than in other states.

While all violent acts in human society are deplorable, the edifice of Western and international law over the centuries has striven to create subtle but significant legal distinctions among them, such as first-, second-, and third-degree murder, manslaughter, self-defense, guerrilla warfare, armed resistance, declared and undeclared war, and even "a just war." Useful definitions therefore need to avoid the term "terrorism" as a sweeping catch-all label for any violent action that someone doesn't like regardless of circumstances. Nearly all national liberation movements of history have engaged in one form of terrorism or another. Political violence is the coinage of politics globally, making blanket condemnation morally comforting but politically irrelevant.

Yet there assuredly is such a thing as terrorism and it must not be defined away into non-existence by legalistic, philosophical, and rhetorical hair-splitting, nor should all response be paralyzed due to definitional problems. Yet many groups accused of terrorism and their sympathizers call for definitions to be established. Their requests are legitimate and not simply aimed at obfuscation. The scourge of terrorism cannot be dealt with either justly or effectively until we know and agree on what we are talking about.

Among the leanest and most effective definitions upon which nearly all might agree is "the *intentional* targeting of civilians, including women and children for political ends."[1] The Qur'an itself clearly condemns such action.

Webster's International Dictionary offers an alternative definition: "the use of terrorizing methods of *governing* or *resisting* a government" [Italics mine] This definition importantly admits the possible culpability of the state in terrorist action as well, skirting the dilemma of the traditional legitimacy granted by the interstate system to "monopolization of the means of coercion" as belonging strictly to the state. This latter definition was largely conceived in the West under conditions of representative, answerable and consensual governance where to use force against the state clearly constitutes rebellion against a consensual order. But in most of the world, regimes are neither answerable nor consensual, raising questions about the legitimacy of indiscriminate use of force by regimes determined to hold on to power at any cost. The fact is that by far the greatest number of casualties of "terrorism" are the victims of terror—illegal violence—applied by the state.[2]

The policies and style of the state, and the *overall political culture* of a country also seriously affect the emergence of terrorism. Islamist movements are predictably more inclined to violence when the state itself practices significant violence against its own citizens—as in Egypt, Algeria, Tunisia, Uzbekistan, and Saudi Arabia, to name just a few. Deeply repressive states such as Iraq can successfully maintain a virtual monopoly on the use of violence through indiscriminate and undiluted brute force, while more open societies constrain the response of the state. The violence employed by the state against its own citizens is a leading source of an environment of violence. Furthermore, in states where no serious form of political expression is allowed and change of the political order seems beyond reach, the average citizen develops a sense of powerlessness and impotence that ultimately encourages a turn for violence—either domestically or against a foreign oppressor.

The issue for Muslims is complicated when the use of the term "jihad" is invoked in Islamist politics or adopted by terrorists. The basic meaning of jihad is "to struggle." In Islam the "greater jihad" is the struggle of the individual to overcome one's own baser instincts; "lesser jihad" is the use of force to defend one's family or the community from non-Muslim attack. But Muslim warriors in the past have used the term in their broader military campaigns even when not strictly correct in religious terms. They have invoked it even in struggles against other Muslims such as Saddam Hussein did against Shi'ite Iraq. Finally, the term "jihad" is used casually or colloquially to mean a great campaign, very similar to the use of the term "crusade" in the West—originally a Christian religious term from the word *cruz*, or holy cross—and applied to such initiatives as "a crusade against drugs."

In religious terms, the Qur'an unambiguously condemns attacks on civilians. Scholar of Islamic law and professor at the UCLA School of Law Khaled Abou El Fadl observes that there are a "number of Muslims who do believe that terrorism, at some level, is justified. It is worth noting, however, that, at a minimum, this belief is at odds with Islamic law. The Islamic juristic tradition, which is similar to the Jewish rabbinical tradition, has exhibited unmitigated hostility toward terror as a means of political resistance.

Modern Muslim terrorist groups are more rooted in national liberation ideologies of the 19th and 20th centuries than they are in the Islamic tradition. Although these terrorist groups adopt various theological justifications for their behavior, their ideologies, symbolism, language and organizational structure reflect the influence of the anti-colonial struggle of the developing world. . . .

It is a well-established Koranic precept that the injustice of others does not excuse one's own injustice."[3]

This analysis too points up the commonalities of a broader anti-colonial struggle in which the Muslim world is just one element.

ROOTS OF ANTI-WESTERNISM IN ISLAMIST IDEOLOGY

Why are there deep roots of anti-Westernism in so much radical Islamist thought? We know that much of historic anti-Western resentment in Muslim society is based on centuries of conflict and rivalry, issues of colonialism, imperialism, neo-imperialism, Western power and hegemony, and Western-dominated globalization. These issues have little explicitly to do with religious or philosophical issues at all. Here Islamism acts as a vehicle for a great many issues not directly linked with the goal of establishing an Islamic state per se, or even with the propagation of Islam. In other words, there is a historically based anti-Western impetus in much of Muslim culture itself *that would likely exist even if the Middle East were not Islamic but simply a regional "Middle Eastern" culture.* If the Middle East were even Christian the sources of *regional resentment* would still exist and would find some kind of name by which to express themselves. Indeed, we need only look at the deep historical tensions for fifteen hundred years between the Western and Eastern *Christian* worlds, still not ameliorated—look at Greek views of Rome—to understand why *regional* differences can be the source of conflict that later becomes ideologized into primarily *religious* differences or intensified by them. The entire history of the eastern, western and North African regions of the Roman Empire is a chronicle of regions adopting heterodox (later declared "heretical") forms of Christianity in part as a *vehicle for expression of regional hostility to the center.* If the entire Middle East were Christian and not Muslim the tensions would not be exactly the same but likely quite similar given tensions over history, oil, power, invasion, and geopolitics.

The point is, the clash of *regional interests* may precede the *ideological clash.* The regional clash will produce its own ideological justification and banner. In Middle Eastern culture today there are anti-Western instincts of varying degrees. Those who feel the issue most strongly have been searching for an ideological vehicle that usefully describes, explains, articulates, and justifies that anti-Westernism. For a long time many of these ideologues signed on to Arab nationalism as a strong vehicle of opposition. Others signed on to communism as a similar vehicle. Both of these secular ideologies failed because they could not address the many problems besetting the Arab world. Indeed, many Arab nationalists disillusioned with the impotence and failure of Arab nationalism came to embrace the new ideological refuge of Islamism. There are numerous cases of ex-communists who today are Islamists across the Muslim world. This is not entirely surprising: they continue to search for vehicles that explain, dignify, and empower their materially-based or regionally-based anti-Western grievances. This is one why Islamism *functionally* has much to do with nationalism. The explanatory framework of each ideology may differ to one degree or another. Between communism and Islamism lie the major polarities of atheism and faith. But otherwise political activists are driven by the same quest for social justice, reform, change, anger at corruption among the ruling classes, anger at impotence, foreign domination, and the West.

But to say that all Islamists are crypto-, would-be communists or nationalists would be simplistic. Most people probably come to Islamism from deeper religious impulses as well, but still they represent an activist mentality that seeks change in the status quo. This may be the most powerful distinction between Islamism and conventional Muslim believers. The Islamists seek bold change, while the traditionalists avoid struggle or confrontation. And they may differ on means of change as well.

Among Islamists themselves we see different visions of change, as they proceed from differing perspectives, intensities of conviction, and political psychologies. Some are driven to peaceful visions of social harmony and the creation of a better world. Others are angry at existing conditions. Others would love to see the deep spiritual values of Islam better informing the sad state of governance and society in the region today. Others want to see the Muslim world strong.

It is critical, then, to make distinctions, and to understand first the *psychology of politics and then the psychology of terrorism.* The psychology of politics relates to complex questions of the origins of political belief itself: is our own personal political philosophy purely the product of rational consideration? Or does the mind follow the impulses of the heart, helping justify what our emotions feel first? What makes one person a liberal, another conservative, another radical? Individuals emerging from virtually identical conditions and identical education regularly divide along ideological lines. What makes U.S. Supreme Court justices regularly divide 5–4 on issues in which they are all immensely knowledgeable and all exposed to the same facts? Personal psychologies differ.

At the extreme, what makes a man or woman become a terrorist? A variety of complex impulses come into play—with material, social, cultural, and psychological foundations all affecting individual human behavior. It is differences in personal psychology that lead one opponent of abortion to write articles, another to demonstrate, and a third to bomb a clinic. Some social activists with a cause will organize demonstrations; others form movements, throw rocks at police, shoot at cops, or even bomb a police station or a corporation. Some Palestinians will call for passive resistance, others for a massive informational campaign, for armed confrontation, for carrying the struggle to the civilian population of Israel. These are not hard-wired political preferences but deep personal predispositions that are further swayed by circumstances and environment. A peaceful struggler can turn to violence if provoked sufficiently. And some contain dark violence deep in their hearts from early events of personal psychological formation. We should note as well in our own personal psychologies differences that determine the severity of punishment we advocate for murder: some are hard set on capital punishment, while others find the death penalty repugnant. What makes a hard-liner on social issues? The reality that harsh conditions overall tend to produce harsh responses is part of this psychological equation.

Even the package of psychological impulses that shapes a latent terrorist still offers that same terrorist a choice of differing extremist vehicles for expression—fanatic religiosity, extreme secular nationalism, murderous and amoral anarchism, rabid fascism, or zealous communism—to suggest a few. Thus some Muslims are by instinct more upset, more angry, more disturbed, more moved by the panoply of frictions between the West and the Muslim world than are others. They will seek appropriate vehicles for the expression of those concerns. Their personal psychological makeup will determine whether they will reach for the sword, work through a political system, or dedicate themselves to propagating ideas and values to change the human heart. Islamic society and culture is no different in this respect than any other. People living under harsh conditions will routinely produce a higher degree of violent individuals than do comfortable societies. The reality is that the Middle East is a harsh place. The individual already psychologically predisposed to radicalism encounters many more daily causes or reasons that impel one toward embrace of radical action. In today's Muslim world it now happens to be extremist Islam that offers the most compelling vehicle for action in response to oppressive state governance and the perception that the U.S. policies harm

Muslim interests and humiliate Muslims. Thus the terrorist is demonstrably driven by more than simply "Islamist ideology."

As Eqbal Ahmad observed years prior to 11 September, the emergence of serious terrorism today is the technology that enables massive damage to be done by individuals who also have the ability to travel, communicate ideas, and coordinate with like-minded individuals. Much of modern terrorism is the globalization of psychotic discontent. Its alleviation involves the same answers that have always been adduced to lessen any kind of social grievance and discontent: reduction of the proportion of the population inclined toward violent expression. More importantly, it involves reduction of the *atmosphere of support and adulation* that accompanies those few reckless souls who adopt the vehicle of terrorism. Few in American today will applaud, even secretly, an act of terrorism in the name of much of anything. Our social and economic conditions are good enough, and generally fixable enough, largely to exclude terrorism as a vehicle for the attainment of anything. In the Middle East there is little ground for belief or hope that the existing political orders will fix much of anything. Terrorism thus finds sufficiently fertile grounds for acceptance or even popular adulation, even if the vast majority of the population does not itself actively participate.

But to understand terrorism is not to eliminate it. Terrorism is indeed a scourge that affects much of the world and is likely to be the instrument of the weak against the powerful indefinitely. Neither the United States nor any country can remain passive in the face of the challenge. The Bin Ladins and al-Qa'idas of the world must be tracked down and neutralized. International cooperation must make the movement and planning by terrorists as difficult as possible. The struggle will be ongoing. But the limits of the struggle are set not just by military or intelligence capabilities but by the willingness of the world and its populations to cooperate. And the degree of that cooperation will be determined in part by the perceived justness of the U.S. cause and the justness of the (U.S.-dominated) international order in the eyes of most of the rest of the world. Americans may seek their own justice for 11 September and feel fully righteous—properly so—in doing so, but that does not mean that it necessarily represents justice for others. At some point we reach a tradeoff between continued unilateral American campaigns and the counterreaction of the world as it weighs U.S. interests in the balance of its own interests and sympathies.

And among the most important elements in the War Against Terrorism are those of the "silent majority" in the Muslim world. The silent majority is really that great majority that never becomes deeply engaged in the struggles of the era. Its members are well aware of the shortcomings or outrages of their political, social, and economic order. They applaud and support (perhaps tacitly) those who take radical or even violent steps to change these outrages. They grasp the extremism of those taking violent, even shockingly immoral action, but they understand their motivations, even if they do not approve of their means. This is the silent majority. It is caught between repressive dictatorship at home, intrusive Western policies through the War Against Terrorism abroad, and the massive violence of a Bin Ladin response. With little to choose between, and limited ability to change the existing order, sullen passivity and applause for the current Robin Hood is the result. Western demands that the Muslim silent majority speak out against extremism should first consider this panoply of existing grievances and work for its alleviation. Otherwise striking out against the offenders of the moment will result only in a generation of more offenders in the future.

ISLAMISM IN POWER
IRAN, SUDAN, AND AFGHANISTAN

ASSESSING ISLAMISM IN POWER

When all the theoretical discussion about political Islam is put aside, one of the ultimate touchstones is how political Islam actually behaves in power. We have only three such cases to date: Iran, Sudan, and Afghanistan. Judging by these three limited examples, the depressing reality by general standards of judgment is that the experience of Islamist governance to date has not been encouraging. But how conclusive should these cases be in prompting broader conclusions about Islamism in power in general?

Some caution is in order. First, three cases out of hundreds of movements represents a narrow data base. More importantly, in all three cases Islamists came to power through *non-democratic processes*—social revolution, military coup, and civil war. In Iran and Afghanistan, political Islam *replaced* authoritarian regimes, while Sudan over decades has demonstrated a pattern of military coups alternating with democratic governance. The reality is that accession to power through force, by any group or party, invariably creates an authoritarian structure and legacy of violence that impedes evolution toward moderation and rule of law. Regrettably, resort to force is a classic pattern across most of the developing world. In this regard, these three states are hardly exceptional given the political culture across the region.

We have even less evidence to go on when we come to the question of how political Islam might function when it achieves power democratically. Virtually all Islamist parties are denied access to participation in the political order under the authoritarian regimes that dominate the Muslim world.

Given the inauspicious founding of these three regimes, the critical issue is to assess their success or failure. Different actors judge these regimes by quite different criteria. For some Islamists, merely being able to achieve power is a notable accomplishment—a Leninist perspective. By this measure, Islamists in Iran, Sudan, and Afghanistan have "succeeded" where other Islamist movements have failed. Obviously this is an unsatisfactory criterion for judging success since it completely ignores assessment of the uses and results of power. A second criterion might be the level of popular support for an Islamist government. Some hard-line Islamists will argue that the creation of an Islamic state is an "obligation" inherent in Islam and is unrelated to public opinion. Most Islamists, however, would reject any potential contradiction between the general public welfare and the requirements of Islam and instead see them as integrally linked. Indeed, one classic school of Islamic thought insists that the public welfare (*maslaha*) is the key measure of Islamic correctness and good governance. Increasingly Islamists must come to terms with factors of public opinion, popular support, and the public interest in administering an Islamic state.

And *who* is to judge their performance—the citizens of the state or the "international order"? More pointedly, if Washington does not like the policies of the regime in question, does that constitute de facto regime "failure"? Domestic and international acceptance should not be mutually exclusive, but perspectives can differ considerably: Muslim public opinion might welcome an elected Islamist government in Egypt, for example, while Washington will not. The fact is, however, that none of the three Islamist regimes enjoy majority support from their populations (and the Taleban were overthrown by the United States in 2001.) This absence of popular support is sadly true of a great many other non-Islamist regimes across the Muslim world as well.

To be sure, Islamist regimes have been in power for relatively brief periods of time, making longer range judgments more difficult. In Iran we have two decades of dramatically evolving political experience; Sudan has had only one decade; the Taleban in Afghanistan had barely half a decade. Few regimes of any kind in the Muslim world can demonstrate great signs of success, but they are tolerated in the West as long as their policies are generally not seen as seriously damaging to Western interests.

Political correctness should not paralyze United States from evaluating Islamist regimes from Western perspectives of what constitutes good governance, but we must also recognize that such U.S. judgments contain more than a few subjective elements. The United States frequently applies harsher standards of judgment to its adversaries than to those states with unpalatable policies whose cooperation it seeks for geopolitical reasons. Inconsistent standards of judgment are routine in U.S. foreign policy.

Rational analysis of Islamist regimes is immensely complicated by superheated American domestic politics that often permit little nuance and promote demonization of offending regimes, as has happened in the case of Iran and Sudan. In the end, the wishes of the populations themselves should be the determinative criterion of how these regimes have fared. Yet we must also note how difficult it is for regimes under Islamist rule to be judged "objectively" if they pose significant challenges to aspects of the Western-dominated international.

Furthermore, given the negative experiences the West has had with these three Islamist regimes, a popular distrust of the idea of any "Islamic state" has now developed. Any movement or party is generally condemned out of hand if it reportedly seeks to establish an "Islamic state." Yet, in reality, no one actually knows exactly what an "Islamic state" should be. An Islamic state has never existed in history in the sense of a *modern state*—except for the attempts of the three self-proclaimed states under consideration here. Muslim states throughout history never felt a need to declare themselves "Islamic"; such a label historically seemed superfluous in the Muslim world where the reigning political culture was always Muslim and where Islamic law was applied to one extent or another over a millennium and a half. The concept of an "Islamic state" in modern times is a reaction to the jettisoning of most traditional concepts of Islamic statecraft and adoption by governments in Arab and other Muslim states of Western codes of law, usually under colonial pressure. The very use of the term in modern times establishes a major precedent in the history of Islamic statecraft and refers to a pioneering effort by Islamists quite self-consciously to create an unprecedented kind of state that would find accord with both modernity and the Muslim identity.

Ironically, the supreme influence upon all Muslims engaged in politics today, including Islamists, is the concept and nature of the Western state. The power of the model of the Western state—an example of contemporary power and success in comparison to the current impotence and failure of most Muslim states—cannot be ignored. Thus two of the three states, Sudan and Iran, both show heavy influence of Western constitutional principles: an elected legislature (even if not always fairly run), and separation of powers (partly corrupted in practice). Neither of these principles is present in traditional Islamic thinking about the state, and both are rejected outright, for example, by Saudi Arabia as "foreign."

Thus, these states represent three early efforts at creating something new. Of the three, only Iran has genuinely broken new intellectual and ideological ground that suggests an evolving experiment that may yet yield some useful precedents about how Islamic government might function.

THE NATURE OF AMERICAN CRITERIA

We require some degree of objective criteria, such as the degree of popular support from these regimes, in judging their record. Yet the reality is that any critique of Islam in power tends to be dominated by the charges leveled by the United States against these regimes. These charges are partially justified. But they also reflect certain subjective U.S. geopolitical concerns, not necessarily broadly shared in the region or even in Europe. Key American concerns have been the existence of anti-Americanism, Israel's security, the Arab-Israeli peace process, development of weapons of mass destruction, and terrorism. The main problem is Washington's tendency to single out these states selectively for high-profile accusations when their policies often differ little from those of many other states in one or another objectionable respects.

It is a reality that some degree of anti-Americanism marks all of these Islamist regimes. But we are confronted with a serious chicken-and-egg problem here. Iran, for example, was born in the full flush of anti-Americanism, a legacy of Washington's overthrow of the first popularly elected Prime Minister Mossadegh in 1953, along with heavy backing for the Shah's autocracy and his ruthless intelligence organization Savak—policies that contributed to producing the Iranian revolution, seizure of the American Embassy and the hostage crisis in 1980, followed by heavy U.S. support to Saddam Hussein in his war of aggression against Iran in the 1980s. Popular anti-American attitudes molded the character of the Islamic Republic of Iran from the outset, becoming an ideological foundation of the clerical regime. Ironically, popular dislike of the policies of the clerics twenty years later has led to the growth of a measure of pro-U.S. attitudes.

The Taleban initially had no views on the United States or on foreign policy in general, although they came out of an ideological tradition of suspicion toward the West. They were quite prepared to work with the West, but for good reasons the United States soon found their harsh and discriminatory policies distasteful—even if many of these social policies differed little from those of U.S. ally Saudi Arabia. In the end it was the Taleban leadership's persistent provision of refuge to Usama bin Ladin and al-Qa'ida that terminated all possibility of cooperation. Bin Ladin aside, the United States would probably not have otherwise chosen to overthrow the Taleban.

The Sudanese Islamist government that came to power in 1989 did not have a deep anti-U.S. agenda, but it initially offered refuge to many Islamist *mujahidin,* graduates of the anti-Soviet jihad in Afghanistan, who were hostile to many regional regimes. Ideologues in the ruling Islamist movement, led by Hasan al-Turabi, also strongly supported the cause of Palestinian liberation and convened several "anti-imperialist" international conferences, even though the official policy of the Sudanese government stated support for any solution that satisfied the Palestinians. But by 1996 the regime was moderating, and under pressure from the United States, turned over "master terrorist" Carlos to France. The former U.S. ambassador to Sudan states that the regime in 1996 first offered to turn Bin Ladin over to Saudi Arabia and then to the United States in return for the lifting of sanctions but the offer was refused. By 1997 Sudan offered unconditional cooperation and willingness to share data on anti-terrorist issues and the U.S. Secretary of State proposed an upgrading of relations, but it was overruled by the White House on largely domestic political grounds.[1] The Clinton administration was committed to a long and unsuccessful effort at overthrowing the regime through military pressure from neighboring states.

The Sudanese government itself has rarely taken an overtly defiant posture toward the United States, even though it pursued a number of policies distasteful to Washington, including perpetuation (and worsening) of the long ongoing civil war that predated the Islamists, and a cancellation of the democratic order.

Relations with the three Islamist regimes is thus a complex equation in which seriously flawed regimes were subsequently demonized by Washington, which exacerbated the situation—and this in contrast to the far more measured tones Washington has employed with other states pursuing quite distasteful policies such as China, North Korea, Burma, Syria, and Uzbekistan. When Washington is perceived to be supportive of regimes that crush Islamic movements, Islamist hostility and suspicion in return cannot be surprising. Washington is indeed right to expect at least initially a frosty view toward U.S. policies from Islamists who come to power. And this expectation often leads Washington to try to prevent their coming to power at all. The perceptions of each side feed the other.

A core problem is the reality that many U.S. policies are highly unpopular in the Muslim world, and governments that would fully reflect public opinion are likely to adopt a harsher stance toward the United States than current authoritarian regimes that look to American support to stay in power. This is the dilemma of democratization in the Muslim world: the more representative governments become, the more likely they are to collide with U.S. interests, at least for an initial period. Islamist states thus tend to reflect much of the angry anti-U.S. sentiment inside these countries and do not simply manufacture it.

Each of the three Islamist regimes—Iran, Sudan, and Afghanistan—came to power under dramatically different conditions. Each had immediate impact upon both regional and even international politics and thereby exacerbated the problems that had existed before they came to power.

THE CASE OF IRAN

The Islamic Republic of Iran is unique in a number of respects. First, it came to power through a genuine social revolution, rare in modern history. At the same time its revolution brought down one of the West's closest allies, the Shah, and expunged what was once a key seat of major American influence. It has subsequently been one of the few states in the region unbeholden to the United States for either economic or security support to the regime, and therefore willing to publicly oppose U.S. policy in the region. Iran's ideology has facilitated, but not generated, this anti-American posture. Witness neighboring Iraq, with no shred of Islamic character, which adopts similar geopolitical postures in the name of secular nationalist ideologies. On the basis of its revolution and willingness to resist the United States, Iran has won the respect of most Muslims for its feisty independent-mindedness and for its progress toward democratic rule. As the first modern state to call itself Islamic, Iran has established a historical precedent that confers upon it considerable ideological importance, regardless of how successful its political, economic, and social policies have been or will be.

Iran is furthermore perceived by many Muslims to be "truer to its Islamic culture," partly defined by its independence from the United States. It has adopted a number of institutions that mark its bold experiment in seeking to apply Islamist thought. It is the first Muslim state in modern Middle Eastern history to be actually ruled by clerics—an innovation in Islam—and a critical step that is still under debate, interpretation, and evolution. Its largely Western-style constitution including democratic elections sets a precedent for what other Islamic governments might be in the future—flying sharply in the face of some other radical Islamists who have rejected Western models or democracy entirely.

Iran further created the position of Supreme Leader (*Rahbar*), a major innovation, designed in principle to embody the highest level of religious qualification and moral leadership to stand above and oversee the general political process. He represents the highest power in the state. The Supreme Leader is not elected but rather selected by a clerical commission of senior ayatollahs who are charged with selecting the cleric with the highest moral and juridical qualifications to ensure the ultimate Islamic correctness of state policies. The position in one sense resembles that of a president in a parliamentary system who is above daily politics and whose role is to focus on the broader welfare of the political order. This office in theory represents a fusion of two differing ideals: democracy at the working level of politics, and unelected moral leadership designed to protect the Islamic nature of the state. In other words, democracy is not an unlimited value but one bounded by Islamic values.

The position of the Supreme Leader of course structurally weakens the functioning of the democratic process since he can legally overrule democratically-based decision-making processes of government and is not answerable to the general public since he is not popularly elected. This position perhaps also partially resembles members of the U.S. Supreme Court who are not elected but selected for life by the president on the basis of their jurisprudential capabilities in protection of the Constitution—in principle over and above politics.

A profound debate is under way in Iran about whether such a Supreme Leader should not in fact be popularly elected rather than selected strictly by clerics supposedly qualified to make such a determination. As in any political order, the position of Supreme Leader has become quite politicized and in effect represents an autocratically empowered player in the middle of a democratic political arena.

Democratic principles are enshrined in the constitution, even if they are sometimes abused. Despite the abuses, this is no "show-piece constitution"; its provisions and workings are deeply and publicly contested. More important, the vast majority of clerics view Iran's democratic parliament as entirely compatible with Islamic concepts of *shura* or consultation. Islamic Iran has remarkably adopted some of the most open and honest elections in the Middle East. If honest, they are not fully fair, however: a Council of Guardians judges the acceptability of all potential candidates before they can run, based allegedly on whether the individuals are upright citizens by Islamic criteria. While every country places certain minimal constraints on who may run for office (non-felons, native-born citizens.) in Iran this process of "moral vetting" has in fact been politicized into a process designed primarily to maintain the power of the hard-liners. Reformist candidates are often routinely disqualified. Nonetheless the elections have been remarkably free and vigorously contested by candidates, and despite hard-liner interference, they have produced parliaments with ever greater numbers of reformers. Government and society are marked by growing diversity as restrictions placed by the government are eroding.

The state has not yet permitted free establishment of political parties, although this principle too is under public challenge as certain well known "tendencies" and networks among candidates, precursors to political parties, are forming. The Islamic Republic still shows an Islamist preference for corporatist thinking that seeks to homogenize the interests of all national elements in the interests of a national harmony, placing society above the individual. The regime seeks internal compromises, hoping to avoid what many Islamists view as the negative and divisive character of adversarial politics. This vision is rapidly breaking down in the face of universal political realities.

In terms of human rights and civil liberties, Iran is probably actually above par for the region, with a distinctly livelier press and an unusually high level of national debate and discussion. Prospects for evolutionary progress toward genuine democratic process are promising over the longer run.

The situation in Iran is thus dramatically and rapidly evolving, and its dynamism distinguishes it from so many autocratic regimes in the Muslim world. But what is particularly important is the "ideological progress" that Iran's Islamists are achieving. The country is in the throes of defining or redefining major issues of Islamic jurisprudence and ideology as they apply to governance. Iran's lively debate over the nature of modern Islamist governance is religiously and politically more creative than anything taking place elsewhere in the Muslim World.

From the hindsight of several decades hence, how will history look back at the Iranian experience? A first possible narrative would show that after several decades of rough and rocky developments following the revolution, Iran evolved toward relatively democratic, stable, and responsible governance. Iran will have succeeded in creating modern governance based on Islamic heritage and contemporary interpretations of Islamic values and institutions—the first country to create a serious synthesis between Islamic principles of government and universal values of democracy, pluralism, and tolerance. Iran will thus have played an immensely important role in the history of innovative reinterpretation (*ijtihad*) in Islamic theory of governance, exerting great impact on other Islamist movements.

An alternative narrative would show that Iran's theocracy simply led to intensified repression, authoritarianism, and eventual collapse of the Islamic Republic, giving way to either military rule or Western democratic leadership. The Iranian experience will thereby have demonstrated not only the disastrous character of clerical rule but the folly of attempting governance based on dated Islamist principles of governance, however conceived. Iran's failure will have had a debilitating effect upon other aspiring Islamist movements in the Muslim world.

While Western criticism of the failings of the Iranian regime is well known and will be discussed in another chapter, it is interesting to observe Islamist criticisms of Tehran's failings. A strong ideological defender of the Iranian regime, Dr. Kalim Siddiqui—a Sunni of Pakistani origin who was director of the Muslim Institute in London until his death in 1998—observed that Tehran early on fell into the trap of Iranian nationalism, thus negating some of the universal qualities that an Islamic state should possess. He also criticized Iran for maintaining a bloated bureaucracy, whereas an Islamic state in his view should be lean and minimalist. Siddiqui faults the Islamic Revolution for having failed to undertake revolutionary land reform as part of a program of social justice, due to the long-standing historical ties between the landowning aristocracy and the clergy. He sees the Iranian regime also drifting too heavily toward particularistic Shi'ite doctrine in some respects, thus belying its own aspirations and claims toward universality and damaging unnecessarily its relations with the Sunni world.[2]

But for many Muslims, the Iranian regime gained its greatest credibility and acceptance through its ability to defy the West. A record of defiance, of course, is insufficient to constitute success in governance. Iran has also paid a considerable price in U.S.-imposed isolation as a result of these policies, from which it began to emerge only in the very last years of the twentieth century. Nonetheless, many other Muslims and Islamists who would like to see their own states stand up more boldly to Western and especially American interests find much to respect in the foreign policy of the Islamic Republic. Other Islamists, mostly Arab, ignore the Iranian experience entirely, dismissing it as Shi'ite and hence irrelevant to Sunnis.

In one sense, Islamism as presently conceived by the hard-line ideologues has already failed in Iran. The younger generation in particular is cynical about the clerics and their incessant invocation of Islam to justify repression and imposition of stifling social policies. Indeed, many clerics are concerned precisely about the damage being done to Islam itself in the eyes of a public that may now judge Islam more by the failures of the regime than as an eternal faith. In short, power has corrupted religious institutions and discredited the idea of Islamic values in government. The disillusionment of youth is already well advanced and very serious. Boredom and frustration may surpass repression as the chief grievance of youth.[3]

The Iranian regime has furthermore inadvertently demonstrated one of the central tenets of Shi'ite faith, namely the corrupting character of government and power. The Shi'ite clergy over history had largely avoided association with power, preferring the role of moral critic of the ruler. Yet with Khomeini's ascension to power and the proclamation of clerical rule, the traditional Shi'ite fear was vindicated: the clergy indeed did become corrupted by both money and power, losing its moral authority in the face of the public.

What is fascinating today is that Islam today *is* the framework of nearly all political debate. Conservative, liberal, right or left, clerical rule versus secularism, democracy versus authoritarian institutions, socially restrictive or permissive, statist or civil libertarian, free market or centralized economy—the entire debate is encompassed within the vocabulary, frame of reference, and coinage of Islam.

On the one hand, this framework is artificially imposed: in the absence of freedom to assault clerical rule and its authoritarian implications head on, the battle must be engaged on Islamic turf, the arguments adduced from the Qur'an, the Traditions of the Prophet, and the annals of Islamic jurisprudence. The Islamic vocabulary thus provides cover for the arguments even of those who are not committed to the Islamist cause, such as leftists, who must resort to a textual basis in arguing for a more liberal approach. Yet this imposed limitation of arguing politics within the framework of Islam has nonetheless produced major contributions to the evolution of Islamic political thought. Probably nowhere else in the world has Islamic thinking been "force-marched" at such a speed in the field of political and social theory—opening new ranges of argumentation on all sides about the nature of politics and its relationship to Islamic thought.

Equally notable in Iran, women have been playing an increasingly public role. For all the debate over what the position of women should be in Islamic society, Iran has never had doubts about women's role in politics—in which they have occupied positions of vice president, cabinet members, and a considerable number of members of parliament—and academia where they hold more university teaching positions than do women in the United States. Significantly for an Islamic Republic, Iran has totally abandoned several key features of Shari'a law, especially law relating to women on issues of inheritance, divorce law, and child custody.

While women are widely employed and make up over half of the university student body, social codes regarding women's dress in public are relatively strict, but they are weakening. Public culture is repressed by highly conservative interpretations of public behavior of men and women together, quite similar to Saudi Arabia, although Iran has movie theaters whereas Saudi Arabia does not. (Indeed, Iran is internationally recognized as possessing some of the most brilliant cinematic directors in the world.) Since 1999 a process of gradual liberalization has been underway in all these areas as the regime recognizes it cannot afford to continue enforcement of its originally draconian cultural regulations that once even banned Western music.

Spasms of repression have accompanied even the advancement of reforms: several political murders of opposition figures forced the resignation of the Minister of Interior, arbitrary arrests of numerous other leading political reformers and even parliamentarians have incensed the public and raised tensions within the country. Journalists are threatened, jailed, later acquitted or released early; newspapers are shut down, often only to reopen under new names and sponsoring major revelations of political struggles. Political lines are drawn ever more clearly, and the massive political struggle between hard-liners and liberals (to oversimplify the issues) is conducted with remarkable transparency, including the front pages of the press, which finds no parallel almost anywhere in the Arab world.

The Iranian economy has been a signal failure. Corruption and statism hobble the economy, unemployment is high, and most workers must maintain more than one job to make ends meet. Inflation has been consistently high. The weaknesses of the Iranian economy, of course, are also due in part to the devastating effects of the eight-year Iran–Iraq War (begun by Iraq but perpetuated by Iran), followed by American-imposed sanctions that have served to cripple needed investment in the energy sector.

Education under the Islamic Republic has flourished and surpassed the levels attained by the Shah. Large numbers of students are sent abroad, including to the United States.

In short, the Iranian record is a mixed one. By regional standards, including such U.S. allies as Egypt and Saudi Arabia, Iran has a more open political order, with a lively intellectual life that has few analogues in other regional states. It still has some major distance to go before becoming a genuinely democratic state, but it has outpaced most other Muslim states in the region except Turkey.

THE CASE OF SUDAN

Islamism in Sudan presents several important characteristics that make it worthy of special attention. Sudan is the largest country in Africa, bordering on nine different states. With its extensive and fertile agricultural lands, it is a potential breadbasket for all of Africa. Sudan is only the second Islamist state to appear in the Muslim world (after Iran), and the first Islamist state that is Sunni and Arab. It is also the first country in which an Islamist movement came to power by military coup.

Sudan is especially important because of its location on one of the important cultural fault lines of the Muslim world. Sudan is not a homogeneous Muslim state at all; indeed, it has 597 tribes that speak over 400 different languages and dialects.[4] Fault lines exist between northern and southern Sudan not only between Arab (45 percent to 60 percent of the population) and non-Arab, but between Muslim (55 to 65 percent of the population) and non-Muslim. Major cultural differences exist even among Muslim tribes in the north and the west. The southern population is mainly animist and, despite the impression given by vociferous Christian advocacy groups in the United States who oppose the regime, only very slightly Christian (3 to 4 percent).[5] Because Sudan historically represented the southern borderlands of Islamic civilization, successive Arab-dominated governments in Sudan have felt a special "Islamic manifest destiny" in spreading both Arab culture and Islam into southern Sudan and deeper into black Africa. This mission has intensified opposition among populations in the non-Arab, non-Muslim south. These ethnic and religious splits have confronted Sudan with an armed confrontation considerably predating the Islamist takeover, with strong separatist overtones—a genuine civil war—that have almost destroyed the very integrity of the state.

Sudan's long and bloody civil war raises major humanitarian issues; the war's brutality and violation of human rights, on all sides, are unprecedented in Sudan's history, creating massive refugee flows both within and outside the state since the latest round of conflict began in 1983, six years before the Islamists came to power. The ethnic and racial character of the war also affects parallel racial and religious tensions in bordering states with their own minority problems.

THE PATH TO POWER

Sudan's major Islamist movement has been the National Islamic Front (NIF), loosely linked to the Egyptian Muslim Brotherhood. The NIF's path to power through military coup may represent a successful Leninist model of taking power, but in doing so it casts doubt upon the democratic avowals of other Islamist movements. The process provides some lessons. The longtime leader of the Sudanese Islamists and the acknowledged ideological leader of the regime, Dr. Hasan al-Turabi, planned for many decades the transformation of his minoritarian movement into a vehicle capable of attaining power. The stepping stones for Turabi's march to power lay in three main areas: financial, educational-ideological, and military. Turabi first built a powerful economic base with the indispensable assistance of external money from Islamist banking systems, especially those linked with Saudi Arabia. As Minister of Education he gained significant control over the educational system, enabling the NIF to identify sympathetic students and to place them into the university system and the military academy, thus building a cadre of loyalist followers. Finally, the NIF's support within the military grew over time, ultimately enabling key sympathetic officers to pull off a coup d'etat in 1989 during a period of failing coalition politics.

The ability of a limited ideological movement to seize power suggests that the slow process of building cadre support within the armed forces and other branches of government can be a fruitful route for Islamists elsewhere in the Muslim world. (Indeed, radical Islamists by 1979 had infiltrated the Egyptian army to the extent of being able to assassinate Egyptian President Sadat.) The military officers who carried out the Sudanese coup, linked with the NIF as the force behind the scenes, are a significant element of the power core of the Sudanese Islamist regime today.

One of the most disheartening features of the Sudanese regime has been the role of its chief ideologist, Dr. Turabi, with his erudition and deep Western education (Sorbonne and Oxford) and his oft-stated commitment to democratic process and liberal government. Yet, once in power, the NIF with army support adopted a se-

ries of policies that immediately provoked considerable international disapprobation and isolation. The regime early on imposed harsh methods of political suppression throughout the country, especially in the non-Muslim south, but also in
the Arab north. It crushed most political opposition, purged the ranks of the military, and extended the workings of the intelligence and security apparatuses more
widely than ever before. Civil liberties, always frail, were further reduced by a more
efficient, centrally controlled regime. There are no legal or constitutional impedi-
ments against the regime's wielding almost absolute power. Turabi was reportedly
under pressure from more hard-line elements within the regime but nonetheless
has been part of process of authoritarianization.

Serious opposition movements were eliminated in the north, and most potential opposition was exiled. The regime is more entrenched than previous regimes
have been, seemingly less susceptible either to military coup or popular uprising.
NIF members privately acknowledge that they probably would not yet be able to
win in genuinely free elections, partly because of the continued dominance of traditionalist Sufi "parties," based on religious brotherhoods whose members are
unswervingly loyal followers of their leader, regardless of the issues.

Despite its Islamist character, it is important to note that the NIF nucleus in
government is highly educated and professional, with large numbers of doctoral
graduates from U.S. universities. It is described as the most professional government in Sudan's history, even if it is lacking in political experience. It is interesting
that over the past twenty years only two parties, the communists and the NIF,
commanded the support of much of the Sudanese educated class as the only two
forces with a "modern" and fully national outlook, that is, one that sought to move
away from the traditional rural patronage system that had always dominated politics and that did not identify with tribal politics. It was also the weakening of the
Communist Party that was among the key factors that led to the strong rise of the
NIF among many elements of the educated Sudanese, students, and professionals.
The NIF quite candidly admits that it learned much from its competition with the
communists in the seventies since it was challenged to learn the techniques of becoming a mass party with a clear-cut national program.

NIF POLITICAL FAILURES

The Sudanese Islamist regime has been sharply criticized by the West, often de-
servedly: inexperience in politics, numerous serious miscalculations and mistakes
in the early years, maladroit policies, a determination to hold onto power, the
elimination of democratic practice, an early dalliance with international Islamist

revolutionaries of all stripes, the intensification and ideologization of a long-standing brutal civil war, and the alienation of nearly all neighbors. Committed to its international ideological vision, the regime also fell afoul—without adequate recognition of the full international implications of some of its actions—of numerous major international political forces that have intensified the attacks upon it: first from the Egyptian, Saudi, Israeli, and Kuwaiti governments and then, more importantly, from Christian-dominated governments south of Sudan, Christian missionary groups in the West, the Christian right in the United States, U.S. human rights groups, and U.S. counter-terrorism policies. It is nonetheless noteworthy that in 2001 President George W. Bush's War Against Terrorism impelled Washington for the first time in a decade to take up Sudan's long-stated willingness to cooperate on terrorism that has lead to a less adversarial relationship and an end to U.S. efforts to overthrow the regime.

Twelve years of fighting against southern separatism under the Islamist regime have resulted only in stalemate, with the economic and political costs of the war exacting a debilitating price, forcing upon the regime the recognition that it must finally put aside the ideological goals of Islamization and work to achieve a genuine negotiated settlement. Some Islamists are seemingly torn between abandoning the Islamist goals of the revolution in order to maintain the unity of the country on the one hand, and preserving the goals of the Islamist revolution in the Muslim north even at the cost of losing the south to secession.

There are now few grounds for optimism about the long-term prospects for Sudan's territorial integrity—under almost any regime. Sudan shares the pan-African challenge of massive, nearly unmanageable religious, ethnic, tribal, and cultural differences that few states can survive. Sudan's problems have been exacerbated by an ideological struggle, both national and international, between Christian and Muslim missionary activism for the conversion of animist peoples in southern Sudan and Africa more generally. Since Islam as a religion focuses more on state structure and legal organization than does Christianity, and it will probably enjoy the backing of a broad range of Muslim states, the chances are good that Islam will be the strongest contender for new converts across Africa. That ongoing process will also complicate the future geopolitics of the region as Islam gradually moves southwards, meeting with opposition from Christian states who seek backing from the West and from Christian groups in the United States. This has become one of the more emotive domestic issues surrounding debate over U.S.-Sudanese policy in the United States.

A major element of the regime's economic failure flowed specifically from purely political choices early on in the regime that alienated patrons such as Saudi

Arabia and damaged its economic standing on an international basis. The war in the south has bled the economy. The regime was forced to fall back on self-sufficiency, probably a blessing in disguise. Sudan's main problem is capital starvation, which hinders major restructuring of the economy and prevents the undertaking of more ambitious economic projects. Interestingly, the regime accepted from the beginning the recommendations and restrictions of the IMF and worked hard to implement them; it has not engaged in leftist denunciation of a "Western-imposed neo-colonialist international economic order" that radical Islamist rhetoric might have suggested. The current leadership reflects a considerable degree of pragmatism that over the long term could offer Sudan a brighter future.

LIBERALIZATION

In the last few years of the nineties there has been a gradual but clear move away from the "internationalist" and ideological wing of the NIF in favor of the "nationalist" or more pragmatic leaders who focus on trying to recover from Sudan's disastrous international isolation and economic damage that resulted from ideological adventurism. This shift has significantly weakened Dr. Turabi's position within the government, and he has been under house arrest for several years.

Encouraging efforts at regime liberalization and reform efforts have also been underway. Key political leaders in exile have returned and are now negotiating for some restoration of electoral politics—a major risk for the generally unpopular NIF regime but one it recognizes it must deal with. Improvement of ties with the United States after 11 September 2001 may also assist this process.

Any visitor to Khartoum is struck quickly by the relaxed and relatively non-ideological feeling of the country. The Sudanese regime is almost certainly less of a police state than many other Arab regimes, despite its poor human rights record. The social restrictions, despite Islamism, are far fewer than those found in Saudi Arabia or even Iran.

Dr. Turabi is considered by many Islamists in the Muslim world as a better thinker than a politician. He is a modernist (not his term) in Islamist thought and is attacked by many Islamist conservatives for his more dynamic approach to understanding Islam under contemporary conditions. He is considered a "liberal" in his views on the absolute necessity of liberation of women and their role in politics; he rejects the hard-line view of apostasy in Islam that calls for the death penalty, he opposed Iran's death sentence *fatwa* against Salman Rushdie; he believes that many Islamist organizations are too focused on narrow historical debates and behavioral issues of what should be forbidden, at the expense of focusing on the grand issues of economic and societal development and Muslim backwardness; he believes that modern reinterpretation of Islam (*ijtihad*) is essential and cannot be the narrow prerogative of any special class or professional group (like '*ulama*) but the privilege of everyone in determining their own lives; he opposes traditionalist religious authority that encourages blind and unconsidered obedience among followers. He opposes the elitism of many Islamist movements that are distant from the majority of the population. He believes it is essential for Muslims to develop a comprehensive vision of what is required to face the future. He stresses the need for broad modern education in all subjects. He believes that an Islamic approach to economics must be developed in which moral issues are embedded: the necessity of focus on ecological issues, the attack against corruption within the economy, the need for economic development, and the centrality of social justice within the economic order.[6]

All of these issues, of course, are presented on the theoretical level; clearly how they are understood and applied is the heart of the issue. One might point out that contemporary Islamist Sudan has not yet demonstrated major success in many of these areas, even if the vision is there. Either Turabi's liberalizing influence has been blocked or he has been forced to abandon many of his precepts in the face of the realities of maintaining power.

At the heart of the problem for all Islamists in power—or indeed for any party with a clear vision and program—is the reluctance to give up power until the program is implemented. It is easy to rationalize why a new regime "should be given time" to implement its programs before being judged at the polls. But how much time? The NIF unquestionably feels frustrated that it has been the object of economic sanctions and destabilization for a variety of reasons. The NIF argues that it has been condemned and marginalized by the West and Sudan's own neighbors who fear the spread of Islamist ideas or who do not wish to see Islamist Sudan succeed. All of these arguments have some elements of truth to them.

A collision course benefits neither side. While international pressures can be justified to force Sudanese recognition of certain international norms of behavior, the United States could have done much more to encourage the regime to evolve. For many years the leaders of Khartoum have been clearly rethinking the costs of past adventurism and have been seeking more pragmatic policies and ties with Washington, but they have been consistently rebuffed for many of the reasons already mentioned, including domestic U.S. politics. Yet it has also been evident that Washington for many years has wanted not to see improved ties, but rather the total collapse of the regime. This reality has been driven by a powerful anti-Sudan lobby in Washington that has spearheaded a virtual no-negotiation policy that has struck many observers, including former U.S. president Jimmy Carter, as willful and unproductive. It has helped build and perpetuate an exaggerated, sensationalist, and one-sided picture of Sudanese realities including quite distorted claims of slavery—a historically rooted curse of southern Sudanese tribal society in war. The real problems of the country are bad enough without the hyperbole of many groups to serve parochial ends. U.S. policies consisted almost entirely of sticks with no carrots, and they gave little recognition to areas where significant progress has been made, as noted by a past American ambassador to the NIF regime.[7]

If Khartoum can continue its efforts toward liberalization and reform it could present a second case of an Islamist regime that has moved toward a more open society. In such a case it could in the future serve as a moderating force among Islamist movements, in its examples of mistakes and lessons learned. It could serve as intermediary and moderating force with other Islamist groups. It may be establishing some important principles about how and how not to apply Shari'a law in practical ways in a modern state; this experience could affect the attitudes of less flexible Islamist movements not in power. Unfortunately, however, at least some conservative Islamists, such as those from Saudi Arabia, are inclined to write Dr. Turabi off even as a "non-Muslim" for his more liberal interpretations of Shari'a application.

If the problem of Khartoum is seen in the broader context—that is, the problem of dealing with the "first Sunni fundamentalist state" in the region, then more is at stake than simply the fate of one among many distasteful regimes in the Middle East. It is highly desirable that its weaknesses be visible to all, including other Muslims and Islamists. It will be the past mistakes and failures of the Sudanese regime that will highlight for other Islamist groups the realities and problems of Islamist politics and policies in the world today. In this sense, a direct Western confrontation with Khartoum that suggests that Islamism itself is the problem—as opposed to certain specific policies by Khartoum—is not desirable. Let confrontation come at the regional level and into the full light of publicity about conditions in Sudan. The regime's record is a mixed one, quite similar to that of other regimes in the region. Western support for intervention to end the regime will only help perpetuate the Islamist mystique. The new dialog between Washington and Khartoum starting in 2001 may be the beginning of greater wisdom on both sides, may assist Khartoum in overcoming past excesses and may break the mold of seemingly automatic confrontation between Islamist states and Washington.

THE CASE OF AFGHANISTAN

The Taleban regime of Afghanistan was in power for six years before being overthrown by U.S. military forces in November 2001 for its support to terrorist Usama bin Ladin and the al-Qa'ida organization. By almost any standards, the

Taleban regime in Afghanistan has to be judged as the worst of the three Islamist regimes. It enjoyed a terrible international reputation, becoming almost a byword in the West for primitive, harsh, medieval, intolerant policies—virtual Hollywood stereotypes of fanatical Islam. Despite the media hype, many of these epithets were deserved. But however ignorant and ill-conceived many of the Taleban's own policies were, the Taleban also came to preside over a country already in a state of immense misery and civil war—the legacy of twenty long years of warfare, ten of them against a Soviet superpower. Afghanistan in 1997, just after the Taleban takeover, already had ranked high on the UN's "misery list," The United Nations' so-called Human Development Index placed Afghanistan 170th of 174 countries, "the least developed country in the world outside of Africa in terms of illiteracy, infant and maternal mortality, massive internal and external refugees malnourishment, destruction of cultivated land by war, drought and ten million landmines."[8] The Taleban thus inherited a state already in a high state of wretchedness and proceeded to worsen it in several respects.

Despite the spectacular victory of the *mujahidin* over the Soviet occupation, supported by massive aid from the West, the euphoria quickly deteriorated as the country descended into civil war among the *mujahidin* groups, accompanied by the emergence of local warlords and an increase in poppy production; banditry, brigandage, lawlessness, and extortion flourished. It was hardly foreordained by Afghan conditions that the Taleban would come to power—indeed, several other Islamist movements were also contending, many of which were far more moderate and sophisticated. But the mere fact that the Taleban initially brought a restoration of law and order, however harsh and austerely applied, was welcomed in 1996 by much of the population, anxious to be free of the horrors of civil war, warlords, anarchy, and chaos. Taleban social policies were not the major concern of most of Afghanistan's population—food, water, shelter, medicine, and ubiquitous landmines were the dominant issues outside of the few major cities.

Given their ignorant, narrow and inexperienced nature, the Taleban were almost doomed from the start in their accession to power in what was a downward spiral: they took over a highly underdeveloped country after twenty years of warfare; while equipped with no previous experience and limited education or knowledge of the world and few skills, they fell heir to administering a government. Their first task was to restore law and order out of anarchy; they then introduced extremely austere social and legal policies that reflected traditional Deobandi thinking (an austere and literalistic South Asian school of Islam with some resemblance to Wahhabism in Saudi Arabia.) They were heavily imbued as well with Afghan tribal Islam that was as much tribal tradition as it was Islam. They inherited an economy based on rampant poppy production going back at least forty years; inherited large numbers of Islamist *mujahidin* from around the world who sought to maintain training camps for themselves after having helped expel the Soviets; they were quickly drawn into international conflict on resulting terrorism issues, and as a result drew down sanctions upon their heads. This was the special blend of circumstances that produced one of the most unpleasant regimes in the contemporary Muslim world, in a country whose backwardness and isolation were already legendary. The Taleban, facing a steep learning curve, did little to improve the situation and never managed to establish functional and responsible national government. This is the context that formed the nature of the Taleban regime in Afghanistan.

While the West focused on the problem of the Taleban's primitive Islamic interpretations, for the bulk of the Afghan population the most salient reality was the fact that the Taleban were almost exclusively ethnic Pashtuns—the single largest ethnic group (perhaps 38 percent of the population) in the country—who had controlled multiethnic Afghanistan for several centuries. Other ethnic groups—Hazara, Tajik, Uzbek, Turkmen, and Nuristani—were unwilling to accede to renewed Pashtun domination of the country following the participation of all Afghans in the anti-Soviet struggle.

All over Central Asia conditions existed and still continue to exist that provide ideal conditions for the growth and expansion of Islamist movements: corruption, bad governance, repressive political orders that crush all political opposition, several key ongoing national liberation movements (Uyghur, Chechen, and Kashmiri) that naturally employ Islam as part of their identity and ideological impulse against oppression from non-Muslim authorities. Afghanistan lies at the epicenter of this turmoil. As a result, important external forces that shared a stake in Afghan events were disturbed at the implications of a Taleban takeover: Iran because the Taleban were fiercely anti-Shi'ite and treated the Shi'ite Hazara population with extreme harshness; and Russia, Uzbekistan, and Tajikistan because they feared the Taleban would turn their sights toward expanding Islamist movements north into Central Asia. India too, geopolitically sought to deny Pakistan strategic dominance in Afghanistan, which a Taleban victory would represent. Washington was initially neutral and hoped, with Pakistani urging, that the Taleban had no anti-U.S. agenda, could at last unify the country so long wracked by civil war; could facilitate the passage of Turkmen gas pipelines through Afghanistan to the Indian Ocean, skirting Iran; could impose control over the rampant poppy production and crack down on the presence of Muslim guerrillas and training camps in the country since the anti-Soviet jihad.

Twenty years of warfare and the breakdown of the state system also made the theological schools or *madrasas* virtually the only education available in the countryside, remote villages, or refugee camps.[9] These *madrasas* are privately run, especially under the tutelage of the large Islamist *Jama'at-i Ulama-i Islam*, (The Association of Islamic 'Ulama or JUI), a highly conservative Islamist movement inclined toward hard-line *salafi* interpretations of Islam.

Quite unlike Iran or Sudan, the Taleban rejected outright the concept of republic as non-Islamic and adopted the official title of Islamic Emirate of Afghanistan from early Islamic history with its implications of sharply delimited power of the state mechanism beyond assuring a moral society.

WESTERN CONCERNS OVER TALEBAN POLICIES

Obviously Western and specifically American concerns over Taleban policies became the determinative factors placing pressure upon that regime. U.S. objections focused first on women's rights, then overall human rights, drug trafficking (a continuation of forty years of Afghan life), and finally and most importantly, the Taleban's links to terrorism and especially support to Bin Ladin.

The Taleban originally had no guerrilla or terrorist agenda of their own—they were strictly intent upon establishing their control over the country and simply inherited the *mujahidin* training infrastructure that had existed for fifteen years. The Taleban gradually began to acquire some stake in the guerrilla groups already in the country, which assisted them in extending control over the country. The Taleban's acquiescence to Islamist terrorism reached its pinnacle when it granted asylum to Usama bin Ladin after his expulsion from Sudan in 1996. The *mujahidin* training facilities of Afghanistan enabled Pakistan to support international *mujahidin* groups to fight in Kashmir. Taleban support for Bin Ladin became the proximate cause of the U.S. overthrow of the Taleban after the 11 September attack on the United States.

The Taleban did no more than to perpetuate the permissive policies of previous Afghan governments toward poppy cultivation going back forty years, despite long-term efforts by the United States and the West to curtail it. The welfare of a large portion of the impoverished population depended on poppies as virtually its sole source of reliable income. Surprisingly, however, in 2000 the Taleban did actually implement a ban on poppy production for the first time in Afghan history.

The Taleban's social policies, some of the harshest in the whole world, immensely discredited the country. Women in particular were the key victims of their policies: the refusal to allow women to work, some of the most restrictive clothing policies for women anywhere, requiring full coverage of all skin, and the closing of all schools for girls. Men too were compelled to observe dress codes and wear obligatory beards. Music, games, kite-flying, and photography were also generally banned and the regime adopted a near-Luddite ban on television and VCRs as potential carriers of morally unsuitable material, distracting people from religious contemplation. The politics of intimidation spread into the neighboring Pashtun regions in Pakistan where a million and a half Afghan refugees still live. Groups affiliated with or sympathetic to the Taleban tried to impose their social and political values and practices upon the Afghan refugee community in many areas, employing various forms of intimidation or punishment, including murder.[10]

In one of their most outrageous cultural acts of all, in 2001 the Taleban—seemingly at Bin Ladin's urging as well—ordered the destruction of the giant, ancient standing Buddha statues in Bamyan, a world class cultural monument. The justification was that "idols are offensive to Islam." This act won massive disapprobation from around the world, including from leading Islamic authorities. The Taleban pointed out that the West was faster off the mark to protect statues than it was to rescue Afghans from famine.

But however ill-conceived Taleban policies were, they cannot be dismissed as irrelevant to the Islamist experience simply because "this is not true Islam." Taleban edicts represent an authentic extreme of Islamic interpretation and practice, much more so than the actions of al-Qa'ida. The Taleban believed they were very much indeed practicing Islam. While all mainstream Islamists condemn their policies and interpretations of Islam as reprehensible and foolish, the Taleban were not literally "deviant" (munharif), but fairly consistent—while ignorant and harsh—within the extremely austere and narrow interpretations of Deobandi Islam. In the end, the Islamist ideology of the Taleban, whatever it was, was not able to administer the country or even keep Afghanistan together.

CONCLUSION

The three Islamist regimes that have emerged to date have not been able to demonstrate the superiority of Islamic government over previous regimes. All three came to power by force, typical of most of the region. Each conceived of Islamic government in different ways. Islamists have not been able to move beyond the classic weaknesses of the political culture of their respective countries. In the case of Afghanistan, the Taleban were worse than preceding regimes. These regimes have demonstrated no distinctively new features that mark significant departure in their approach to managing their domestic and foreign policies.

Neither Iran nor Sudan began with any acceptance of genuine democratic practice, but Iran's Islamist government began to make impressive progress after fifteen years in power. Islamists in Sudan after ten years in power may be moving toward some early liberalization. But neither state could afford fully open, fair elections without probable loss of power. All three are likely to fall without having persuaded their populations that Islamic government brought major new benefits.

Each regime has pursued highly conservative cultural and social policies, the Taleban most of all, Sudan the least. The Iranian Islamic regime has been the most nationalist, and in future histories written in Iran are most likely to be commended for having restored genuine national independence free of previous U.S. domination and for having restored a degree of national dignity that is respected across the Muslim world. All three have run afoul of U.S. policies due to their extreme nationalist stance toward U.S. power and policies. All three have been sympathetic to one degree or another of Islamic national liberation movements and have supported selective violent Islamist movements, at least initially. Both Iran and Sudan continue to move toward moderation.

It is probably useful to view these three early experiences in Islamic government as just that—initial experiments to try to bring some degree of Islamic principles into government, however understood. Their intense nationalism vis-à-vis the United States is probably their major common feature; this characteristic will likely resemble the increased nationalist expression that will characterize most future regimes in the Muslim world after the fall of authoritarian regimes that now look to the United States for support.

None of these regimes offers much encouragement for the future of Islamist governance *that attains power by force*. Indeed, apart from a prickly nationalism, they resemble non-Islamist authoritarian regimes in the region. The experience of Islamism in power is still in its early stages of historical development and is likely to develop many variations. The real test of future Islamist governance will come when Islamists attain power by democratic means and operate within that milieu. The first such step in that direction has now taken place with the election of a moderate Islamist party to power in Turkey in late 2002.

ISLAMISM IN POLITICS

ISLAM AND THE EMERGENCE
OF THE MODERN STATE

For most of the colonial period *Islam as a faith, for all its inherent political dimensions, was largely excluded from opportunities to affect the evolution of politics in the modern Muslim state.* Thus the relationship between politics and Islam simply never had the chance to evolve "normally" as it would have been able to do under conditions of sustained and unbroken sovereignty.

Colonialism set most of the new institutional groundwork for the modern Muslim state, reflecting contemporary European values and institutions of the period. But *these institutions were rarely organically related to the political culture, experience, structure, and society of Muslim populations.* As a result, the grafting on of Western institutions was invariably awkward, partial, artificial, and temporary. In fact, one might argue that *one of the key projects of Islamists today—intentionally or unintentionally—is to formulate a reconciliation between traditional Muslim philosophy and practice of statecraft on the one hand, and those Western institutions and practices already on the scene on the other.*

Even though they had been mainly excluded from politics earlier, Islamic organizations in most places did come to extensively participate in the final national liberation struggle against colonialism. Yet the anti-colonial struggle generated a set of new, usually quite Westernized leaders to preside over the newly liberated state in a distinctly secular spirit: Atatürk in Turkey, Bourgiba in Tunisia, Sukarno in Indonesia, Jinnah in Pakistan, Nasser in Egypt, Reza Shah in Iran, Ben Bella in Algeria. Nearly all of them looked to secular nation-building and even socialism as the key tasks at hand. Islam and its institutions were viewed as largely irrelevant, negative, backward, competitive, or possibly even hostile to the cause of a new forced march to modernity and national power. Thus to Islamic intellectuals, the new postcolonial independent state represented a new and positive threat to their outlook and aspirations, as the forms—but not usually the substance—of Western culture were grafted onto Islamic society. This process was carried out in the name of broadened state power with few restrictions upon the legal abuse of that power. Traditional middle and lower classes who feel uncomfortable and distant from this Westernized lifestyle have provided much of the backing to Islamist movements with roots in local culture.

While today Islamists are among those contesting for power within the state, Islamist movements earlier were not directly engaged in politics; they conceived of the Islamist project initially as operating largely outside the structure of the state. It was only after the state so heavily corralled and even marginalized the Islamists that they turned to the political arena out of self-defense, in what had not been a traditional role for clerics in the past.

A key turning point came in the 1941 when a young Indian Muslim journalist, Abu al-A'la al-Mawdudi, conceived the idea of forming a political party specifically to promote the Islamic agenda. This was a major innovation in the relationship of Islam to contemporary politics: Islam had previously been mobilized to serve the state. The Muslim Brotherhood in Egypt in the 1920s had called for political action in the name of Islam, but Islam had never functioned as a player in the form a political party in the arena of modern politics. No political party had existed before which *institutionally* linked politics and Islam. Thus, Mawdudi's *Jama'at-i Islami* (Islamic Association), which later took root in Pakistan, broke new ground and served as the forerunner to a series of Islamist political parties to be created later in the Arab world.[1] "Islamic politics" in the modern sense had been born.

ISLAMISTS AND POWER

The first challenge to Islamists is to define their relationship to power. While all movements seek influence, how is "power" attained? Through suasion of the public? Or through acquisition of the means of coercion through control of the state? And if influence over the state is a desirable goal, how is it achieved?

The broader the range of the state's intrusiveness into society, the greater the incentive becomes for the Islamists (or any other opposition) to take over its widespread powers and deny them to others, simply because the state can determine all. The decentralized state is far less susceptible (or even attractive) to total takeover by opposition forces and less effective than a corporatist state at imposing its goals, and thus it represents less of a threat to those outside it. It is the dictators of the world who encourage the winner-take-all nature of local politics.

The entry of Islamist parties onto the political scene has also elicited a range of external observations about the Islamists' "true agenda," that "it's not really about Islam at all, but about power." While perhaps initially persuasive, this remark upon examination really has little content: all political groups with ideas seek the requisite power to implement them. Do we assume that craving for personal power prompts ambitious political leaders simply to canvass available ideologies and adopt the one that seems to offer promise? Certainly opportunists exist on the political scene, and politics is the art of mobilization and compromise. But the price many Islamists have paid personally for their beliefs indicates their sincerity of conviction. We cannot brush away the ideological foundations of any movement as simply "instrumental" to the process of acquiring power. Such a vision strips all parties of intellectual content if we attribute the adoption of their ideas to mere transient electoral appeal. Indeed, the more ideological a movement is, the harder it is to call it purely "power-oriented" when its political success or failure may ride on its maintenance of those very principles. Ideas may be altered and tailored to meet changing circumstances and reality because that is what makes politics responsive to society's needs. Indeed, it is not the ideological party at all, but perhaps the personality-driven party that can be charged most easily with mere quest for power. What is striking is how consistent Islamists have been in their message, a consistency no doubt due in part to the consistently poor performance of existing government.

The state is furthermore not simply a vehicle or "prize" for Islamists. Islamists, as other parties and groups, seek power to be represented in the system, to gain voice, to protect themselves, to influence the social process, and to implement their vision of the ideal society. Control over the state is not an end but a means to the attainment of a program or agenda. And not all Islamists even agree on the wisdom of seeking influence through politics, as we shall see.

ARE ISLAM AND DEMOCRACY COMPATIBLE?

No religion is inherently "compatible" with democracy: Judaism, Christianity, Buddhism, and Islam are all concerned with issues that have little to do with democracy. The closest most of these faiths come is in reference to just governance, and Islam explicitly talks about the necessity for the ruler to "consult with the people." Indeed, Islamists find in this concept of consultation its modern functional equivalent in representative institutions like parliament.

The argument that Islam is not compatible with democracy is based upon particular quotations from the Qur'an or the Traditions of the Prophet and the belief that Muslims possess an inflexible, religiously driven vision in which "God's word cannot be challenged." Islam is not a fixed thing, able to be skewered like a butterfly specimen and placed in a box on exhibit for all time. Islam is a living phenomenon of Muslims who constantly interact and evolve with the world around it. Indeed, the real question is not whether "Islam is compatible with democracy" but rather what is the relationship between *Muslims* and democracy. *We are discussing not what Islam is, but what Muslims want.* Virtually all Muslims seek a voice in the determination of government policies that affect their own lives and welfare. And most Muslims proceed with confidence that their faith is indeed compatible with the benefits of modern governance and society.

THE ROLE OF ISLAMISTS
IN THE MODERN STATE

ISLAMIST POLITICAL OPTIONS

Islamists who operate in closed political orders that permit no political activity at all have few options open to them other than armed struggle or underground organizational activities. But Islamists who operate in states that do permit some degree of democratic activity have at least four broad political options open to them in advancing their cause:

- *da'wa* (literally a "call"), missionary, preaching, or propaganda work among the Muslim population;
- the building of Islam-oriented civil institutions, organizations, or NGOs;
- the establishment of formal political movements;
- the founding of political parties.

These are not necessarily mutually exclusive options: a political party, for example, is capable of engaging in all four of the activities, whereas a *da'wa*-oriented group might not go beyond the specific phase of missionary work among Muslim communities. The borderline between these various activities is often blurred. Furthermore, Islamists themselves do not set all their own options; the state itself largely determines what range of political and social activism are permissible and subjects them to control and manipulation.

POWER OR ISLAMISM FROM ABOVE

Some Islamist movements have come to perceive power as essential to achieving the Islamic state, Islamism imposed from above. This argument is made on at least two grounds. First, in an era in which the state has set itself up as the all-powerful pharaoh (an image of godless power often used by Islamists), the Islamist movement is largely helpless against the repressive power of the state. This requires the change of the repressive state. Second, the state can be positively used by Islamists once they come to power to establish the kind of Islamic state they envision. In short, missionary work (*da'wa*) is valuable, but control of the state is far more effective in this view in achieving political and social goals. This is not sinister in itself. All political parties function with similar rationale—only the range of their ambitions varies.

But power by what means? Imposing Islam from above clearly represents an authoritarian agenda. It is tempting to leaders who fear that democratic means to power are either barred or unavailing—where even in free elections the public will not elect them. Such was the case of Islamist leader Hasan al-Turabi in Sudan, who acquiesced—or even helped plan—a military coup in 1989 in recognition that his forces could not win an election. The concept of Islam from above is essentially Leninist. Liberal Islamists, however, criticize this approach to power through force as deeply flawed, producing subsequent popular antagonism against the Islamist movement and its leadership, and perhaps dooming it to failure in implementing its policies. They would argue too, on solid Qur'anic grounds, that religion cannot be imposed. Whatever the problems of the strategy of Islam from above may be, few movements—of any ideological stripe—will be able to resist it in unstable states if they see the chance for power arising.

ISLAMISM FROM BELOW

Islam from below involves working to win the public over to some kind of Islam-oriented outlook. This process can come through a political party or political movement, or through a non-political movement. It is linked to *da'wa*—missionary or proselytization work, to change the attitudes, beliefs, and religious behavior of the public through education and propagation of a particular message of Islam. By this rationale, once their hearts have changed, the public itself will eventually bring about the necessary change in laws and governance to accord with their Islamic beliefs.

This approach avoids the dilemmas of engagement in politics. It maintains the movement as a moral force, a debating platform, a voice of conscience, a force in civil society, a lobby, but one always keeping to the message and eschewing tactical maneuvering in transitory political situations. This approach also has the virtue of avoiding direct confrontation with the state since the challenge is only indirect and long term. Nonetheless, in Turkey, for example, the military and the security forces seek to root out even the proselytizing and *da'wa* aspects of the moderate apolitical Nur movement out of fear that the approach from below over the long run poses a more sinister threat to the rigid secular order than the more outward approach of an Islamist political party or even a violent group that can be crushed.

ISLAMISM AS POLITICAL CATALYST

Islamism may well not achieve the goal of coming to power in many states. Yet Islamism can still exert major influence as a crucial catalyst to political change and reform in the Muslim world by spearheading ideas of the illegitimacy of current authoritarian regimes, the need for change, liberalization, and democratization. Islamists may serve as a more effective conveyor belt to bring these ideas to the broader public than any other organization, preparing the groundwork for other parties and political activities that may or may not politically benefit the Islamists in the end. While playing this role is not a goal of their movement, it could be one of the most important influences of Islamism on the political process in the Muslim world, achieved by simply framing the issues in a new light.

WHOM DO ISLAMISTS CHALLENGE?

As Islamists move into the political arena, they contest the role and power of at least three forces: the state, the traditional *'ulama,* and other political parties including other Islamist movements.

Islamists by their very existence pose a challenge to the state, just as any opposition political party does. Islamists seek to change the nature of political discourse in the country, to weaken the state monopoly over policy, to influence state decisions, to gain a voice in the conduct of state affairs, to work toward removing or changing powerful elements within the state who oppose them, and ultimately to have a dominant voice or even control over the exercise of state power itself. They regularly work against the establishment *'ulama* whom they perceive as instruments and servants of the state, lacking commitment to the Islamist cause. This is indeed often the case. In recognition of this some *'ulama* have abandoned the umbrella of the state, becoming Islamists themselves. Overall these developments represent a profound threat to the authoritarian state.

THE IMPLICATIONS OF ISLAMIST RIVALRY

Islamist movements can and do pose challenges to other Islamist movements. Once an Islamist movement emerges onto the political scene, it faces an immediate ideological problem: if the group claims a comprehensive vision of Islam, logically it must claim a monopoly on the correct understanding of Islam and is the bearer of truth. Relating to other Islamist organizations thus becomes problematic. Are they mere ideological rivals with whom one can disagree, or are they deadly distorters of the real Islam, masquerading as the purveyors of truth? The emergence of diversity among Islamist movements marks a creative turning point in the history of Islamism, *for it represents the first appearance of pluralism—intentionally or not—within the context of Islamism in modern politics.* This is a thoroughly healthy development, because the existence of alternative views among Islamists makes clear that there is no monopoly on truth and that Islamist groups in competition certainly cannot all have a monopoly upon the truth. In fact, most Islamist organizations quickly recognize that serious differences exist among various organizations on leadership, tactics, and goals, which does not suggest that their rivals are un-Islamic. With competition the door is open to multiple understandings of Islam and the legitimacy of debate.

Thus *the existence of a reasonably open political system places a greater onus on Islamist organizations to accept some kind of ideological flexibility, moderation and pluralism—characteristics easier to reject when the system is closed.* But will they cooperate or perceive each other as bitter rivals? The local situation may be the key determinant, but the phenomenon of rival Islamist organizations deserves greater study.

Diversity of Islamist organizations is surely the wave of the future as political orders grow more open. Today we see multiple Islamist organizations across a broad range, both violent and peaceful, at work in Egypt, Turkey, Morocco, Algeria, Yemen, Indonesia, Pakistan, Kuwait, and Palestine. In most cases the relationships among rival Islamists have grown less dogmatic and more pragmatic.

TYPES OF ISLAMIST MOVEMENTS

1. PURSUIT OF ARMED STRUGGLE OR TERRORISM

The armed struggle is, of course, the supreme rejection of the existing political order. It purveys a revolutionary and revisionist vision, usually utopian in character. It almost surely excludes any elements of democratization on two grounds: first, utopianism cannot accommodate itself to the political compromises inherent in democracy, and second, the use of violence almost fatally twists the content of the program itself. The medium inevitably informs the message. Achievement of power by force places few restrictions on new leaders in their subsequent exercise of power.

Adoption of terrorism or armed struggle furthermore automatically exposes any movement to the full repressive instruments of the state and even those of the international order. This has been most vividly demonstrated by the massive and crippling international military and police effort against the al-Qa'ida movement in the wake of the 11 September attacks. Terrorism cannot by itself bring any movement to power. Some violent movements may opt for armed violence in the hopes that greater state repression in response will intensify public opposition to the state, or to the United States, thereby hastening crisis. Few if any armed movements can be certain of gaining sufficient public support to bring about a coup, much less to foment the collapse of the state through social revolution. The mere attempt can be disastrous. In even the most oppressive of states, such as Iraq, armed struggle has been of little avail against the power of the *mukhabarat* (security services) state and its army of informers.

A significant exception to the futility of force is Islamic armed struggle in the name of national liberation of Muslim minorities under non-Muslim rule. Here armed Islamist groups seek to forge genuine *national* movements that the state cannot suppress—as in Chechnya, Kashmir, the Philippines, and Palestine. This kind of Muslim armed struggle against a non-Muslim state has greater chance of success than the struggle by Muslims against Muslim states. Repression of Muslims by a non-Muslim state usually only increases discontent and determination of the population to separate.

Armed struggle as a strategy will not likely entirely disappear from international politics as long as the state is either excessively repressive or feeble. Coup planning is also a possibility where Islamists infiltrate the military as occurred in Sudan and Egypt. While the armed struggle can furnish a movement with resistance credentials useful for the future, it is not usually a productive vehicle in most cases to induce regime change. Nonetheless there are states whose brittle character still renders them vulnerable to social revolution and potential armed takeover by Islamists including Egypt, Pakistan, and possibly Morocco, Algeria, Libya, Saudi Arabia, Syria, and Indonesia.

2. *DA'WA* AND NON-POLITICAL MOVEMENTS

In essence, *da'wa* (literally, a summons or calling to Islam) is the classic strategy to change society from below for the creation of a more truly Islam-oriented society. It suggests that change and reform of personal conduct in the direction of greater religious observance will over time lead to improved social conduct that will eventually change the political order itself. But *da'wa* is not directly involved in bringing about political change. *Da'wa* is in fact a basic responsibility of all Muslims—to help propagate the faith. It involves preaching the word in the broadest sense, not only formally in the mosque but also in working among the community and among one's personal associations. The moral character of the missionary *da'i* (summoner) to Islam is important in lending moral strength to the movement.

Da'wa in its traditional sense actually implied the missionary task of calling *non-Muslims* to Islam, but it could also imply bringing Muslims themselves to renewal (*tajdid*) and repurification of their faith. With the emergence of modern Islamist movements *da'wa* now places almost exclusive emphasis on Muslim individuals whom Islamists perceive as only nominally Muslim or who pursue an erroneous conception of Islam: to bring them to a fuller and more proper understanding of their own faith in a new political and social sense. (Note the parallels here with Christian evangelism that focuses on changing Christians.) To conduct *da'wa*, of course, requires funds, institutions, organizations, staff, and materials—educational activity within society.

The largest and most prominent *da'wa* movement in the world is the *Tablighi Jama'at* (Association for the Propagation of the Faith), based in Pakistan, backed by a membership in the millions with branches around the world, but especially in South Asia. *Tabligh* literally means propagation (of the Faith), a word closely linked to *da'wa* in meaning. The Tablighi Jama'at is characterized by a resolute determination to stay outside of politics and to dedicate itself exclusively to *da'wa* among Muslims. It has no distinct ideological message or intellectual content beyond the propagation and purification of Islamic teaching and the betterment of Muslims. While its members may participate as individuals in politics, the organization refuses to speak out on any political issue, even about the establishment of Shari'a law. Its body of beliefs is quite traditional and socially highly conservative, especially on women's issues; it also incorporates many features of pietism and folk Islam. It believes that devoting a few weeks each year to participation in the pious task of itinerant preaching among the people at their own economic level is a form of worship and moral improvement for the message-bearers themselves.[2]

The Tablighi Jama'at particularly galvanizes Muslims at its annual meeting in Raiwind, Pakistan each year when it brings together over a million people. This is the second biggest Muslim convocation in the world after the *hajj*. Such a massive ceremonial event raises consciousness about the faith and the *umma*, with indefinable influence upon the broader political environment and other Islamist political parties. In principle Tablighi Jama'at is above criticism by the state since it remains scrupulously outside the political realm. Yet the ramifications are major: its attitude toward power implies subtle criticism of the un-Islamic character of many regimes in the Muslim world. The Tablighis furthermore have the effect of broadening the space and salience of Islam within the thinking of the community—a kind of softening-up process that, even if not politically exploited by the Tablighis themselves, facilitates the advance of other Islamist groups that might explicitly seek to politicize the Islamic consciousness raised by the Tablighis. It is not inconceivable that the Tablighi Jama'at could at some point in the future decide to adopt a more overt political role or even to create a political wing, especially in Pakistan, but no such plans are now evident.

A second important example of dedication to *da'wa* work is the Nur (Light) movement (*Nurcu Hareketi*) in Turkey, founded in 1926 by Bediüzzaman Said Nursi (1876–1960), a largely self-taught and widely read Islamic scholar from Eastern Turkey. Today the movement is often referred to as the Gülen movement, or *Fethullahçilar* (Fethullah followers) after the name of its largest and most influential wing led now by Fethullah Gülen. The Nur movement has been on the scene for over seventy years, is by far the largest organized religious movement in Turkey and one of the largest in the Muslim world. Gülen in particular dedicates the bulk of the movement's energies to an educational effort, including the founding of schools and study circles to propagate a modernist approach to Islam based on broad moral teachings that are nearly universalist in character. The focus on study reflects the movement's belief that education and knowledge in all fields, including science and technology, can never contradict religion but only serve to reveal God's presence and grand purpose in the universe. The movement strives to create a higher level of moral consciousness in society, thus leading over time to more enlightened governance. Classic Shari'a does not play a central role in the thinking of the movement; indeed, Shari'a is understood in a broader sense as "the way" (the literal meaning of *Shari'a*) to fulfill the broadest goals of God. Nur members describe even the law of gravity, for example, as one of the elements of Shari'a. The movement employs a considerable degree of *ijtihad* (interpretation) of Islamic texts, designed to understand them not in their literal prescriptions but in the context of their original application, interpreted in light of today's new contexts. In this sense too, the movement is thoroughly modernist in outlook.

The Nur movement states that the three greatest enemies of Islam are ignorance, poverty, and discord. It eschews violence because violence produces injustice. The movement does not engage in political activity, has no party, and believes that any legal government must be accorded respect. Politics *within* the religious movement are viewed as the source of dissension, discord, and rivalry leading to compromise and hatred among members. Furthermore, "Islam attaches no importance to the external form of the government. Nursi did not focus on the shape and name of political structure in government. If it works for the benefit of society and it promotes Islamic ethics, it is acceptable to Nursi."[3] It respects the law as a bulwark against dictatorship, which is seen as a threat to Islam; it supports democratic governance.

The Nur movement is rationalist in its views and places great emphasis on tolerance toward all other religious (and even non-religious) views within a pluralist society that express the multi-faceted panoply of God's creation. In its emphasis on knowledge as the path to God, the Nur movement reportedly has established 236 primary and middle schools in Turkey, 280 schools abroad, especially in the areas of the former Soviet bloc, offering good quality secular education in English and Turkish. Some 200 religious foundations (*vakif*) and 211 commercial companies financially support the activities.[4]

While such a movement should be viewed as an ideal model of modern Islam, enlightened Muslim thinking, and a non-confrontational approach to politics and the state, it is in fact the source of much controversy inside the Kemalist state that fears its long range potential to bring back Islam into the hearts of Turkish citizenry in ways that might affect the state-controlled secularism of the state.[5]

The movement is culturally very Turkey-oriented, nationalist in outlook, and broadly supportive of the Turkish state. It has long had a strong anticommunist bias. The movement is not technically a brotherhood (Sufi *tarikat)* since it does not have a formal shaykh, although Gülen is the indispensable intellectual force behind it. It shares some views with the powerful Turkish Nakshibendi (international Sufi) brotherhood, but is not directly linked to it. It is quite critical of Turkey's main Islamist party Welfare (*Refah)* Party and its successors, Virtue (*Fazilet)* and Justice and Construction (*AK*), which it perceives as having damaged the position of Islam in Turkey through engagement in politics and confrontations with the Turkish military, casting a negative pall over the state's relations with nearly all Islamist organizations. To some degree the friction between the apolitical Nur Movement and mainstream Islamist political party Refah/Fazilet/AK reflects the familiar and widespread Sufi-versus-Islamist rivalry, but inside Turkey such rivalry is rather muted, albeit stronger among Turks in Europe.[6]

While the Nurcus have no intention of creating a political party, the movement's leadership does offer non-binding advice to its multimillion following on how to vote on key issues. Its members are represented in several different traditional Turkish political parties and only modestly in the Islamist parties. For all of the Nur movement's apolitical nature, Turkey's radical secularists, particularly the military leadership, regard the Nur movement as subversive and even dangerous in what they allege is a long range intention to infiltrate the state with religious activists with an eye to eventual takeover. They fear precisely what the Nurcus advocate—the gradual Islamization of society from below through change in people's hearts. Consequently, Nurcus are regularly purged from the military and state organizations, and the movement and its institutions are harassed and persecuted in the courts.

SUFI MOVEMENTS.   More broadly in the Muslim world, many Sufi (mystical) brotherhoods (Arabic *tariqa,* pl. *tariqat* or *turuq)* are an important part of *da'wa*-oriented movements. These movements usually do not establish political parties or even true political movements as such, but as social movements dedicate themselves to raising the level of Islamic consciousness and religio-social cohesion among their followers, usually under the leadership of a charismatic shaykh with religious authority. Many are involved in building nonpolitical institutions. Others can be quite politically oriented and exert considerable political influence through their willingness to support political parties at the ballot box by offering the votes of their followers: for example, as in Sudan, the Sufi-like Ansar movement votes as a bloc for its leader, Sadiq al-Mahdi, who has long been deeply engaged in politics. Sufi movements are frequently the target of Islamist movements that see them as representing traditional, impure, superstitious, and even non-Islamic practices such as saint-worship that for Islamists carries overtones of polytheism (*shirk*). Turkey's mainstream Islamist party Fazilet, however, emerged right out of a branch of the Turkish Nakshibendi brotherhood.

3. BUILDING CIVIL ORGANIZATIONS AND POLITICAL MOVEMENTS

Civil society as a political concept is quite new in Islamic thinking, although forms of civil society have historically been a well-established feature of Muslim life where the state traditionally performed limited functions. Today, many Islamist movements have turned their focus on civil society for several reasons. First, the state has often closed the door to more overt political activities, thereby requiring the movement to find alternative vehicles of activity. Second, social work within society is an excellent way to gain both a following within society and experience in organizing community activity around a religious focus, thereby showing up the state for its failures in serving the public, and creating the groundwork for a future political challenge to the existing regime. Third, such activity in itself has religious validity in its service to the community through the creation of benevolent organizations (*munadhamat khairiyya*). The Muslim Brotherhood in Egypt, Jordan, and Palestine (Hamas), and Hizballah in Lebanon have extensive programs of social services including clinics, educational assistance, women's support groups, and youth activities. The same is true of most other large Islamist movements (Fazilet in Turkey, Jama'at-i Islami in Pakistan, Muhammadiya and Nahdatul Ulama in Indonesia, PAS in Malaysia, and FIS in Algeria) that are able to garner the necessary financial support for their work, usually from donations from pious and wealthy businessmen or from external contributions. The borderline between charitable and political work is often blurred, and indeed many of the movements referred to above are also formal political parties as well.

It would not be an exaggeration to state that *Islamists are probably more focused on civil society and the creation of institutions within it than any other political force in the Muslim world*. They have deeper grassroots organizations due to their intimate links to neighborhood mosque networks and hence are among the primary exponents of the benefits of civil society.

THE STATE RESPONDS

The state does not take all these challenges lying down, however. It leans on its own tame state-employed *'ulama* institutions to defend the status quo against the more dynamic views of Islam presented by Islamists. In many cases the state has attempted to preempt the Islamization process itself, to bring greater religious legitimacy to the regime, to steal a march on the Islamists, and to attempt to control Islamization to its own benefit. Pakistan is one of the most prominent cases of *state Islamization*. Most Islamists would charge that the several Pakistani regimes that advocated Islamization, most notably General Zia al-Haq's (1977–1988), imposed only symbols and not the spirit of Islamization. Whatever one may think of General Zia's regime, he did undertake a program of quite serious Islamization in many spheres, probably more than under any other regime except Iran and Sudan. He both sought to use Islam to bolster his own illegitimate means of gaining power (military coup) and to control the Islamists themselves. As Vali Nasr notes in a fascinating study, "the state had made the institution of ulama central to Islamization. It had initiated the ulama into the Islamist discourse and by doing so had *universalized Islamism as Islam.*" [Italics mine.][7]

Thus the state served to transform the *'ulama* into an Islamist movement in their own right, both to gain their support and to attenuate the strength of the lay Islamists—"amounting to competition between various Islamic and Islamist institutional and intellectual traditions for the control of the Islamization process."[8] But even these *'ulama*-based movements pose a danger to the state because their new "Islamist" status lends them a degree of independence and a more critical view of the state.

In sum, Islamist movements may not always engage in direct politics, but they are exquisitely tuned to the political implications of their activities and their relationship to the state. Control of the educational process and the establishment of linked *madrasas* provides the opportunity to train whole cadres of committed activists who then carry the work forward at different levels. Building influence within the bureaucracy provides a powerful alternative to a direct political bid for formal power through elections. All political movements, of course, seek to place their own people within institutions that can influence policy on national issues. Regimes on the defensive often refer to this Islamist effort in the darkest conspiratorial sense as "infiltration" and not surprisingly are particularly vigilant about the presence of Islamists in security organizations or the military—the main bastions of regime support and loyalty.

Indeed, regime fears about Islamist infiltration are not always ill-founded; all would-be coup plotters of any political stripe seek to infiltrate the military. In Sudan the National Islamic Front consciously undertook a policy of building cadres within state institutions, including the military, that ultimately created the groundwork for a military coup against the state in 1989. In Egypt, infiltration of the military by extremist Islamists led to the assassination of President Anwar Sadat. In Pakistan the military has for over two decades at the least had a major presence of Islamist-oriented officers within its ranks, right up to the top with General Zia.

4. ESTABLISHING POLITICAL PARTIES

Few states in the Muslim world ban outright the establishment of political parties in principle; Saudi Arabia is the primary case and is far more honest about its views on this matter than the many so-called republican regimes that permit only one ruling party and at best one or two regime-controlled and regime-friendly "opposition" parties such as in Iraq, Syria, Libya, Tunisia, and Uzbekistan. These states are harshly authoritarian in character, leaving little or no room for legal Islamist social or political movements. Even when the state is slightly more open, it does not always give room to Islamist parties. A number of states grant relatively free reign to some political parties, but ban those political parties organized on religious principle.

- **Turkey**, for example, within the confines of its rigidly secularist legislation, bans parties that "threaten the secularist order"—as broadly defined by the state—but in fact has periodically played brief cat-and-mouse games with several clearly religiously oriented parties, each one eventually banned. In 2002 however, a new incarnation of an older Islamist party explicitly denied being Islamist and was allowed to participate and win a national election—major progress for Turkish democracy and the annals of Islamist politics in general.

- In **Algeria**'s 1997 legislative elections—in the middle of a brutal and bloody civil conflict with Islamists who had been denied the fruits of an electoral victory in 1991—the military junta that dominated power decreed that no overtly religious or ethnically based parties (i.e., Berber) would be permitted to run; in the event, however, the Algerian Hamas (unrelated to the Palestinian Hamas) and al-Nahda movements (both moderate Islamist) were allowed to run under new non-religious names, but not the banned Islamist FIS.

- **Egypt** does not permit religious or ethnically based parties, but it has been willing in the last two decades to permit the Muslim Brotherhood movement to exist and let members run as individuals on the lists of other non-religious parties, thus permitting at least a few Islamists to be elected as individuals to parliament, with no overt formal party mechanism behind them.

- **Kuwait** permits political movements to exist but not formal political parties, although there is discussion of changing this legislation at some point in the future. Islamists have won up to one-third of parliamentary seats under this arrangement.

- Until the overthrow of Suharto in 1998 **Indonesia** permitted a handful of religiously oriented parties to participate in politics, but only within the confines of a strictly state-controlled umbrella Islamic party that effectively stifled their political voice. Since Suharto's fall, Islamist parties have been freer to organize.

Movements, of course, contain many characteristics similar to political parties, and as proto-parties they are engaged in many organizational activities that can facilitate their subsequent transformation into political parties. Movements are also able to engage in civil society activities described previously, thus strengthening their social base and gaining control of mosques. While there may not be major differences between political movements and political parties, it is evident that the state finds advantage in making these distinctions and setting certain limits for purposes of control.

THE TRADEOFFS IN FORMING A POLITICAL PARTY

Should an Islamist movement move beyond the phase of a social movement to seek direct involvement in the political order? The choice to enter politics is fraught with problems, particularly since it requires compromise—in all senses of the word—of ideological beliefs, preferences, modus operandi, and even goals. *Indeed, the decision of an Islamist leader to enter politics represents by definition not only an abandonment of ideological purity, but a supreme act of* ijtihad *(interpretation of Islam) in itself.* It represents an acceptance that the political order is legitimate enough to work with, that politics represent a valuable vehicle for the promulgation and implementation of Islamic ideas, and that power-sharing—pluralism by definition—even with groups whose views are different is acceptable. Political involvement signals abandonment of abstract ideals and marks entry into the murky and dissatisfying world of compromises and partial goals.

The Islamist leader in politics must constantly make choices about how to apply his own understanding of Islam to concrete messy realities that offer little room for pure ideological principles. *Through entry into politics, an Islamist party implicitly recognizes that political priorities will often supercede the religious, that compromises in belief and ideology will inevitably have to be made, and that daily decisions will require choices between Islam or the interests of the party—all outside the framework of a pure ideal. Indeed, by entering into politics an Islamist party is signaling a dramatic break with rigid ideology or theology.* For this reason, many Islamist leaders have been highly wary of the risks that entry into politics entails. Over time we may see many Islamists abandoning the political arena precisely because the political requirements are too compromising.

If Islamists find they are unlikely to be able to attract enough votes to win an election (as has been consistently the case in Pakistan, for example), they must consider accepting the role of permanent political opposition. Such a task might entail adopting the role of ethical and moral keeper of the precepts of Islam within the political order as critics of the system. For some Islamists that role might perhaps be safer and less compromising than assuming the burdens of power, which would require making compromises on issues of principle and running the risk of failure in their policies.

In principle an Islamist party might tailor its policies simply to win an election and then proceed to violate them and impose a "hidden agenda." But we have no case in the Muslim world so far in which an elected Islamist party rejected the democratic order that brought them into power. The data base is admittedly small to date.

Just what are the tradeoffs between principle and pragmatism, ideology and expediency? A leading moderate Tunisian Islamist cleric in exile in London, Shaykh Rashid al-Ghannushi, asks whether Islamists should give priority to changing society, or to gaining power. He notes that the two are not mutually exclusive since

Islam wants to Islamize politics and society simultaneously. But he notes that "if the interests of social missionary work (*da'wa*) contradict political interests, social interests must be put before anything else. It has been proven that what is achieved socially is more permanent and better than what is achieved politically."[9]

Several other controversial issues also arise for Islamists, or for any kind of political opposition. A number of regimes insist that if Islamists (or others) are to be permitted to participate in politics, the Islamists must commit themselves to "playing by the rules of the game," naturally as set by the state. Such a position by the state presents a dilemma to the Islamists, complicated by the determination of many regimes to permit no real challenge in the end to their monopoly on power. In genuinely functioning democratic orders the "rules of the game" are of course important since the rules represent a true national consensus on politic process. But in authoritarian political orders to play by the skewed rules of the regime's game is often tantamount to abandoning any prospects of change. *It is the very rules of the game that represent the problem and node of contention.* Slow incremental change within the political order is a possible scenario and has in fact taken place in many states during a long and constant political tug-of-war across the region. But many Islamists see the rules of the game as constituting a trap for any political parties that seek to introduce reform, greater transparency, democratization, and ultimate displacement of the entrenched ruling party. Other political parties usually agree.[10]

Regimes have so structured the system that any efforts to dislodge the ruling group are by definition subversive and outside the rules of the game. To participate risks dignifying and perpetuating the skewed rules of the game, thereby lending it legitimacy. Islamist parties that have broken their teeth in trying to work within skewed systems are often frustrated and less willing to play the game in which the regime always wins by shaping the rules.

THE PROBLEM OF COMPROMISE WITH PRINCIPLE

Olivier Roy early in the 1990s observed that fundamentalists essentially reject the political arena entirely, precisely because they perceive the Western democratic political order, including elections and parliaments, as *kufr* or infidel practice, placing the sovereignty of Man over the sovereignty of God.[11] This is the most basic objection that some Islamists might level against the political process—that it is all religiously unacceptable according to their own narrow reading of Islam. But even these groups, now a distinct minority among Islamists, have been forced to rethink the wisdom of a sweeping religiously based rejection of politics, particularly since it can lead to costly exclusion from the process of distribution of state resources.

Some elements of the Muslim Brotherhood in Jordan have made just this case in debates over the wisdom of the participation strategy of its political wing, the Islamic Action Front party. Regular state manipulation of the electoral rules by the Jordanian government in order to strengthen pro-government candidates and weaken the Islamists has raised further doubts about playing the game. The Kuwaiti government has employed similar tactics vis-à-vis its own opposition groups, including the Islamists. Based on their experiences, might not the Islamists be better off remaining simply as a movement, able to attract and educate followers, propagate their ideology and political positions, criticize the state, and maintain the purity of their ideals by remaining outside the political order? The debate will continue, but failure to play in the skewed game usually is more costly than participation.

Shaykh Rashid al-Ghannushi gets to the heart of the issue:

> The Islamic movement must not have the government as its first priority. Takeover of government should not be the biggest achievement possible. A bigger achievement would be if the people would love Islam and its leaders. . . . *The most dangerous thing is for the Islamists to be loved by the people before they get to power and then hated afterward.* . . .
>
> Until Islamists are ready to develop realistic and viable alternative programs, the best gift these autocratic regimes can bestow upon them ironically may be hindering them from accession to power at this stage of Islamist political development—which obviously varies from state to state. [Emphasis mine][12]

An alternative political strategy involves indirect influence upon the political order: let the movement influence the public through its organizational activities and political messages, but let its followers enter the political system as individuals, working to push their agenda through other existing parties. The Muhammadiya movement in Indonesia under Suharto's autocracy had long opted not to become a political party under those conditions but simply to remain a movement of political influence; it bade its members to implement their ideas through joining the political party of their choice. (This posture later changed as the Indonesian political order opened with the fall of Suharto.) The apolitical Nur movement in Turkey at election time often makes its non-binding political preferences clear to its followers. The Nakshibendi brotherhood in Turkey also exerts considerable influence over the political order through its members in different political parties.

THE PRICE OF FAILURE

When Islamists actually succeed in coming to power—by whatever means—a series of challenges face them. They must be ready to assume responsibility for the serious if not overwhelming problems that beset so many of these societies. They must possess the trained professional cadres within the party capable of thoughtful response to national demands. If they cannot do so, what is the price of failure? Broad Islamist popularity is based on their role out of power, as a fresh, principled, and untested element on a tired and corrupt political scene. Many of the votes they attract come as protests against existing discredited parties rather than a vote of for Islamism per se.

The price of failure may be the loss of many voters in the next election who found their performance disappointing. Voter disillusionment might be fatal to the party over the longer run. Worse, if the Islamists do fail, does this reflect on Islam itself in the popular mind? Political failure cannot, of course, truly tarnish Islam itself as a faith, but it will certainly discredit Islamists and their failure to successfully apply broad Islamic precepts to politics. They run a haunting risk: the association of failure with Islam, or what has been called "the Islamization of failure." The broad public may conclude that they have now "tried Islam" and that it "did not work." (Similarly, one hears some Muslims claim they have "tried socialism" or "tried nationalism" and these ideologies were found wanting.)

But as Ghannushi points out, the most terrible result is for the public to come to hate Islam. That risk has been fully apparent in Iran, Sudan, and Taleban Afghanistan; there, if the anger has not been directed at Islam itself, at least those who utilize it for political dominance are resented. These societies can only respond with cynicism to future political calls in the name of Islam. Such setbacks could be very serious for the long-term success of Islamist parties, and they give pause for thought about seeking to gain executive responsibility within government.

THE TREND TOWARD PARTICIPATION

Whatever doubts Islamists may entertain about the costs of working within the system, they still opt for political participation where permitted, despite potential disadvantages. It is hard to find a case of a serious Islamist party opting out of political participation because of disadvantages inherent in the rules of the game or the compromises required. *Not to participate* is to lose out to rival forces in society. In short, the lure and the logic of joining the political process are ineluctable and the cost of abstaining grows.

Whatever the limitations or unfairnesses of the system, Islamists see that they are not alone in this process, that other political parties also suffer from discrimination from the system, offering opportunities to form political alliances or cooperation. This is, of course, the essence of the democratic parliamentary process, which demonstrably provides Islamists with some chances for genuine gains despite "compromise" of principle. Those Islamist parties insistent upon maintaining ideological purity and unwilling to work with non-religious opposition groups are quickly marginalized and doomed to irrelevance, obscurity, or even a turn to violence, as has happened in Algeria or Egypt.

Where Islamist movements have created political wings or parties, in some cases they have sought to insulate the movement from the party so as to diminish potential negative impact on the movement itself from any failures of the party. Thus the Muslim Brotherhood in both Jordan and Palestine has created separate political parties (the Islamic Action Front and Hamas) that are staffed by Brotherhood members but that represent those elements in the movement more committed to political party activity and do not include those who are less happy with direct participation in politics. In the case of Hamas, the Brotherhood does not disavow but seeks a higher degree of insulation from the armed guerrilla and terrorist operations of the organization's national liberation struggle. In Indonesia, the leaderships of both the major Nahdatul Ulama and Muhammadiya movements have created political organizations that are distinct from the movement themselves, preserving them from automatic politicization.

Many regimes frequently justify their refusal to liberalize the system out of concern that "the Islamists will take advantage of the system." Regimes have real grounds to fear loss of power if the political system is opened up; nearly all of them would lose in free elections to the Islamists who would be the single biggest gainers, especially in initial elections. But there has not been a single case to date yet in which Islamists have democratically come to power and then put an end to the democratic order. The charge "one man, one vote, one time" is no more than a slogan wielded by authoritarians and Westerners who fear Islamist power at the ballot box.

STATE MANIPULATION
OF THE DEMOCRATIC ORDER

Among major Muslim states with existing democratic processes, politically active Islamist parties are functioning in Algeria, Bahrain, Egypt, Bangladesh, Indonesia, Jordan, Kuwait, Lebanon, Malaysia, Morocco, Pakistan, Turkey, and Yemen. While the progress toward liberalization in the region is encouraging, the state is typically deeply engaged in manipulation of the political process in order to disadvantage the

Islamists—and usually other parties as well. Even among states with more advanced democratization, the state employs a number of common devices to ensure that there is no level playing field when it comes to political competition. (Some of these devices, such as gerrymandering, are not exactly unknown in democratic states in the West either.) While these devices clearly tarnish the democratic process, one cannot deny that the state in the Muslim world, for all its manifold failings, is sometimes sharply challenged by groups that are extreme or even practice violence. Repression of such groups on occasion may be partially justified.

Suppressive devices employed by the state include the following:

- Restriction of access to media: the state places restrictions on the ability of the Islamist parties to reach the general public during election campaigns (Egypt, Pakistan, Yemen). The state can facilitate purchase of the media by individuals close to the regime who ensure that the mainstream press does not confront the state (Turkey, Egypt). The state can manipulate the supply of newsprint to opposition newspapers to encourage compliance, or it can manipulate the distribution of major advertising monies from state-owned corporations to reach only friendly or compliant newspapers. TV licenses can be quite narrowly distributed: in Yemen, for example, the state allows a considerable degree of press freedom but quite firmly controls TV access—the prime instrument of influence upon the masses. Radio licensing can also be similarly politically influenced.

- Co-optation: Regimes seek to co-opt leading Islamists by offering them positions in the government or by suggesting that they can avoid intimidation through cooperation. Algeria has used this effectively with the most moderate Islamist leaders. Co-optation, of course, is a time-honored democratic device that can also serve to strengthen democratic consensus through inclusion.

- Libel and security laws: The state passes libel legislation designed to punish anyone who "damages the image and prestige of the state" or "attacks the national ideology," "threatens the national security," "attacks the person of the president," or "encourages hatred and division among the population." Such practices are widespread across the Muslim world.

- Gerrymandering: the state shifts boundaries of voting districts to strengthen state support or weaken opposition support in specific areas (Kuwait, Jordan).

- Limitation of parties on ideological grounds: The government can forbid the establishment of political parties along religious lines (Turkey, Egypt, Indonesia, Algeria). The government can also require that parties not oppose the state ideology (Kemalism in Turkey, the Five Principles (*Panj Sila*) in Indonesia under Suharto.) In Iran, already an Islamist state, a constitutionally designated Council of Guardians passes on the qualifications or "fitness" of candidates to run for office, tailored to favor the hard-liners.

- Manipulation of electoral procedures: The state can change electoral procedures to favor the state and its candidates by raising or lowering the numerical thresholds for small parties to qualify for entry into parliament (Turkey, Pakistan, and Indonesia, among others.)

- NGO controls: As Islamists establish non-governmental organizations for charitable, educational, or professional purposes, the state has moved to establish tight controls over the membership, voting procedures, or qualifications for NGO registry, which can serve to weaken, discourage or eliminate Islamist-linked NGO groups. In 1999 Egypt, for example, passed quite restrictive legislation in this regard to weaken the Islamist voice in professional organizations in which they had been strongly represented.

- Distribution of state largesse: Incumbent governments possess huge advantages in the distribution of state largesse, particularly around election time. All states with relatively democratic elections in the Muslim world use this device as well in order to strengthen the ruling party versus the opposition.

- Harassment and arrest: The state detains, arrests, or even places on trial leading politicians on certain charges near election time so they become disqualified for participation in that election, or disbarred from politics for longer periods of time. (Turkey, Egypt, and Iran). Street beatings or even assassination by "unknown individuals" of Islamist or other opposition leaders is also commonplace. The state can also intimidate candidates through investigations into politicians' lives and activities.

I should note that most of the states singled out for mention here are actually among the more democratic in the Muslim world. We are talking about manipulation of the political order by relatively more democratic states in which techniques of repression must be ever subtler and more indirect. Turkey, as the most democratic Muslim state, therefore has a longer list of political devices to marginalize Islamists than any other state since cruder techniques so commonplace in most of the rest of the Muslim world are far less acceptable there.

ISLAMIST COALITION BUILDING

Islamist cooperation with other political forces is the nearly inevitable—and desirable—result of life within a parliamentary system. Such coalitions weaken ideological rigidity within the movements and impel them toward greater pragmatism.

The ability of Islamist parties to work with other parties is the surest sign of moderation of ideological stance and greater tolerance for the reality of diverse social views. We see serious coalition building in Kuwait, Jordan, Egypt, Bangladesh, Turkey, Algeria, Sudan, and Pakistan.

ISLAMISTS AND THE ROLE OF THE STATE IN THE FREE MARKET

Islamists are ambivalent on the role of the state in the economy—a disparity between theory and practice. On the one hand, political Islam broadly supports the concept of a liberal economy. Classical Islamic theory envisages the role of the state as limited to facilitating the well-being of markets and merchants rather than controlling them. Islamists have always powerfully objected to socialism and communism, not only on the basis of communism's atheism or socialism's tendency toward secularism, but also on their insistence on rigid control of society and free markets. An Islamist state in principle strongly supports a liberal economy and the autonomy of the individual to operate freely within it as long as they do not damage the overall welfare of society. Islam has never had problems with the idea that wealth is unevenly distributed, so long as basic principles of social justice are observed.

In reality, however, present conditions of Muslim states and societies place pressures upon Islamists to adopt more statist economic policies. First, Islamists are consistently wary of economic liberalization if it opens Muslim society to damage from powerful external competition through globalizing forces. These views reflect a kind of economic nationalism. Over the past half century certain leftist concepts linked to international socialism have crept into the language of some Islamist thinkers, such as the Iranian 'Ali Shariati who perceived the West as perpetuating a long process of economic as well as political exploitation of the Muslim world. These ideas dovetail with Islamist rhetoric against the broader neo-imperialist inroads of the West on the cultural level.

Second, Islamic thought sets high priority on social justice that in contemporary terms is taken to imply state involvement in the establishment of some kind of "just" economic order—however interpreted. In recent decades Islamists have discussed concepts of "Islamic economics," an entirely contemporary creation. What is Islamic economics? At bottom it focuses upon the classic issue of "who gets what, when, and how." For Islamists, Islamic economics is not descriptive but prescriptive, calling for some moral dimension of justice in the process of distribution. "Justice" does not equate to egalitarianism—Islam readily admits of social differences in wealth and position—but prioritizes concern for the overall welfare of society rather than the abstract "state of the economy" or the individual economic freedom of the individual. Islamist writing often refers to Islam as the "third way" between capitalism and communism. Rather than referring to an entirely new kind of economic order, this approach addresses the component of social justice in economics that suggests greater state intrusion into economic policy than the laissez-faire orientation of traditional Islamic thought, while avoiding the extremes of socialization of the economy.

Practice also varies. Iran has been heavily statist in what is the most leftist Islamic movement of all. Populism is a key part of its policies as well. But in Sudan the regime has employed conservative economics and has not rejected market forces in the formulation of state policies. Islamists both in and out of power show marked reluctance to adopt austerity policies and decreased subsidies that will place hardships on the poorer segments of society, even in the interest of economic reform. Islamists have opposed IMF austerity measures in Algeria, Jordan, Egypt, and Pakistan and have avoided cutting the state budget and salaries in Turkey, for example. The problem is as much foreign (Western) intervention in the local economy as it is austerity. But the Islamists' position is clearly evolving as they grow more sophisticated about national and international economic issues. My sense is that Islamist policies will move toward an economic populism that will strengthen rather than diminish state involvement in the economy.

CONCLUSION

Islamists are new to democracy, elections, governance and policymaking, as are most in the Muslim world. Their thinking already demonstrates evolution over the past several decades and is likely to evolve further as they gain experience. In the social realm, Islamists will remain conservative and sometimes even obstructive on issues relating to public morality and the role of women in society, but women are playing increasingly greater roles within Islamist movements under democratic or quasi-democratic orders such as Turkey or Egypt.

Islamists out of power will be strong supporters of democratization and human rights—key forces for political liberalization. In power Islamists will face the same dilemma that all other political parties do—the temptation to hold onto political power as long as possible. In states with well-defined democratic processes, Islamists will likely conform to existing norms. In states with shaky democratic traditions and norms, the Islamists will be no more or less trustworthy as guardians of democratic process than most other parties. What is important is that Islamists must share and participate in the growing socialization of all Muslim and Third World societies into democratic practice. They should not be viewed as representing a different order of problem even though their goals may present challenges to society, just as those of many other parties also do.

ISLAMISM
AND THE WEST

HUNTINGTON AND THE CLASH OF CIVILIZATIONS

The term "clash of civilizations," coined in the early 1990s by Professor Samuel Huntington of Harvard, has taken on a life of its own, becoming a shorthand phrase for summarizing issues involving Islam and the West. We are exposed to regular images and statements from the Muslim world carrying an anti-Western, and especially anti-American, message. How much does anti-Westernism permeate Islamist thinking, and why?

Samuel Huntington's writings on the "clash of civilizations" identify culture or civilization as a key source of future international friction in the coming century. The key flaw in his many thoughtful observations is that he conflates the *vehicle of conflict* with the *source of conflict*. All societies prefer to ennoble their conflicts through justification at the highest level of moral cause. Thus, few will go to war in the name of capturing territory, destroying a rival, exacting revenging, gaining geopolitical hegemony, or seizing economic assets. Instead, war is waged in the name of Christian values, the proletarian revolution, the master race, the war to end all wars, the free world, the forces of history, manifest destiny, or whatever. The banner raised is not really the actual cause of conflict; it rather springs from quite concrete issues, grievances that are more susceptible to solution than lofty abstract concepts about "clashes of civilizations."

To seek refuge in primordial explanations like "clashes of civilization," and "Islam versus the West," and "they hate our values" is in one sense to abdicate responsibility, to writhe in the grip of apparently overwhelming abstract forces. It is a convenient cop-out since there is really nothing anyone can actually do about forces so cosmic; they thus absolve United States of any need for self-examination of our own responsibilities. To understand and deal with sources of conflict requires examination of the real, concrete, grounded, and workable issues on both sides, including psychological legacies. In any discussion of "Islam versus the West" Western grievances will include issues such as terrorism, proliferation of weapons of mass destruction, Israel's security, oil, and strategic instability. The Muslim side will include the familiar issues of Western imperialism, an American-dominated hegemonic world order, Western interventionism, U.S. indifference to democracy in the Arab world, and indiscriminate U.S. support for Israel. Thus the ideologized "Islam versus the West" conception can and must be reduced to these real component parts that are both understandable and manageable. Until then political Islam will remain the preeminent *vehicle*, and not the preeminent *cause*, of these grievances on both sides to which the West has contributed.

Let's examine in this chapter some of the *concrete* issues and the nature of frictions between the Muslim world and the West that should not be simply swept up into "intercivilizational conflict."

THEOLOGICAL SOURCES OF CONFLICT WITH THE WEST

Among religions of the world, Islam is quite remarkable in its conscious foundation upon two earlier faiths, Judaism and Christianity. Christianity, of course, accepts the Old (Hebrew) Testament and its early prophets who first preached monotheism. But Christianity eliminated most of Jewish religious law and radically reconfigured the faith by basing it on the person of Jesus as the literal Son of God and his message of love and forgiveness. Islam too accepts the Old Testament prophets as an essential element of God's gradual revelation of his message to mankind over time. At the same time Islam shares with Christianity the basic critique of the Jewish faith that the Jews misunderstood the message as being relevant only for themselves as the Chosen People. Similarly, Islam accepts the virgin birth and venerates Mary as the mother of Jesus and the basic message of Jesus as a great prophet of God's revelations who universalized the earlier revelations of the Jewish prophets, emphasized new elements of love, and directed the message to all mankind. Christians went wrong, in the Islamic view, only in accepting Jesus as the literal son of God, or as God himself, instead of the great human prophet that he was. For Muslims, God "neither begets nor is begotten" and direct worship of Jesus himself and the elaboration of the Trinity thus fatefully strays from the concept of strict monotheism.

Lest some contemporary Christians find Muslim insistence upon the strictly human nature of Christ to be blasphemous, let's recall that such a view of Jesus was widespread among great numbers of Christians themselves in the Near East for many centuries before the birth of Islam. Debate had raged within Christianity for many hundreds of years as to Jesus' true nature, leading to several Church councils that attempted to establish a firm theological position on the Trinitarian view of Jesus, weaving a fine line of political and theological compromise between different schools of thought across the Roman Empire. Indeed, the Islamic view of the non-divinity of Christ strongly parallels the views of what Rome had earlier ended up denouncing as the Monophysite heresy—views that nonetheless persisted across large parts of the Near East right up to the birth of Islam.[1] Indeed, the presence of these Christian theological views on the non-divinity of Jesus dramatically helps to explain the theological readiness of so much of the Middle East to accept the Islamic vision of Jesus in the seventh century when Islam emerged as a faith.

But Islam makes clear that the Prophet Muhammad, at the end of a long series of prophets of God, represented God's final revelation, its final perfect and complete synthesis and expression, a seal upon the historical process of revelation. Otherwise Islam's "problems" with Judaism or Christianity *in theological terms* are in fact remarkably limited. In principle Islam has less of a problem with the earlier two faiths than either of those two faiths have with each other or with Islam.

Muslims do bear some residual resentment about early rejection of the Prophet by Jewish communities in Mecca and Medina when blood was shed, and there is negative language in the Qur'an about the Jews in this context. Some fundamentalists quote this as indicating permanent hostility to Jews, but nearly all modern Islamic theologians state that this language was directed at a specific issue at a specific time and was not meant to constitute a criticism of Jews as a people for all time. Apart from these early incidents, Muslim relationships with Jews were marked by a far higher degree of tolerance and acceptance than Jews ever encountered in the West. Unfortunately any latent frictions with Jews were rekindled, redramatized, and intensified 1,400 years later by contemporary hostility between the modern state of Israel and the Muslim world.

Fundamentalist Christian and Jewish movements have similar problems in reaching *theological* compromise with other faiths if they believe that compromise is theologically unacceptable. For many Christians, a number of these theological differences themselves constitute precisely the necessary preconditions of salvation, that is, belief in Jesus as the literal Son of God and God himself. The Catholic and Lutheran churches, for example, both have recognized serious problems, even within the spirit of ecumenism, in accepting other faiths as *equally valid paths* to salvation. For example, Christian evangelist leader Franklin Graham, Billy Graham's son, declared in November 2001 that "the God of Islam is not the same

God. He's not the son of God of the Christian or Judeo-Christian faith. It's a different God and I believe it is a very evil and wicked religion."[2]

In sum, there are significant *theological* differences among Islam, Judaism, and Christianity. What is important, however, is how communities and leaderships have actually *acted* upon these beliefs, and *why*. Ironically, it may be precisely in the *political realm* that religion may be able to act more flexibly toward other religions than in the theological realm, since in politics followers are interested in pragmatic political results and not just in justification of theology.

HOW LEADERS USE THEOLOGICAL DIFFERENCES

Theological differences between Islam, Judaism, and Christianity, then, *when they coincide with other non-religious frictions and conflicts,* are only as important as their followers want them to be in accordance with their political goals. Theology is otherwise not the major source of the problem between the Muslim world and the West. *This is not about Jesus Christ and the Prophet Muhammad at all.* Religious doctrine itself is rarely the main source of communitarian conflicts in which actual concrete frictions come to be clothed in religious terms.

We are familiar with the Christian Crusades to capture Jerusalem from the Muslims (killing Jews and trashing the Christian Eastern Orthodox Empire on the way.) And we know of the Ottoman Empire's conquest of Christians in the Near East and the Balkans. The geopolitical confrontation of the two faiths in the last 1,500 years has been frequent and often bloody. But it should be remembered that religious wars among Christians within the West itself were even more common. Few historians would suggest that it was primarily theological differences that actually impelled the multiple princedoms of Europe to savage each other during the Thirty Years War, for example. Far deeper reasons existed for war: rivalry in the political and economic sphere, the need for rulers to control religious ideology as a source of power, rivalries for power between personalities, imperial expansionism, and so on—all of which sought ideological vehicles. To become Protestant was, even in name, an act of defiance against the Catholic state; Protestantism was an attractive ideology for expressing serious grievances with the Catholic state.

So we should attach limited emphasis to theological differences as the source of conflict between East and West. It's more important to look at the *psychological legacy* today of the many centuries of warfare between the Muslim and Christian worlds. Lest we single out even these tensions as specific to the Middle East, let's recall that the West itself is just barely overcoming the legacy of 1,500 years of constant warfare among the various European peoples as well. Conflict—military, ideological, and psychological—between the Eastern Orthodox world and the Western Catholic and Protestant world has still not been tempered to a level of comfortable coexistence. In 2001 the Greek Orthodox Patriarch in Athens refused to have dinner with visiting Pope John Paul II, saying it was "premature" in the long process of healing deep historical rifts between Eastern and Western Christianity.

PROXIMITY BREEDS CONFLICT AND CONTEMPT

When you set out south or east from Europe, the very first place you encounter is the Muslim world, the closest immediate arena of potential confrontation among world "civilizations." Before European imperialism and colonialism began to recede, the entire developing world had fallen under European domination, but it was the regions closest to Europe that encountered the most frequent and the most intense imperial and colonial influence. (India and South Africa were key exceptions given their intense European presence.) Western political domination extended virtually everywhere, but its political, cultural, and ideological domination posed greater challenges to Muslim state structures and political philosophies than to most other regions. Islam really represented *the only cohesive, widespread, international, alternative institutional structure in theoretical, legal, and practical terms to the European model.* Neither East Asia, India, nor Africa offered quite as comprehensive a body of enduring alternative civilizational models, and hence there was less violent "cultural clash."

It is ironically Islam's very cultural and institutional success over the centuries that contributes to its intense resistance to an alternative "civilizational order." The legacy of that clash seems still to express a resentment exceeding that found in such other powerful historical cultures as China or India where native models were less successful as contenders for modernity and capitulated sooner. Indeed, in the contemporary era it is still hard to identify a non-Western culture that possesses such a comprehensive and coherent a philosophy of faith, governance, law, and society as does the Muslim world—across international borders for over ten thousand miles. Thus *political* Islam draws its greatest strength from seeking to represent just such a traditional cultural alternative of governance and society to the reigning Western model.

THE JIHADIST VIEW OF THE WEST

The most ideologically extreme part of the Islamist spectrum is the jihadist tendency, that does not constitute a separate sect of Islam, but a radical interpretation of it. The word *jihad* may be familiar but not so the distinction between greater (*akbar*) and lesser (*asghar*) jihad: the greater is the constant struggle within the self against evil impulses that must be overcome to lead a pious life, while the lesser jihad represents defense of the Muslim community against non-Muslims, or external war against unbelief (*kufr*) under various conditions. In Islamic history the term jihad later came to be more casually applied to any war with non-Muslims, but this is not its theological meaning—just as the West sometimes employs the term "crusade" in war, not always in its theological meaning.

The modern jihadist ideology *reinterprets* the concept of jihad against unbelief as central, indeed essential, to the practice of Islam. It seeks the reestablishment of a unified *umma* and believes that the division of the *umma* into local national states directly contravenes the intent of Islam and is hence illegitimate. It inveighs against the Islamic illegitimacy of most regimes due to misrule, oppression, corruption, and consorting with unbelief at the international level.

Jihadist Islamism views the struggle between Islam and the West as implacable. Here is genuine embrace of the concept "clash of civilizations." It rejects all efforts at compromise and reconciliation as no being more than attempts to compromise, divide, and weaken Islam. This view is powerfully and succinctly presented by Maulana Masoud Muhammad Azhar, the Pakistani cleric long active on behalf of jihad in Kashmir as one of the heads of the militant guerrilla group Jaish-e Mohammad. His long, comprehensive, and cohesive argument is a mirror image of Western concerns about radical Islam. I sum up his language and argument as follows:

The West is implacably hostile to Islam both on theological grounds and grounds of power, simply because Muslims are the last group to stand against Western domination of the world. These Western non-believers are determined to eliminate Islam as a force through total Western domination. They have determined that "Fundamentalism" is the enemy to Western domination and global power.

Fundamentalism to the West means nothing more or less than the combination of Islam and Power.

Islam alone cannot be said to "threaten the West" since the West happily accepts, for example, the austere but emasculated non-political form of Islam as practiced in Saudi Arabia, often known as "American Islam." Nor does *power* alone in the Muslim world upset the West unduly because it will deal with the secular PLO as a reality. But as soon as power is combined with Islam, the West automatically perceives the enemy and it makes all efforts to crush it. To destroy Fundamentalism is to destroy Muslim power.

To possess strength is an obligation of Islam. But many Muslim rulers readily join with the West in condemning "Fundamentalism" because they themselves fear this power. Efforts are sometimes made to bring Islam into the political order in order to eliminate the element of Jihad in their belief and thus render them impotent, harmless and content to engage in mere parliamentary debate on social issues. If regimes lack the will and strength to crush the enemies of Islam, they should at least stand aside and facilitate the task of those who will.

The West is thus engaged in a major campaign to weaken and divide Muslims. "The objective of this propaganda is to convince the Muslims that the Fundamentalist Muslims are a different group of Muslims and to destroy them has become a necessity." Civil war among Muslims is the preferred method.

But "Fundamentalists" are not a new conception. "What changes have taken place as to why some Muslims are being labeled as Fundamentalists? Have these Muslims invented a new belief? Have they added a new custom?" Fundamentalists seek to reestablish the original obligation of jihad upon Muslims to restore Muslim power. But the key Western strategy is to turn Islam into a mere exercise of ritual and custom, gutted of political content. "Liberal" Islam has the same effect: excising the vitality of Islam and rendering it harmless and meaningless, no longer a threat to the West. Reconciliation, modernization, and new interpretations of Islam are all designed to destroy its nature and power.[3]

This comprehensive argument yields no quarter. Indeed, in Maulana Azhar's interpretation my own arguments in this book constitute precisely a part of that Western exercise to emasculate Islam, modernize it, embrace its "moderate" elements, tame it, and thereby ultimately render it compatible with and pliant to Western policies. Books like Huntington's *Clash of Civilizations* are welcomed by this school since—in an oversimplified version of his more sophisticated and nuanced argument—Huntington too preaches the incompatibility of these two civilizations and the likely clash between them.

This absolutist argument is blunt. There is no "misunderstanding," "prejudice," or absence of dialog, we are talking about sheer confrontation of rival power. From one point of view Azhar's logic is internally persuasive and reflects facts as seen on the ground by many radical Muslims. Clearly this jihadist view is not open to compromise or evolution. Western power is a threat to it and cannot be otherwise by definition. The West in effect agrees.

Fortunately, most Muslims do not accept the bulk of this argument, although some of it is occasionally attractive in seemingly explaining why Western policies are so urgently directed against all Islamist states and leaders. Most Muslims casually perceive that President Bush's War Against Terrorism, in its net effect, really is a war against Islam. Nearly all Muslims would subscribe to the belief that Muslim power is a legitimate and worthwhile goal, but most do not believe that it has to be on a collision course with the West. But as long as Western power is seen to dominate the Muslim world, the logic of this argument will strike sympathetic chords.

THE PROBLEM OF THE CREATION OF ISRAEL

It is impossible to discuss relations between the Muslim world and the West without examining the impact of the establishment of the state of Israel upon the Arabs, and even the Muslim world more broadly. I fully recognize the political sensitivity of the topic and that to some, any discussion of the reality of Israel is perceived as a subtle argument against the existence of Israel. That indeed is not my intention; I deeply believe the quest for a homeland is a basic right of all peoples. Yet we should not be inhibited from analyzing the immense *impact* of the creation of Israel—that even in Israel itself is the subject of wide discussion.

The creation and role of the Israeli state is the single most emotionally charged and violently contested issue between East and West. Partisans on both sides are often extreme and uncompromising, dedicated to rendering every issue into an ideological litmus test of everyone else's commitment to either the Arab or the Israeli cause. The debate sadly pervades politics, the media, academia, even the government. The basic reality is that the foundation of the state of Israel represents an extraordinary historical precedent—an astonishing and remarkable event in modern world history. Never before *in modern times* did Europeans (European Jews) consciously create an ideology, then a permanent colony and finally establish an independent Western-style state on territory inhabited primarily by a non-European people. (The cases of South Africa and the Western Hemisphere go back several hundred years—with serious ongoing consequences still in existence today.)

Thus for Muslims the case was exceptional and extraordinary, even in the annals of colonialism. Their fixation upon it as an extraordinary political event should not therefore be surprising or dismissed. Nor was its impact limited to a single event, but rather it set off a cascade of other events in ever-widening circles until it has become the central ongoing international conflict of half a century, unrivaled in its impact by any other ethno-religious rivalry or armed territorial struggle. Not only was a state established by Europeans on lands under Muslim rule, but the new Israeli state, in defending its newfound existence against immediate Arab attack, expanded its borders further and drove out large numbers of Palestinians from their homes—creating a huge and ugly refugee problem that still exists and that most Arab states themselves have done little to alleviate.

Muslims find it a supreme irony that they—who have an incalculably better history of treatment of Jewish minorities across their lands for fourteen hundred years than do the Christians—were asked to pay the price for the extraordinary sufferings of European Jews at the hands of European states—as refugees from Europe and victims of centuries of pogroms capped by a chilling European-directed holocaust. That holocaust, furthermore, was built on centuries of earlier discrimination, brutalization, oppression, and ghettoization of Jews across Europe for over a millennium that has no precedent at any time in the Muslim world. It was European persecution that created Zionism.

Thus, while most peoples of the developing world retain some historical memory and grievance from the colonial period, for the Muslim world, and especially the Arab world, the establishment of Israel and its Western-supported dominance remains a source of fierce hostility toward the powers of the West as a form of neo-imperialism. In simplest terms, the Arab world has not let this aspect of the colonial period fade into past memory; Israel for most Arabs is a living symbol and product of the British colonial order that facilitated the creation of Israel while Arab states were still under colonial control. The continued existence of the Palestinian question as an open wound helps maintain anti-Western views at a higher and fresher level than any other political issue in the world, continuously humiliating Arabs in their military impotence and their sense that the Palestinians have been deprived of basic justice.

The creation of Israel and the Arab military confrontation with it, coming at a time when many Arab states were achieving their own independence from European colonial domination, also facilitated the creation of military regimes and a damaging security mentality that remains a significant source of the ongoing disastrous era of authoritarian rule in the Arab world. A parade of despots has cynically used the "Zionist threat" to justify preservation of their own rule through harsh internal security organizations and importation of fascist views. The ongoing confrontation between Arab states and Israel is indeed a geopolitical reality of the region, but it has played to the worst elements within Arab politics, most notably the ideologies of Nasser's Egypt and the brutal Ba'thi regimes of Syria and Iraq.

The Israel issue has been the dominant factor in creating not only anti-Israeli, but later even anti-Jewish feeling in the Muslim and especially Arab world. Israel is viewed by a majority as a Western implant designed to keep the Arab states weak and compliant. Nearly a millennium and a half of tolerant and cooperative Jewish-Muslim coexistence has been shattered as a result. While an eventual peaceful settlement of the Arab-Israeli conflict will begin to remove some of the now-deep antipathies, that day is still not in sight; even more time will be required before genuine normalization of relations are attained. While the rough outlines of a solution are evident to all, the world has lacked the political will to stipulate and impose its final shape. The formidable power of the pro-Israeli lobby and the Christian right in U.S. politics, dominant in the U.S. Congress and further exaggerated in the minds of the Arab world, also serves to heighten paranoia among Muslims about Israel's ability to influence or manipulate all U.S. policy toward the region.

During the second half of the twentieth century the Arab-Israeli conflict has metastasized far beyond its local borders. Dictators jockey to see who can be more dedicated to an anti-Israeli position. Islamists draw lifeblood from the struggle because of its emotive nationalist/religious power and its colonial origins. All Muslims are angered and frustrated at more than thirty-five years of harsh Israeli occupation of the West Bank, which breeds only deepening reservoirs of terrorism. With the status of Jerusalem itself in play, the entire Muslim world now perceives a stake in the issue. Muslim relations with the Western world will long remain under this corrosive and damaging pall until a settlement—one equitable in the eyes of all—has been reached. Even more time will be required for the residual emotionalism of the issue to fall off the political screen.

THE COLD WAR LEGACY AND STRATEGIC THREAT

The Cold War played right into these accumulated grievances and exacerbated them. The Arab world's anger at the West made it a natural target of Soviet interest, while strong Western military support for Israel lent Moscow a ready-made issue and natural role as benefactor to much of the Arab world. In fact, the Arabs were not especially pro-Russian. They had little direct sympathy for the Soviet Union, its communist ideology, or its culture. But unlike some other Muslim states on or near the Soviet border—Turkey, Iran, Pakistan, Afghanistan—where Soviet power posed an immediate threat to their own territorial integrity, the Arab world had no such proximity and therefore less grounds to fear Moscow as a potential invader.

The only states in the Arab world that felt threatened by the policies of the Soviet Union were the conservative states (usually monarchies) that were themselves the object of propaganda attack by the radical Arab states enjoying special support by Moscow as "progressive vanguards of the revolution." Numerous Arab states adopted relatively pro-Western positions as a result of their fear of Arab radical states like Egypt, Syria, Iraq, Algeria, Libya, and South Yemen.

Finally, the West was broadly perceived by Arab progressives and intellectuals as the key prop to the very monarchical regimes that they sought to reform, change, or even overthrow. (Never mind that the revolutionary Arab states were often at least as oppressive of their own people, if not more so, than the conservative ones.) Conservative regimes were seen as instruments of Western policy, protected and perpetuated by the West in order to prevent any serious Arab ability to develop its own defensive/offensive capability against Israel.

PAN-ARABISM

Nearly all Arabs feel a sense of cultural unity with other Arabs. Regardless of differences or rivalries among the states, any Moroccan is interested in developments in Iraq, while a Syrian will closely follow events in Algeria. The entire Arab world shares a common literary language, culture, and, increasingly, an electronic media. All Arabs feel that their division into so many small separate states is the product of colonial rule, and most share a vague yearning for a greater degree of unity even if not a single political state.

At a juncture in world history where ethnic separatism and the breakup of the state is a common phenomenon, it is striking that the Arabs reflect quite the opposite trend, a desire for unity as the preferred or even natural state of affairs. In one sense this is a highly progressive movement consonant with the move toward regionalism in Europe. While no one expects that a single political union will emerge in the Arab world, there may well be some unions in the future based on well-defined historical/cultural regions, such as Mesopotamia, Greater Syria, and a union of peoples of the Arabian Peninsula. Arbitrary and despotic leadership across most of the region is one of the main hindrances to the formation of any greater degree of union since the security mentality of these police states insists on closed borders and is suspicious of outside influences and ideas penetrating the local polity. With greater political liberalization and democratization, moves toward amalgamation will become easier rather than harder and natural regional groupings will emerge.

Pan-Arabism presents yet another political-cultural feature that intensifies potential confrontation with the West. Visions of Arab solidarity nourish an independent regional identity unwilling to automatically acquiesce to Western decisions on the international order. Pan-Arabism strengthens the cultural resistance of Arab peoples, perhaps slightly parallel to the strong cultural nationalism of the Francophone world that cherishes its cultural distinctiveness from an Anglo-Saxon-dominated cultural world. Francophone distinctiveness often leads even to an independence of foreign policy action as well. But Washington has always feared the force of pan-Arabism, partly because it can more effectively challenge U.S. regional policies, but also quite simply because pan-Arabism was generally pro-Moscow, anti-Israel, and often violently and forcefully expounded by expansionist dictators like Abdul Nasser and Saddam Hussein intent on exporting their power. Pan-Arabism thus becomes the nucleus of resistance to the power of the Western order. Islamism has inherited some elements of this mantle since Islamic solidarity and Arab solidarity are mutually self-reinforcing.

THE AMERICAN FACTOR IN FUTURE MUSLIM WORLD POLITICS

The United States will continue to dominate the international arena in nearly all regards for many decades to come—both in policies of omission as well as commission. The combination of U.S. ability to project military, economic, and diplomatic power along with its major edge in cultural "soft power" is rivaled by no other challenger. Nonetheless, the willingness of the United States to maintain a dominant, even intrusive role in the Muslim world over the longer term may be open to question. Even after the 11 September 2001 attacks, the U.S. public is unlikely to be willing to shoulder indefinitely the costs of the rising tide of anti-American attitudes in the absence of immediately demonstrable threats to specific and important American interests. The Muslim world may be in the process of becoming far more hostile, not only to U.S. interests, but to close ties with the United States on many levels.

U.S. policy in the Muslim world has been focused on four issues since the end of the Cold War: protection of the steady flow of energy from the region, the security of Israel, non-proliferation of weapons of mass destruction, and the fight against terrorism. A fifth, generally unspoken, preference is to hinder the emergence of any regional hegemons. Except for the first issue, ensuring the free flow of energy, *the other four goals place Washington on a basic course of opposition toward the perceived longer term interests of most Muslim states.*

These five goals, routinely invoked, deserve closer examination. U.S. policies in each respect are perceived as antipathetic to the Muslim world and will form the geopolitical backdrop to issues that involve "Islam and the West."

First, the essentiality of Middle East energy to the industrialized world is beyond question. But we need to examine the issue with some rigor: what exactly is being protected, from whom, for whom and by whom, and at what cost to the U.S. taxpayer? None of the answers is clear. The free flow of oil rarely seems to have been at much risk in the past, from even the most anti-American of dictators such as Qadhafi in Libya, Saddam Hussein in Iraq, or Ayatollah Khomeini in Iran, all of whom happily sold oil. More realistically, the self-appointed task of "safeguarding the free flow of oil" in reality is designed to justify a U.S. military presence in the Gulf for broader U.S. strategic purposes.[4] As other nations decide that they have no desire to support this questionable task, the rationale for a U.S. military presence in the Gulf begins to weaken and creates long term regional hostility. Indeed, this military presence in Saudi Arabia was the immediate cause of Usama bin Ladin's early hostility to the United States. The political, diplomatic, military and economic cost to the United States of this presence is rising.

Second, the U.S. commitment to Israel's security guarantees overwhelming Israeli military power in the region. It also exacerbates all the attendant frustrations of the Palestinian problem to the Arab and Muslim world discussed earlier. While Israel's security should not be open to question, the near automatic support lent to any of its policies extracts higher costs for the United States in the region. Successful conclusion of a just settlement of the Palestinian problem and creation of a viable Palestinian state is the indispensable condition for even a beginning of lessening of tensions between the United States and the Muslim world. This goal remains elusive, and the situation is seriously worsening, despite some remarkable progress since 1990. The ensuing cost of U.S.–Muslim world confrontation may be serious as the issue polarizes alarmingly under the administration of George W. Bush.

Third, the issue of proliferation of nuclear weapons will remain troublesome indefinitely. It is a virtual certitude that numerous Muslim states, along with most other developing nations, will seek to develop their own weapons of mass destruction—chemical, biological, and nuclear—and many are well along that road. Israel's security is one key factor. While the United States prefers not to articulate it in this way, the basic strategic imperative behind Washington's nonproliferation policy is not only to prevent devastating nuclear conflict from engulfing the region, but even more to discourage major regional powers from developing capabilities that hinder the U.S. role of policeman, peace-keeper, hegemon, balancing force, or intervener of last resort in the region in accordance with its self-perceived interests. The United States will have to determine what price it is willing to pay to hinder or stop the inevitable process of proliferation. If nuclear proliferation cannot be stopped, Washington will be required, as before, to be selectively acquiescent (as it has been with Israel, Pakistan, and India.) We may posit that yet other states, by the logic of international relations and great regional power aspirations, will also eventually seek to join the prestigious nuclear club—such as Turkey, Egypt, Algeria, and Saudi Arabia—apart from more obvious candidates, Iraq and Iran. The reality is that Washington's desire to block proliferation flies in the face of the long-term preferences of *all* regional aspirants to power, a permanent built-in friction point.

Fourth, terrorism, discussed in a separate chapter, will remain a constant source of friction between the United States and the Muslim world for the foreseeable future, especially since the U.S. War Against Terrorism in essence strengthens regional repression and creates deeper anti-American resentment.

Fifth, there is the unspoken goal of preventing regional hegemony of any power. This goal clearly conflicts directly with the geopolitical ambitions of all the major powers of the region—especially Iran, Iraq, and Saudi Arabia—and is not sustainable as a policy over the long run in its attempt to suspend the laws of geopolitics in the region.

Finally, there is the issue of democracy. Despite its rhetorical stance in favor of democracy worldwide, Washington possesses an unspoken sense that representative governments in most Muslim states will be less acquiescent to American interests than the current generation of authoritarian leaders, especially if Islamists should come to power. There is a considerable element of truth to this anxiety, at least over the short term since there is much—indeed, growing—pent-up anti-Americanism that open political processes will release. But there is no escaping the reality that Washington will eventually have to come to terms with both democracy and the reality of highly ambivalent feelings toward the United States in the Muslim world. This issue of political liberalization will therefore remain a point of friction between the United States and the Muslim peoples in the decades to come unless Washington comes to realize the long-term price it will pay by preferring authoritarian "stability" today over the inevitable turmoil of change and reform required to produce ultimately better governance tomorrow.

For all these reasons, then, the character of Islamist movements in the region will be highly affected by the nature of Washington's future activism and interventionism in the Muslim world. Indeed, *U.S. policy will probably be the central external determinant upon the evolution of Islamist movements and governments.* At this stage of development, Islamist movements have assumed the role of the key guardians of the national honor, sovereignty, and "Islamic authenticity" and therefore, by definition, will be among the first forces to adopt anti-American rhetoric in the event of U.S.-Muslim state confrontation. That quasi-nationalist aspect *need not be automatically anti-American, but in reality it is nearly invariably anti-American* in the face of almost all present U.S. policies in the region.

But deep, long-term U.S. activism in the international arena is not a certainty. One should not assume that the United States will remain indefinitely the highly intrusive gendarme of the region and guarantor of the status quo, mirroring the role of the British Empire in the region in an earlier era and maintaining military bases in the region. The imperial role sits less comfortably upon Congress than it did in the corridors of Whitehall; preservation of a highly flawed status quo—in the most repressive and marginalized region in the world—becomes less attractive to American taxpayers, liberals, and even to U.S. military planners—unless it contributes directly to stopping anti American terrorism. To many observers it may, on the contrary, be exacerbating anti-American terrorism.

THE EMERGENCE OF ANTI-AMERICANISM AS AN "IDEOLOGY"

Jihadist Islam demonstrates an implacable Manichaean anti-Westernism subscribed to by only a small minority of Muslims. But the tide of virulence may be spreading, particularly after 11 September. More disturbing, it is undergoing a shift away from generalized anti-Westernism toward an explicit and focused anti-Americanism.

Many people familiar with the Muslim world, including myself, have observed the growth of specifically anti-American sentiments over the years. Along with numerous other specialists on the region, I had concluded—wrongly—that major U.S. military action against Muslims would quickly lead to explosive popular anti-regime violence threatening the present order. Overt reaction to the sweeping character of the early War Against Terrorism—overthrowing the Taleban, hunting down al-Qa'ida elements across the region, making demands on Arab nations to cooperate against Bin Ladin, planning an attack on Iraq, making threats against other Muslim states—has been remarkably constrained. But this does not mean that the Arab and Muslim world remains essentially quiescent, impassive, and lacking any alternative to acceptance of the unpopular American vision of international security. Tensions against local regimes and the United States are growing. But when they will reveal themselves fully, when the glass will finally overflow, remains a key unknown.

While lack of violent reaction to U.S. policies is, of course, the good news, this greater surface political passivity in the face of growing U.S. interventionism and imposition of unpopular policies represents a disturbing new trend—the concealment of anger, frustration, and impotence reflected more openly in the past. Part of the quiescence can be attributed to regime skills in managing and repressing more open expression of violence. But part of it too represents a bitter fatalism that resistance is now essentially futile, that the domestic and international order is so arrayed as to make protest both impotent and impossible. The United States is observed by Muslims to have irrevocably turned a corner in the embrace of a naked policy of hostility to Muslims, their interests, honor, and dignity.

This phenomenon may be the most frightening consequence of the War Against Terrorism—the quiet, sullen bitterness and deepening of broad anti-American resentment across the region that has now taken on the character of an "ideology"—a dominant mindset. This is no longer Islamism but naked anger at the United States, leading to unofficial boycotts of U.S. products, to popular anti-Americanism at the casual social level that even, according to *The Economist*, has included cursing of the United States silently at prayer. These simple visceral attitudes will strengthen both Islamism and any other nationalist forces that may emerge. The consequences are literally incalculable since we cannot determine what form they will take. A slowdown in seeking education in the United States? Diminished travel to the United States and less business with the United States? Both are already visible. It could lead to lessening investment in the United States or purchase of American goods (already happening), or to resistance by states to U.S. policies more broadly. This may be a time bomb waiting to go off against pro-American regimes at some point in the near future. Low-key and unorganized anti-American violence against individuals could emerge. The overall atmosphere bolsters support for jihadist forces around the Muslim world.

The silent impassiveness is the newest and most disturbing feature of anti-American sentiment. It is dangerous to assume that such Muslim anger is basically transient, manageable, and basically irrelevant to U.S. global strategy and deeper U.S. interests in the region. Only time will reveal the dimensions of this smoldering anti-Americanism that need not even take Islamist form. "Secular" anti-Americanism, perhaps of a nationalist or neo-leftist variety, will dovetail comfortably with Islamist perceptions on this issue. Indeed, *it may already be easier for secularists lacking commitment to the moral foundations of Islam to take up unsanctioned violence against Americans.* It may in fact be revealing here that it is Iraq—a rich, educated, and secular country—that emerged at the top of Washington's list of "evil" states.

ISLAM AND THE WEST

The (re)emergence of a "secular anti-Americanism" simply demonstrates more clearly how common the attitude of suspicion and distrust toward America is among the more hard-line Islamists. Muslim experience with the West may have contributed considerably to this attitude, but it does not basically emerge from Islam itself. Anti-Western views emerge from other places in the world: Latin resentments of "Yanqui imperialism," Asian support for "Asian values" against Western domination, Marxist interpretations of politics and economics, and various colorations of Third-Worldism that can be traced back to the non-aligned movement and before. Islamists are just one of many groups willing to give open voice to their concerns, although perhaps with greater religious and cultural flavor than any other group.

What the West faces in essence is a Muslim world rife with a complex of grievances at once historical and contemporary, psychological and material, political and economic, and even structural in nature as they relate to institutionalized differences in power. These grievances have entered the political culture as an existing reality. Western cynics may say the problem belongs to the Muslims—"let them deal with it"; but if the problem is large enough it also belongs to the West. It is indeed large, it consumes a great deal of American energy, and it represents an existing reality that will find inevitable expression in one fashion or another.

A key question is the vantage point from which the West views Islamism. One perspective is based primarily on the often narrowly conceived interests of the West itself. Another would factor in more carefully the stated interests of the *local regimes* as well. A third would also show major concern for the views of the *peoples themselves* of the states involved. None of these should be mutually exclusive. But historically the viewpoint of the people of the region has been far from the purview of U.S. policymakers. *But surely it is significant that the United States finds the greatest political challenge precisely in that region of the world where government is least representative of its people. And where the United States routinely opposes the leading groups that challenge the entrenched status quo.* Here lies a key source of the problem between the West and the Muslim world, including the Islamists.

As a former resident of the Muslim world for nearly two decades and still a frequent visitor there, I come back and forth from the area with a profound feeling of schizophrenia, a huge cultural disconnect between two seemingly unrelated worlds—as if passing through a looking-glass. After absorbing the current range of views, concerns, and aspirations in the Muslim world, within several weeks after each return to the United States I invariably find myself once again overwhelmed by the blanketing, all-dominating Western media and its exclusive view of the world. The powerful immanence and urgent reality of the other world from whence I returned, as a psychological and ideological universe of its own, inevitably is squeezed out even from my own mind under this assault. Under this conditioning, most of the American public has no idea that there even is another world and perspective out there, nor does it care. One invariably gets the feeling of bouncing back and forth like a cultural and psychological ping-pong ball when one sees the CNN view of the world, or even the *New York Times,* and then turns to the Muslim Student Association news or any foreign Muslim TV station or website. It is one thing to disagree on issues, but quite another when we are living in two different universes here, viewing two sides of the same coin. How can such a gap in perception exist for such long periods of time, bridged only sporadically by explosions that thrust the realities of the Muslim world back onto our mental and TV screens until the crisis passes?

We are not talking here after all about the existence of a Soviet-speak from the Cold War days of state-controlled media, but rather about two alternative views existing at the *popular* level of perception. Is the United States sober-minded and real while the other side lives in fantasy and unreality? Or do regional views represent the reality while the United States lives in denial? It cannot be simply a question of right and wrong views of the world. Both sides fail to capture the full reality in front of them, and the gap must be bridged. The gap might even be more explicable if we were simply talking about sad and abandoned parts of the globe of seemingly little significance. But this is a region that rates at the top of international geopolitical and economic attention and concern. Yet the gap of perception is massive—for which there is a price to be paid. And with modern media and the Internet there is no longer any excuse to be globally unaware.

There can be no doubt that the strongest emotions are emerging from people deeply frustrated with their own governments, their own weakness, low standards of living, and lack of voice. These factors provide the main source for the anti-American agenda. Political Islam is one of those vehicles that reflects this reality and that is itself concerned with the welfare of the Muslim world in the face of the Western challenge.

It is in this context, then, that the rigor and forcefulness of traditional Shari'a law and justice takes on an appeal that is invigorating and inspiring to stagnant and troubled societies such as Kashmir, Chechnya, Palestine, Algeria, Nigeria, and Indonesia. It represents a whole series of mindsets that can be expressed in a variety of familiar cliches such as "back-to-basics," "damn the torpedoes," "stiffen your back in a tough world," "stand up to the enemy," "stare down the oppressor," "we will never submit," "blood will demonstrate our seriousness of purpose," etc. These ideas encapsulate the uncompromising stance of any troubled community, clinging to law and tradition for strength, familiarity, and sustenance. It just happens that the tradition in this case is Islam. But it could be conservative Jewish law with its own complex and detailed prescriptions, or traditional Japanese society with its rigidities and strict codes of decorum, honor, and justice in which the rite of *harakiri* or *seppuku* takes on powerful ritual importance.

The West is not required to share all Muslim, much less Islamist values or modes of thinking. But it is required to grasp the source and nature of the gap, recognize its immense seriousness, and begin means to treat the issue before it reaches explosive proportions. Sadly, the gap in comprehension at this point could not be much wider.

U.S. OPTIONS

The United States will have a very difficult time in responding to the breadth and diversity of these problems. Some are beyond unilateral treatment, such as imbalances in world power and the world dominated by Western influence. Any formulations for alleviation of this power imbalance border on the idealistic if not utopian. Nonetheless, a greater sense among Muslims that their states are partners in some kind of greater global process is psychologically and procedurally important if states and regions are to feel either part of a process rather than the victims or objects of its whims. Here U.S. unilateralism, so much the penchant of conservative policymakers, is very much part of the problem. Left untreated, this continuing sense of Muslim world impotence, for multiple reasons, may well lead to increasing violence and terrorism that will itself exacerbate an already serious gap.

There are a number of outstanding international issues that lie at the heart of friction between the United States and the Muslim world, of which Palestine is the first and overwhelmingly most important. The United States has not invested serious muscle in bringing a just settlement to the Palestinians that will over the long run enable Israel to live in a more peaceful environment. This takes a political decision at the highest level, which has not been forthcoming over the decades. Additional issues include the suffering of Iraqis from the U.S.-imposed embargo on Saddam Hussein. While nearly every Muslim knows Saddam is a terrible ruler, his removal by the United States simply exacerbates existing anger that Muslims are the objects and not the subjects of regional policy and U.S. unilateralism. The nature of the cure becomes worse than the disease.

The Kashmir situation has been allowed to drift dangerously for decades without forceful international attention. Palestine and Kashmir both fall into the category of "national liberation struggles" that need separate treatment as a distinct and complex phenomenon involving issues of minority discontent and separatism. The United States has not seriously reviewed the problem of oppressed minorities seeking alleviation of grievance through genuine autonomy or independence. Washington's heavy bias has been in favor of maintenance of territorial integrity and the status quo. In principle this is fine, but the world will see many more, not fewer, struggles by minorities to secede from states cursed with bad and oppressive rule, minorities who, in a new and more democratic world won't take it anymore and see no reason why they should. New criteria need to be established regarding "marriage counseling" for states at risk of internal civil war and collapse, with "divorce counseling" at the end if all other means fail.[5]

Both the Muslim world and the United States require a great deal more dialog with each other on precisely these troublesome issues. Examination of the problem cannot take place only at the level of relations with friendly pro-U.S. autocrats, but needs the participation of Muslim social leaders who enjoy widespread respect within their society even though (or possibly because) they are outside the ruling circles of those societies. The United States can begin to engage overseas Muslims vigorously, including those Islamic clerics who enjoy great respect and authority as men of integrity. Both sides will benefit from a dialogue that initially will reveal deep fissures in thought and approach but that over time may begin to bridge numerous gaps. Many of these clerics represent undeniably moderate forces within political Islam, but their own understanding of the West, though far from uniformly hostile, is flawed and often initially unsympathetic. Many could learn from visits to the United States and dialog with Americans—if ever they were granted visas.

It is worth noting, however, that this process will be fought hard by elements on both sides. The first group of opponents will be the "friendly" Muslim authoritarians themselves, those regimes that stifle critiques from respected independent clerics and restrict their movements. The second group of opponents will come from the United States and will try to discredit the Muslim travelers by pointing to rash statements about Israel they may have made at one point or another. Given the passions aroused in the Middle East by the Arab-Israeli conflict, very few if any prominent Muslim figures will have the kind of liberal record of interfaith dialogue and tolerance that Americans find pleasing and appropriate. That should not disqualify them as potential interlocutors, however. Given the importance of the issues involved and the realities of the situation, the initial litmus test for being included in dialog should be limited to a prohibition on explicit incitement to terrorism and advocacy of war.

At the regional level is the necessity for democratization, a major theme of this whole book, and the single biggest problem of the region that impacts upon it psychologically as well as practically. The United States is well-positioned to stimulate change in this arena, but so far it has been quite unwilling to do so for fear of the election of anti-U.S. voices. Do we believe this situation will improve with prolonged autocracy and repression?

Democratization, of course, is not primarily about just elections but about more open societies and expanded civil societies that help break the totalitarian hold of the state over the life of its citizens. It involves encouragement of freedom of speech, media, association, and rule of law. The Internet can help play a role in this respect by opening up avenues to global thought that can have a purging effect upon domestic opinion. The United States can assist in Internet development.

Education in the United States has long been a key avenue for exposing Muslims to the more positive sides of U.S. life, but the War Against Terrorism has put a severe crimp in this process, not only from the point of view of visas, but from the desire of Muslims to live in or even visit the United States now. Many are reorienting themselves toward Europe, Canada, and Australia.

At the level of Muslim state society and economy, there is much the United States can do, at a tiny sliver of the cost of the vastly expanded U.S. defense budget. Education is a high priority where the United States has already had much experience in its work through AID (Agency for International Development) in textbook projects. This arena is especially important and a place where a new look needs to be taken at the curricula in many Muslim states. The United States can hardly determine the selection of curricula or how Islam is to be taught, but it can help open up curricula to a broader range of materials. The United States can also support high quality state-sponsored or private secular education, now often poor or limited, that would be welcomed by most Muslim families that value U.S. education. This is a highly sensitive cultural area in which unpopular broader U.S. regional policies can impose a high degree of defensiveness upon Muslim educators who otherwise know the problems that exist. The United States would be wise to work on these projects through other Western countries or international institutions that carry far less baggage.

THE IMPACT OF GLOBAL FORCES ON POLITICAL ISLAM

POLITICAL ISLAM faces a wealth of internal challenges to its future development. Islamist movements cannot operate in isolation; rather, they are forced to react to a powerful and ceaseless series of external intrusions—political, military, social, demographic, ideological, and cultural-from a globalizing world.

STATE POLICIES TOWARD ISLAMISM

The state will continue to exert huge impact upon the fortunes of Islamist movements. First, highly authoritarian regimes can continue to ban *all* meaningful political parties and debate, as is the case in Iraq, Syria, Libya, Saudi Arabia, Tunisia, Sudan, Afghanistan, United Arab Emirates, Bahrain, Uzbekistan, Kazakstan, and Turkmenistan. This generally channels opposition into underground Islamist activity. Second, the state can specifically ban political parties organized on the basis of religion, as in Egypt, Algeria, Azerbaijan, and Turkey, for example (although the application of this restriction in each of these states varies considerably.) Third, the state can open up the political order to all political parties but manipulate the system to the disadvantage of the Islamists or other serious challengers to state power, for that matter.

No state order is static, however, and the rules of the game in the Muslim world are evolving, usually in the gradual direction of greater openness, with the notable exception of the severe and brutal repression of Saddam's Iraq. Sudan, Egypt, Tunisia, Algeria, and Jordan have also moved away from liberalization of the 1990s, while Bahrain, Kuwait, Indonesia, Yemen, Malaysia, and Afghanistan show some encouraging liberalization. Unfortunately, the 11 September 2001 attacks on the United States and the subsequent War Against Terrorism gave carte blanche to authoritarian and even semi-democratic regimes to reverse course and begin a crackdown against almost all opposition they dislike.

Indeed, even before 11 September, nearly all Muslim states had been fairly successful in stymieing the emergence of strong Islamist parties and in blocking them, not only from achieving power but from playing any serious role in the political order. As Ibrahim Karawan has pointed out, almost no Islamist organization has been able to withstand the power of the state to ban, arrest, detain, harass, manipulate, and block the activities of Islamist organizations, making it very unlikely that they will come to power short of open elections or the actual collapse of the state into anarchy or revolution, as in Iran in 1979.[1] But even future coups against the state by Islamists are less likely, given the close scrutiny under which military personnel in most countries are placed by governments to deter Islamist "infiltration" (Turkey, Egypt, and Jordan, for example). Islamists have not, however, been seriously excluded from the military in Pakistan, Saudi Arabia, Bangladesh, Morocco, and Indonesia, raising at least the *possibility* of an Islamist coup in the future. Here the impact of the War Against Terrorism is far from clear.

Even if indiscriminate crackdowns against all forms of Islamist politics now occur, the basic problem for all regimes remains: how do they cope with a movement that for the time being carries a greater measure of popular support than any other political force? Deflecting the popularity of those movements is problematic. It is conceivable—but not terribly likely—that continued suppression of all such movements will eventually lead their followers to abandon the Islamists in favor of other ideological movements that have greater chance of achieving political victory in the face of implacable state hostility.

Some states have also adopted a third strategy, sometimes in combination with repression, of preempting the Islamists message by adopting a strong Islamizing agenda themselves, as in Saudi Arabia, Egypt, Pakistan, and Malaysia where to one degree or another the rhetoric of Islamism and other Islamic symbols are promulgated by the state. Here, however, as Louis Cantori comments, "in one sense the Islamists have already won," in that the state has been forced to adopt Islamic vocabulary and much of its agenda in order to preempt the Islamists—thereby yielding to the Islamists' power to impose an agenda.

This phenomenon demonstrates two things: one, that *political power*—for both state and political movement—becomes more important for everybody than the substance of ideological debate itself since each tries to deprive the other of Islamic symbols. Second, when the state has taken great pains to try to establish its own centers of Islamic orthodoxy (like al-Azhar in Egypt), it ends up ceding power in religious affairs to the state's own conservative Islamist apparatus whose own agenda could ultimately come to threaten the state itself. The state is in a trap: while the state-controlled religious institutions must hew fairly closely to the Islamist message if they are to maintain their own credibility with the public, in so doing they are captured by the Islamist agenda and placed in danger of losing control of their own state-sponsored religious institutions. If the state then tries to rein them in, they thereby demonstrate these institutions are puppets and thus strengthen the hand of the anti-state Islamists.[2]

A further byproduct of this state policy of preemption is that top politicians are required to demonstrate public piety—a phenomenon not exactly unknown in politics in other cultures—and to pay some lip service to the concept of an Islamic state. Al-Azhar University in Cairo today is in competition with the Islamists in zealously justifying Islamic bans on social and cultural issues. Very few Muslim rulers can afford to disavow the Islamic agenda as boldly as Turkey's Kemalists, under special historic circumstances, have done. Time, then, has favored the Islamists, and their agenda is advancing even while their parties or movements suffer suppression. Worse, the pressures tend to push the entire Islamic discourse ever further toward narrowness and intolerance—a process that might not happen if other forces of an open civil society were also in play to provide balance in the debate.

The state's victory through this process is Pyrrhic. It has had to resort to repression and extra-legal means to check the Islamists and remains under growing pressure from most of civil society to liberalize the system. As its legitimacy grows ever thinner, any relaxation of authoritarian control and expansion of democratic process can only strengthen the Islamists. How many entrenched current rulers would win truly open and fair elections? As soon as the Egyptian state in the fall of 2000 tried to abandon the rigged elections of the past and operate a fairer electoral process, the Muslim Brotherhood was the immediate beneficiary and the state the first loser. It may be only the specter of overall state failure that will pressure state rulers to yield some voice to other forces, to share the problems. In the longer run pressures for greater democratization cannot be indefinitely resisted. Thus, *even as the Islamists' ability to seize the state by force is weakening, so too is the state's ability to resist Islamist politics in all its forms.*

THE IMPACT OF THE FUTURE WORLD ENVIRONMENT

The twenty-first century will be even more important to the development of Islamic political thinking than the twentieth century was. More opportunities for growth, evolution, and participation in the political arena will emerge for the

Islamists than were ever available to them before in history. Many of these opportunities will undoubtedly come through crisis. Meanwhile, technology is enhancing the freedom, speed, and access to the debate through burgeoning multiple means, from the exploding fields of cyber-Islam to popular Islamic literature.[3] Political liberalization and democratization, however slow it has been in the Muslim world to date, will nonetheless increase, offering greater political options to large numbers of Islamist movements and parties.

Helping shape the environment under which Islamic movements must operate in the future world are several major external trends.

DIVERSITY AND PLURALISM

The future inevitably spells *increasing cultural diversity* for all. People and ideas are on the move, and technology exponentially accelerates the process. Technology can only increase diversification of expression, while migration will be a key feature for nearly all regions, even if they are jarred by international terrorism. This diversity imposes the *reality of pluralism,* in ethnic, religious, social and class arenas, however destructive this may be to maintenance of cultural tradition and homogeneity of social outlook and values. The West is affected as much as the Muslim world.

Political Islam faces a choice here: on the one hand it can champion the rights of the Muslim community exclusively, seek to preserve the "purity" of the Muslim community resident in the West through the erection of cultural barriers and safeguards, and limit the intrusion of foreign cultures into its own societies, cultures, and economies in its own homelands. On the other it can accept and work with this diversity on the basis of more universal cultural values.

So far most Islamist movements are entrenched in lending support to their own Muslim community over the interest of others—as are most other ethnic parties in multiethnic states. But if the Islamists have aspirations beyond their own religious community to any kind of universalism, they need to move beyond their own constituency to appeal to a broader one. We see some clear initial signs of this in Malaysia's PAS, Egypt's Muslim Brotherhood, and Turkey's Justice and Development (AK) Party as they work effectively with minorities at the provincial and municipal level. But many other Islamists are moving toward a more exclusivist view of Islamism that is narrowly communal.

In intellectual terms many Islamists are even more reprehensible. In Egypt, Malaysia, Pakistan, and Bangladesh, they support cries for censorship along Islamic lines and harassment of scholarship. Among Sunni fundamentalists attitudes are hardening toward not only Christians, but toward Shi'a Muslims, or even liberal Muslims. These roads can lead only to religious bigotry, narrowness, discrimination, and racism. Islamist movements do not yet seem fully comfortable with the reality of pluralism even if they recognize the reality in principle. (Traditional nationalist parties face similar problems.) This pluralist challenge is perhaps the single biggest issue confronting Islamism today.

TOLERANCE VERSUS EQUALITY

There are two ways to think about tolerance, which is closely linked to the concept of pluralism. One can accept, support, even welcome the equal rights of others to think and behave differently—requiring a kind of agnosticism or neutrality on the part of the state that will protect all faiths opportunity to blossom. On the other hand, a state or society dominated by an official religious practice may only "tolerate" the pursuit of different practices by others, that is, they will be tolerated, but nothing more—a kind of value judgment in itself that does not extend even legal equality among ideas. For some Islamists the state's accordance of equal validity to all faiths is problematic if not blasphemous. We see the same dilemma elsewhere as Catholics and many Protestants find accordance of equal *validity* to other faiths nearly impossible. The modern Russian state works to preserve the privileged position of the Orthodox Church against missionary inroads from evangelical Protestantism.

Islamist movements are divided on these issues. Certainly Islam historically accords clear-cut rights and protections to religious minorities, but they are not viewed on a par with Islam, they are merely tolerated—not a condition of true social and legal equality. Yet other modernist Islamists are working toward a new concept of pluralism such as Turkey's Nur movement, in which all ideas are tolerated without privileging some over others in the belief that only through true freedom of ideas will human beings ever approach a truer understanding of God and his purposes. These more liberal voices are still in the minority, although they are probably rising.

All Muslims are well aware of the Qur'anic verses that serve as a key justification for pluralism in Islam. Verse 5:48 states: "Unto every one of you We have appointed a (different) law and way of life. And if Allah had so willed, He could surely have made you all one single community; but (He willed it otherwise) in order to test you by means of what He has given you. Vie, then, with one another in doing good works!" A second well-known verse cited to justify pluralism in Islam is "O mankind, surely We have created you from a male and female, and made you nations and tribes that you may know each other" (Verse 49:13). A third verse speaks of God granting each prophet his own "Shari'a" or way to God.

These verses clearly indicate Muslim awareness of the existence of diversity among peoples of the world and within communities. And they suggest that the ability to be pious and do good is the primary criteria for godliness. Other traditions of the Prophet are also cited to demonstrate how he operated within multicultural or diverse societies and sought to bring religious or ethnic truce to warring parties.

While these verses adduce powerful scriptural evidence to support a pluralist position, many more radical Islamists today cite other Qur'anic evidence to justify an intolerance and a determination to seek full homogeneity of thought and practice within Islam as the only true way to respect God's will. Many of these more uncompromising citations are taken entirely out of context, or from the context of Qur'anic description of conflict with non-Muslims under specific historic conditions of warfare, parallel to the absolutism and ethnocentrism of portions of the Old Testament about treatment of the enemies of the Jews in warfare. Many Muslims actually have fewer conflicts with Christians or Jews than they do with heterodox Muslim groups. The *salafi* movement, especially in its Wahhabi form, is exceptionally exclusivistic on this point.

While Islam always extended tolerance to "The People of the Book" (Christians and Jews), they must now recognize the need to extend it to others such as Buddhists, Hindus, Taoists, any number of other native religions, and even atheists. Islam has been pragmatic about this when necessary: when Muslims ruled India under the Mughal Dynasty, there emerged a working de facto coexistence with the Hindu majority even if some clerics disapproved of it, and some Muslim scholars even detected a spirit of monotheism behind Hinduism's apparent polytheism. The PAS government in two states of Malaysia today also deals comfortably with Chinese and Hindus.

Increasing multiplication and diversification of Islamist movements and parties themselves are a further certitude in the evolution of political Islam. Differences among Islamist parties and groups may become at least as great as those between Muslim and non-Muslim political parties. Here we will find a further evidence of "protestantization" of Islamic thinking as increased freedom encourages a greater range of personal religious interpretation of the political and social import of Islam. This should actually lead to healthy debate and to an intellectual sharpening of the issues among them, at least in intellectual terms, even if not necessarily in the political realm. Unfortunately, there has not been as yet major liberalization of Islamist thinking among Islamist political parties resulting from debate and competition among them, except possibly in Turkey, Egypt, and Indonesia. In other areas, such as Pakistan, we witness Islamist parties vying to adopt the most zealous position—to "out-Islam" each other.

As Islamist movements proliferate, the absence of central or definitive authority within Islam grows ever more evident, a further example of the "protestantization" process of diversification and growing dispersal of authority. For a very long time there has not been a single authoritative source of authority in Islam. The Caliph, nominally the supreme religious leader within Islam, quickly evolved into a politicized role in the first Muslim century. Contrary to popular belief, *political and religious authority in Islam in actual practice separated forever in the first century of Islam with religion subordinate to secular power, even if it ruled in the name of Islam for purposes of legitimacy and in defense of Islamic law.* Religious authority has rarely been centralized, with competing major centers such as Najaf (for Shi'a), and senior religious figures in practice competing from Cairo, Baghdad, Istanbul, or other locales with only limited and selective authority outside of the country.

Today, as Eickelman points out, rival claimants as sources of authority in Islam are expanding exponentially, with independent and self-appointed religious opinions being issued through multiple forms of media, including *fatwa* centers all over the world including one in Ann Arbor, Michigan; newsletters, courses of instruction, television programs, books, magazines, audio and video tapes, CDs, and above all Internet sites where one can ask for opinions on any issue from any number of religious authorities, some of whom are not necessarily graduates of madrasas but self-taught Islamic intellectuals. This process has the effect of making it easier to "shop around" for opinions—not all bad in itself since it also forces one to think about the opinions and issues more deeply oneself. (In the West too, people often attend a church in which they are comfortable with the vision of Christianity propounded.)

In other words, a more open intellectual and political environment encourages diversification of thought within Islam. People will be more likely to consider what the *practice* of Islam means to them in practical terms, thereby affecting their approach to alternative Islamist messages. There will be no single voice of authority.

This process of diversification of authority also breaks away from the localization of religious authority, as had invariably been the case throughout most of Islamic history, and transnationalizes it so that one can find religious authority from websites halfway around the world. Today Egyptian Shaykh Yusif Qaradawi, for example, is physically based in Qatar but in reality is now "everywhere" through his successful "Islam-on-line" website, in English and Urdu as well as Arabic (http://www.islamonline.net), where he enjoys far greater authority than he was ever accorded in the intellectually rigid environment of Cairo. Not only are opinions now transnational, but the questions and concerns expressed and exchanged are also creating the "electronic *umma*" or "virtual *umma*" that represents globalization par excellence.[4] That electronic *umma* will also be open to electronic diversity, which will multiply different options and interpretations that were not previously available. So technology both unites and diversifies the *umma*.

THE INDIVIDUALIZATION OF RELIGION

Religion may now be undergoing a deeper revolutionary process, that of individualization. In traditional and immobile societies one's religion was strictly inherited and determined one's social community. But the process of diversification and the ability of the individual to seek a variety of religious opinions not only encourages individuals to think about what the practice of Islam means to them; it gradually moves religion out of the area of a culturally and family-inherited practice and into the area of personal quest and choice. Some Christians, Jews, and Muslims may decry the suggestion here of a "religious buffet" at which one can choose the doctrines that appeal and ignore others. Yet that is exactly what religion of conscience is coming to mean in the contemporary world. The essence of evangelical Protestantism, for example, involves conscious individual choice of faith and leadership, not practice of an inherited faith. Large numbers of other believers in the West reflect some personal tailoring of each person's own religious belief influenced by a variety of sources—choices made specifically because the believer *cares* about his or her faith and explores books and teachings of various traditions that help to define it. This is no longer strict perpetuation of inherited family tradition.

How valuable, some believers will argue, is an inherited faith if it remains unexamined? Is not a quest for a dynamic personal faith all the more meaningful if it is personally derived from reflection and study? These features reflect the evolution of much religious thought in the West today, interpenetrated and irrigated by other faiths. Hence we witness the impact of Buddhism on some major Christian thinkers, or enrichment of Christian spiritualism through reference to other spiritual traditions in a new ecumenical spirit. This phenomenon would seem to emerge directly out of the contemporary conditions of multiculturalism. It is bound to affect Muslims as well, particularly as they come to live in different societies or accept different cultures within their own.

Now, such "ecumenicism" is fiercely resisted when a religiously defined community feels existentially threatened and thus clings more intensely to the essential faith as an assertion of community and personal identity. (A leading Jewish rabbi in the United States has suggested that America may pose more of a threat to Jewish culture than Auschwitz because it encourages intermarriage and a comfortable and ongoing loss of Jewish identity.) We see in all these communities a move toward greater orthodoxy as an assertion of identity rather than pure expression of religious preference. Individualization of faith may be fine from the point of view of personal conscience and the intensity of personal belief, but many Muslims will feel that individualization of faith leads to the weakening of community solidarity and identity. Yet where identity in a multicultural society (or world) is not threatened it is more open to external influence and two-way influence. A sense of existential and cultural comfort on the part of Muslims will be one of the keys to a greater liberalization of the community.

MINORITY AND MAJORITY RIGHTS

The reality of pluralism raises further questions about the imposition of will on a minority by a majority, and whether Muslims—or any majority—can seek to enforce sociocultural legislation unique to their own preferences. Islamic jurisprudence certainly understands that a Muslim minority cannot be expected to legislate aspects of Muslim religious law or impose their views on a non-Muslim majority. On the other hand, if Muslims constitute a small majority, such as Malays in Malaysia with some 54 percent, how much does this change the legal situation? Islamic law—and even the understanding of this concept varies over place and time—is supposed to be a universal concept, so how can it be dependent upon numerical proportions for its validity and importance, especially in Islamist eyes?

The question frequently arises about imposition of Shari'a law, even in a democratic country under a Muslim majority. The majority, of course, will always determine legislation. What of minority rights under these circumstances? Let's look at some of the complexities of the issue. Shari'a law is not, of course, supposed to apply to non-Muslims, but the situation is blurred when Muslims and non-Muslims are both involved in a legal issue, or where society might choose to ban alcohol. Comparable issues arise in the United States with states and counties that have long been free to pass "dry laws" affecting the conditions of sale of alcoholic beverages or even banning them outright. If we seek a more serious example, what about the death penalty? If in Texas a majority votes to implement the death penalty while Minnesota eliminates it, are the rights of a minority of citizens in Texas violated in potentially lethal ways? Do objectors move to Minnesota? What is the place for minority rights in Texas for those who oppose the death penalty? When the community sets its own legal standards by referendum, the minority has no option but to accept it or depart. All legislation on social issues, such as abortion and euthanasia, vitally affects the rights or sensitivities of others. The reality of developing pluralism highly complicates the Islamist agenda and will require broad new thinking about the nature of Islamic law, Islamic practice, majority rule, and minority rights. Islamists are now beginning to tackle some of these issues.

RISING ETHNICITY

Reassertive ethnicity, ethnic and religious separatism, and minority ethnic rights top the list among the greatest challenges of all governance in the twenty-first century. Islam as a faith and religious ideal recognizes neither tribalism nor ethnicity as a factor in making up the Islamic *umma,* or in relations among Muslims. But Muslims, like all other human societies, face practical issues of ethnic differences within their own societies as well as in their relations with non-Muslims.

Issues of ethnicity within Islamic states so far demonstrate that Islamists have not yet developed a workable theoretical and practical policy to handle these problems. Even in states where most of the population is Muslim, there are still ethnic problems among Muslims—in Afghanistan (Pashtuns, Tajiks, Hazara), Algeria (Berbers), Indonesia (Acehnese, Minang), Iran (Kurds, Baluch, Azeri), Iraq (Kurds), Jordan (Palestinians), Morocco (Berbers), Pakistan (Baluch, Sindhis, Punjabi, Pashtun), Sudan (Nubians), Turkey (Kurds), and Uzbekistan (Tajiks). Islam in principle should be able to rise above nationalist ideologies and provide much of the ideological glue to keep the nation together in the face of ethnically based differences, but Islamists have not yet found the formula.

In states with non-Muslim minorities, Islamists have a strong tendency to support the welfare of the Muslim community with limited interest in non-Muslims. They usually have not thought beyond issues of the Muslim community yet. To be fair, when Islamists have come to power so far in regional or municipal governments they have shown concern for the welfare of their non-Muslim constituents as well (Turkey, Algeria, Malaysia). Out of power they are tempted to play ethnic politics.

In summary,

- In states where *religious and ethnic fault lines coincide,* Islamism powerfully reinforces the identity of the Muslim ethnic group.
- In states where Muslims make up the *majority,* Islamists functionally support Muslim community rights versus non-Muslims;

- In states where Muslims are in a *minority*, Islamism always supports Muslims versus the majority and generally supports Muslim ethnic aspirations toward autonomy or national liberation;
- In states where the whole population is Muslim but *sectarian* differences exist among them (Shi'a and Sunni), Islamist groups generally organize along strictly sectarian lines (Lebanon, Afghanistan, Turkey, Iran, Pakistan).

The regrettable conclusion to be drawn here is that political Islam has not so far shown much success at handling the problem of multiethnicity and pluralism across ethnic or religious lines. While the Islamists have never sparked ethnic conflicts between Muslims, neither have they resolved them. Islamists are hardly alone in this failure: few other political parties have shown much success in this arena either.

To conclude, political Islam might be in trouble if it takes too much time in coming to terms with these key ideological challenges of the contemporary world—pluralism, democratization, minorities, and secularism. The reality is that if Islamist movements themselves do not take significant new directions in finding viable answers to these challenges, the external world will generate its own policies and pressures, often in a self-serving way and try to impose them through human rights groups, minority appeals to the UN, feminist movements, religious groups, and others. These external pressures will limit the creative options available to political Islam, effectively denying it the luxury of evolution in quieter domestic contexts and forcing it into constant unproductive reactive modes. This is one of several reasons for Western caution in not weighing in too heavily in the region, burdening and supercharging the debate over the practice of Islam with tangential issues relating to power, Muslim dignity and impotence, and the sovereignty of the Muslim state.

INDIVIDUAL FREEDOM AND IMPOSED VALUES

Most *modernist* Islamists perceive the relationship between an individual and God as a matter of personal decision and conduct: ultimately it is God and not some human instrumentality who will judge the conduct of each believer. But when personal behavior also affects society it must involve *a social contract as defined by the community according to its norms and understanding of Islam*. And if the individual chooses not to live by that community norm, he or she should be free to do otherwise as long as actual laws are not broken. But the community and not some individual or unelected regime should be the arbiter. Islamists or clerics may wish to exhort certain interpretations of Islam and their application, but they should have no *legal* power to do so in the view of most modernists.[5]

In the real world, of course, the "tyranny of the majority" and its values in any community seems unavoidable. In a small, tight, highly homogeneous community any individual courts problems by choosing to live differently from the norm. But in large, diverse, and pluralistic societies, individuals have broader choices and tend to create their own social circles. The more diverse the community, the harder it is to achieve community consensus on norms. Muslim communities will naturally seek to build certain kinds of institutions and structures for the preservation of certain values and ways of life ("current community standards") either legal or customary, and will seek to impose their consensus to some extent.

In the end, attempts to *impose* a specific moral order in the twenty-first century beyond a sense of "current community standards" appear hopelessly anachronistic and doomed to failure, whatever the religious justification might be. Such an attempt will fail on two grounds: a narrow and exclusivist vision of morality cannot win broad support for long, and an effort to impose it is not sustainable. The case of Iran itself demonstrates this—a reality now vividly clear to Iran's religious thinkers.

What can an Islamist do, then, in a contemporary pluralist society in which not all people are Muslim, nor all Muslims the same, nor all Muslims even religious, and where the religious themselves do not agree on the interpretation of Islam under contemporary conditions? Islamists may simply find that their greatest contribution and strength lie in keeping the moral agenda alive in front of society's eyes so that it remains a living and vibrant point of reference. Islamists will not be alone in this: society will produce other bodies, some secular, that also assume the role of moral critic: human rights groups, democratic watchdogs, anti-corruption watchdogs, and others. But Islam-oriented groups can regularly provide a broader moral critique of society on the issues of the day for community consideration, much as various churches do today in the West. If Islamists can succeed in maintaining Islamic ideas as part of an active ongoing debate in society, they will be fulfilling the greatest role possible for the promulgation of Islamic thought.

A closed, inflexible, non-dynamic vision of Islam, such as we witness in Saudi Arabia, in some circles in Pakistan, or in Afghanistan under the Taleban, will lose a great deal of its appeal and grip when individuals attain the freedom to make choices. And if the kind of Islam being promulgated there loses relevancy in the eyes of Muslims on the major issues facing them, then there is patently something wrong with that particular vision of Islam.

Only lively and intelligent interpretations of what the spirit and message of Islam are all about under contemporary circumstances will ensure that Islam is alive and central to contemporary debate. Islam or any other religion lives only as long as it has meaningful things to say on pressing issues of concern to the population, especially under conditions of freedom. Freedom, then, becomes the essential prerequisite for the successful and creative application of Islam's message to mankind. Only freedom can create the environment in which each individual can discover a personal relationship to God and join freely with others to propagate a moral vision.

THE WEIGHT OF SECULARISM

For Islamists the supreme challenge of the century is coming to terms with secularism, one of the grand forces of Western intellectual life for four hundred years. It is by now increasingly entrenched in globalized life. It is often a key target of many Islamists, primarily because they misunderstand the term.

In Western intellectual history secularism is generally taken to mean the rational pursuit of *objective knowledge* in disregard of any non-scientific values including religious belief. In Anglo-Saxon, and especially American juridical usage, secularism denotes strict separation of church and state, insisting that each should stay out of the other's business. There is also a French version of the term, *laicisme*, a product of the French Revolution, whereby the state controls or even suppresses religion and its institutions in the name of the scientific and positivist values of the state. It is the French conception of secularism that has gained widespread salience in the modern Muslim world, most prominently with Mustafa Kemal Atatürk in Turkey, where the state took over full control of religion and all its institutions. The state ideology of Kemalism, which views Islam as essentially reactionary, obscurantist, and obsolete, alone determines how religion will be used in the service of the state's agenda. This approach was perpetuated by Bourgiba in Tunisia and Muhammad Reza Shah in Iran where religious institutions or movements were suppressed and put at the service of the state. It is this form of "secularism" that Islamists find intolerable, since they see it as tantamount to anti-Islamism and suppression of religious institutions.

With the challenge of Islamism to regimes across the Muslim world today, "secularism" in its state-controlled form is a handy and seemingly modernist formula for the crushing of religious opposition. Muslim authoritarian rulers rush to assure Washington that they are "preserving secularism in the struggle against fundamentalism" or, more recently, "in the struggle against terrorism." But in recent years some Islamists have issued calls for adoption of American-style secularism— whereby the state keeps its hands off religious organizations entirely, enabling civil groups to retain autonomy or have "civil space" in society. Indeed, the Islamist Virtue Party in Turkey in 1999 suggested that it would be ready to sign on to the principles of secularism in the American sense but opposed a "secularism" that places religion and its civil practice four-square under state control and subject to manipulation and persecution.

Other Islamists, however, perceive Islam in a holistic sense (hence the insightful French term *intégrisme*) in which Islam is more than a religion—"a total way of life" or *din*—infusing all aspects of life. Certainly from a religious point of view one can perceive God's presence as permeating all things, as an immanence that lends a joy and sacred quality to all aspects of daily existence in celebration of God's creation and will. Such ideas suffuse most mystical and religious outlooks on life. It is another thing, however, for Islamists to stipulate that the sacred quality of all existence requires all human institutions to be subordinated to strict religious treatment, or that their parties, doctrines, and even programs are above debate because of their link to religion. In a modern rationalist society there must be independent secular space that is not linked to the sacred, that can be examined, discussed, and debated without passing judgment on religious values themselves. While one may personally perceive God's work in all things, human institutions and constructs cannot therefore be viewed as automatically sacred. So while Islam certainly offers views on economic justice, the discussion of graduated tax law is not in itself sacred. To declare everything sacred is to trivialize the concept and make rational debate impossible. Indeed, the sacralization of everything essentially results in the sacralization of nothing.

Most "secular" regimes in the Muslim world have given secularism a bad name by associating it with Western-supported autocracy, corruption, subservience to the West, rigid state control of religion, and discrimination against all Islamists, virtually synonymous with atheism. Unfortunately, Westerners freely invoke the term, usually unaware of the reasons for the negative connotations of the word to most Muslims. Today, under exposure to Western and especially U.S. society, Islamists are beginning to recognize that secularism properly speaking denotes no attitude toward religion other than its separation—and independence—from the state. Indeed, Islamists now are beginning to appreciate it can mean *protection* from the intrusive and often self-serving power of the state.

Whatever their legitimate grievances with pseudo-secularism at home, Islamists still must recognize the reality that the force of secularism is growing globally. It protects large numbers of activities conducted by Islamists and their organizations. At the same time it also limits in advance the ability of Islamists *in power* to impose their own state domination over the role of religion in society and law.

Recognition of the force of secularism is growing easier for Islamists, especially as many of them working in professional fields contemplate their faith in the context of contemporary society. As Turkish scholar Nilüfer Göle points out, "the more the Islamists acquire a professional identity, as engineers or intellectuals, the more the realms of the sacred and the profane will be separated. Thus, becoming a member of an elite activates a process of secularization, independent of the intentions of the actors, that leads to the separation of the two realms."[6]

THE CHALLENGE OF WESTERN "MATERIALISM"

Islamists routinely charge the West with being under the thrall of "materialism." All religions are, of course, concerned with obsessive materialism as a barrier to the spiritual life, and Islam is no exception. But many Islamists regularly trot out the claim that Islam represents a "third way," rejecting both communism and Western capitalism and materialism. Their rhetoric seems to have little clear understanding of the issue and poses a false dichotomy between "East and West" here.

The primary historic sources of Western affluence have been capitalism, the "scientific spirit," technology, liberty, wealth derived from colonialism, a beneficent climate and abundance of the raw materials of wood, water, iron, and coal. That affluence, often slipping over into conspicuous consumption, has indeed produced a Western consumer society that earns the admiration, envy, and even resentment of inequities in much of the world's have-nots. The West itself generates its own periodic warnings on excessive Western consumption of the world's raw materials, arguments that have been absorbed by the Islamists. Such critiques trace back at the very least to Old Testament references to worship of Mammon, the obsessive pursuit of material goods that blind one to spiritual values and even to the very purpose of life.

Islamists use the term "materialism" in a dual sense, first as a description of philosophical thought in the scientific age that generated skepticism about the existence of God, at least as based on the inability of religion to scientifically demonstrate it. In the eyes of pious Muslims, this philosophy produced a trend toward Western irreligiosity that eventually reached its acme in spawning communism and its philosophy of dialectical materialism, concepts that not only were explicitly atheistic, but also aggressively propagated atheist campaigns that nearly destroyed religion—including Islam—in the Soviet Union and China. Materialism in this sense—irreligiosity as the product of the scientific revolution—is thus antipathetic to Islam and other religious faiths.

But Islamists also face the challenge of materialism in its more traditional sense—human attraction to the material goods. Here materialism becomes the

"Western ideology" of consumerism, the belief that technology permits life to get better and better, and that material possessions serve to make life vastly more enjoyable. Indeed, these things undeniably do exactly that. But Islam is not anti-material per se, and it is well grounded in concepts of the social well-being of individuals. It lacks even the starkly ascetic traditions of Buddhism, Hinduism, or Christian monasticism. Islamists cannot pretend that Muslims too, don't actually seek the same material benefits that Westerners enjoy, benefits that spark ambitions to work harder, make money, and meet other material needs. Of course, individuals can become consumed and driven by materialism, but the existence of consumerist pleasures need not militate against religion, for two reasons. First, few religious-minded people would wish to suggest that religious faith can be strong only in the presence of hardship and deprivation. Such a line of thought only lends credence to the Marxist aphorism that "religion is the opiate of the people." The poor and the hungry are not necessarily more spiritual, except when religion is escape from the despair of this world. Few would argue that escape from conditions of material despair is a healthy basis for religious faith, and when it is, such religious views are generally exceedingly fatalistic.

Second, the drive for material improvement is arguably even more natural among the poor and deprived than it is among the affluent. One might even posit that a certain minimal level of affluence—decent nourishment, housing, health, education, safety, employment—is required before one can turn one's sights away from material concerns to look toward satisfaction of one's deeper spiritual longings and quests. In short, an obsession with material needs may be the fate of most peoples living in hardship and deprivation, a condition that can be alleviated only when certain minimal material levels of life are attained.

Islamists will have to cope with the rising attraction of the *material* aspects of the Western lifestyle. Muslim publics, especially youth, are often sick of politics—Islamic or otherwise—and its scanty provision of concrete benefits. They very much hope to make money, wear interesting clothes, listen to music, watch films, and meet with members of the opposite sex—more simply, to have more "fun" in life. The youth of the Islamic Republic of Iran fully typifies this quest, even when reared under Islamist ideology.[7] Islamists should not blame on the West the existence of these aspirations among Muslim youth, since whatever their shallowness, they are also universal human aspirations.

How will Islamists handle this supreme challenge from the West? Ayatollah Khomeini dubbed the West "the Great Satan" not simply because he perceived it as evil, but because it was *alluring*—the true mark of diabolical threat. Will Islamists retreat to a permanent litany of what is *haram* or forbidden in this world, or will the focus be on building a meaningful spiritual life in the acceptance of material benefits and the quest for a better life. Need "fun" be incompatible with faith and morality? Indeed, the more demanding religious challenge requires the individual to be morally fortified enough to be able to make personal moral distinctions between what is alluring and what is ethically and morally proper. Surely deprivation will not constitute sufficient basis for successfully winning mass adherence to an austere Islamist lifestyle. There may be problems with consumerist mentality in any society, but a so-called "Western ideology of materialism" is not one of the genuine faultlines between the West and Islam.

GLOBALIZATION

The forces of globalization—the technology of communications, media, transportation, international commerce, style, culture, travel, and migration—are an evolving global reality owned by no one. Muslims themselves were once one of the great globalizing forces and could be so again if they wish. Even today Muslim culture affects architecture, food, clothing, music, literature, art, and thought around the world. Globalization is also the source of growing multiculturalism and modernization in all senses—another challenge to Islamists. Globalization is a morally neutral force with benefits and disadvantages, winners and losers. Any Islamist program that fails to come to terms with globalization, to work to shape it from within rather than trying to stop it, will be a failing program and will bring discredit to Islamic societies. Globalization need not be a zero-sum game. Like capitalism, globalization is an engine that needs to be controlled for it to function at maximum advantage for all and for its inevitable injustices to be rectified as much as possible. To be global is also to compromise. Islamists cannot hope to preserve homogeneity of Islamic culture, values, or lifestyles, if it ever was even possible in the past. An Islam of prohibitions is devoid of the creative energy to forge a new synthesis between Islam and modernism.

PUBLIC "TUNING OUT" FROM IDEOLOGY

Islamists wishing seriously to insulate Muslim countries from the world can do so only if they accept economic stagnation and marginalization as the price. Islamist regimes that pursue such policies will find internal opposition developing quickly. The broader public, as the example of Iran demonstrates, simply becomes alienated and turns a deaf ear to the regime's ideological exhortations. In Iran today it is ideological apathy as much as hostility to the regime's ideological outlook that is undermining the authority, legitimacy, and even the effectiveness of the regime's ability to control the situation. This is especially true of younger generations.

In Egypt and Pakistan, for example, many younger people, particularly at the professional level, are weary of ideology. They are often inclined to tune out the grand ideological issues of war and peace, Arabs and Israel, Islam and the West, and are simply looking to make money, survive, or even profit from new global economic trends. Only major regional clashes and tensions return their attention to the political realm and the Islamist agenda. This manifest loss of state influence over public thinking could presage a grim future for all regimes and serve as a warning to would-be Islamist authoritarians. While serious hardship will periodically fuel radical responses in poorer countries with skewed social orders, the pure Islamist ideal is highly unlikely to provide long-term emotional and psychic nourishment for the broader population that still confronts real material needs. In short, populations will close their ears to irrelevant and strident messages that do not address real concerns of the public. The Islamists will have to fight for relevancy, especially in more peaceful times when people are not distracted by foreign policy circuses.

THE WEST: THE NEW DAR AL-ISLAM?

The ultimate irony is that the West today may now constitute the most vibrant center of modern and creative Islamic thinking—*ijtihad* in intense daily practice as Islamic society becomes part of the rapidly developing trends, both positive and negative, of the West. This emerging importance of Western Islam is not surprising when we look at the stultified and closed nature of political and intellectual life in large parts of the Muslim world today where either the state or conservative Islamic establishments intimidate and crush most new Islamic thinking. Egypt represents the heart of the problem: al-Azhar University—a renowned center of Islamic learning—has grown extremely cautious and narrow in its interpretations, rivaled in intolerance and restrictiveness by Islamist groups that seek to embarrass the state for alleged insufficient vigilance in maintaining the purity of Islam. Legitimate scholars of religion, most notably in Egypt, Pakistan and Iran, have been hounded out of the country, arrested for blasphemy, or have their welfare or even lives threatened. Others, like Abdol Karim Soroush and Abdol Muhsin Kadivar in Iran, were forced to tread exceedingly carefully to avoid arrest or public beating before giving up and seeking refuge in the West. Many of these creative and liberal Islamists—and a few quite radical and intolerant ones—have been able to live and write freely and in safety only in the West where institutes of Islamic thought have proliferated, free to research and expound a great variety of ideas about Islam in modern life.

In one sense, states in much of the Muslim world have transformed their own societies into a kind of *Dar al-Harb*—the "Zone of Contestation," historically the designation of *non*-Muslim territories under religious contestation in the period of the spread of Islam. It is in these areas that new Islamic thinkers now find ideological war waged against them. At the same time it is the West that provides the intellectual, social, and political freedom to become in some ways the modern version of *Dar al-Islam* (Abode of Islam) where Muslims live in political and social peace without ideological repression. Of course this flip-flop in the use of these traditional terms is exaggerated, even offensive to some, but its usage says much about the current state of religious freedom of inquiry in much of the Muslim world. In fact, as Olivier Roy has suggested, seriously practicing Muslims living *anywhere* may come to constitute a minority, even an oppressed one.

Indeed, it is the Muslim in the diaspora today who may represent a more intense and thoughtful strain of Islam, with powerful implications for the faith. First, Muslims in the West become far more aware of their own faith precisely because they are living in a non-Muslim environment. To pray, to attend mosque, to fulfill other Islamic religious and social rituals, and to lead an observant life become acts of conscious will far more than in a Muslim society where they are part of the ambient social scene.

Second, Muslims in the diaspora often no longer live in the same ethnic community that characterized life in the old country. They encounter, live, share problems, and pray with Muslims from all over the world, creating a new and revitalized sense of *umma*. Indeed, some observers have suggested that being Muslim becomes a new "ethnicity" in its own right, because of the shared values of a community as perceived by those both inside and outside the community. Thus to be Muslim in a non-Muslim society heightens the centrality of Islam in one's life, elevating it above any ethnic distinctiveness. Islam in the diaspora is immediately internationalized and sheds its regional characteristics.

Third, the presence of Muslims in the West is voluntary. The creative Palestinian thinker Isma'il al-Faruqi, who spent many years in the West, envisaged migration to the West as akin to the Prophet's *hijra* (migration) to Madina where he built the first Muslim community; al-Faruqi saw migrants as "ambassadors of Islam" in the first phase of spreading new moral ideas in a non-Muslim environment in the West, in the grand old tradition of missionary *da'wa*. "We want to live as if we were . . . companions of Muhammad from Mecca to Madina. This [West] is our Madina, we have arrived, we are here. Now that you are in Madina, what is your task? . . . Your task is . . . the saving, and salvation of life, the realization of the values of dignity, of purity, of charity, of all the nobility of which humans are capable."[8]

It will be Muslims in the diaspora who have the occasion, the freedom, the impulse, the stimulation, the ability, indeed the necessity to rethink the meaning of Islam in a contemporary secular world—that is, the world of the future. As we have noted, to be secular in no way implies non-religious; on the contrary, the secular environment provides the space and the protection for all faiths to practice, flourish, and spread. Indeed, Muslims of the West may play a decisive role in bringing change and clarity of thought back to the old world from whence they came while perhaps bringing new meaning to religious impulse in the West itself. Many Muslims believe that Islam rightly practiced will eventually make Islam powerful in the West. "Muslims in the West will be better Muslims than most Muslims in the East," I have often heard Muslims say. Whether the West will eventually become Muslim or not, the sincere and exemplary practice of Islam by the Western Muslim community will influence Western perceptions of Islam and will stimulate a new synthesis of understanding within the triadic Abrahamic tradition of Judaism, Christianity, and Islam. But Muslims also face an uphill struggle at present when an Usama bin Ladin sadly does more to define the image of Muslim to Westerners than do thousands of pious Muslim citizens.

THE POTENTIAL IMPACT OF EVENTS IN THE MUSLIM WORLD

What regional developments or forces might loom large in affecting the behavior of regional states and Islamist movements within them?

THE SUCCESS OR FAILURE OF EXISTING ISLAMIC REGIMES

The major success or failure of existing Islamist regimes will necessarily impact upon all existing Islamist regimes and movements. The Taleban in Afghanistan already represents spectacular failure by Islamists—primitive ones—in power. Sudan has made serious mistakes, sharply isolating itself from the Muslim world, but conceivably it could be on the way to correcting these mistakes and demonstrating a learning curve by Islamists. Iran may yet emerge as a successful model both in democratic terms and as a model of a state in Muslim eyes that will stand up to the United States in defense of its own independence—a valued commodity among Muslims.

Whatever these regimes' records, other Islamists can easily claim that these regimes committed many unnecessary mistakes that later Islamists need not repeat, and that their failures do not represent the final word on Islamist rule. Of course this is true. Thus the simple evolution in any direction of any of these regimes will certainly not put an end to the Islamist experiment. But when I query Islamists about possible models of emulation for Islamist development or governance, they claim they find none yet that they are willing to endorse. Over time this fact in itself should prove sobering. For that matter, most Muslims can name few if any regimes in the whole Muslim world that they find worthy of emulation.

A MAJOR NEW ISLAMIST REGIME

The emergence of a new Islamist government in another major state in the region would also have significant influence upon other parties. The possibility of a new Islamist regime coming to power—even peacefully—exists most prominently in Algeria, Egypt, Saudi Arabia, Iraq, Libya, Turkey, Indonesia, Jordan, Yemen, and Pakistan, for quite different reasons in each state. Such a development, especially if Islamists come to power by the ballot box, could strongly impact the broader political scene. Indeed, this prospect is a distinct possibility over the next decade, as many of these states face major political or succession crises in the years ahead. The following scenarios could emerge:

- In Turkey, the weakening of its outmoded state ideology and the non-credibility of most establishment right-of-center parties has already given way to a public willingness at the ballot box to try the democratic Islamist "alternative," the most popular party according to polling.
- In Iraq, the collapse of Saddam Hussein and an end of the Ba'th party, coupled with the resurgence of the Iraqi Shi'ite majority, could open the door to Iraqi Shi'ite Islamists playing a role in a democratic government.
- In Saudi Arabia economic and managerial crisis and the discrediting of the al-Sa'ud dynasty in the face of powerful demands to yield to constitutional monarchy or step down could give way to more Islamist-oriented officers coming to power, or to respected independent Islamist clerics coming to rule with military support.
- In Egypt a failing economy coupled with a growing gap in income and living conditions, and demands for opening the political order could open the way to elections in which the Muslim Brotherhood could win a majority, or a military coup could appoint a senior Brotherhood figure to act as national leader.

- In Algeria a continuing refusal of the regime to open the system to the Islamists during continued unemployment, corruption, low living standards, and ongoing civil conflict could eventually compel the regime to permit the return of Islamists back onto the political scene through elections.
- In Indonesia rising ethnic and religious conflict, provincial disorder, terrorism and economic hardship under a government unable to find sufficient ideological glue to hold together its disparate peoples could tempt the public to try the Islamists, possibly the only group with the legitimacy to crack down on Islamist radicals.
- Pakistan, facing government failure, corruption, geopolitical weakness after the Afghan war and pressures from India, sectarian violence, and lack of leadership may well turn to Islamist parties as an alternative in time of crisis; or a military leader could appoint an Islamist to head the government.

THE SPREAD OF DEMOCRACY

Conversely, an Arab state that demonstrated major progress toward successful *liberal democratic rule* could offer an entirely new political prospect and model to the Arab world, unleashing unpredictable forces for change, including the formation of new blocs or a strong move toward greater political unity.

INTRA-MUSLIM CONFLICT

I have sometimes tended to treat the geopolitics of the Muslim world in this book as a unit vis-à-vis the rest of the world. In reality, of course, we are not speaking of a monolithic Muslim world at all. The Muslim world will continue to demonstrate certain shifting natural divisions and splits, reflecting differing interests, leaderships, and local dynamics. These various differences will inevitably impact the fortunes of the Islamists.

First are the *traditional geopolitical rivalries*—not predetermined, but abiding— among such well-defined regions as Greater Syria, Mesopotamia, Egypt, Libya, the Indian subcontinent, Central Asia, the Arabian Peninsula, Iran, Turkey, and North Africa. Second, *ideological differences* will certainly continue to exist across the region—Islamist, nationalist, socialist, and liberal. Divisions will emerge between more democratic and authoritarian states, radical and moderate, and between those with either close or prickly relations with the West. *Differing economic interests*— those with oil and without, statist versus free market economies, degree of dependence upon diaspora labor force, degree of linkage to the globalizing economy—all serve to differentiate Muslim states. *Leadership personalities* also exert their own particular fickle and transient chemistry upon more abiding geopolitical relationships.

Such differences could well translate into *informal alliances* that would divide the Muslim world, not necessarily into hostile blocks but at least into groupings that perceive their interests differently. Some states will retain closer ties with the United States for political, economic, and security reasons (such as Turkey). Others will be distinctly cooler, but not automatically hostile, toward the U.S. role, such as nationalist or Islamist governments. *A geopolitical breakthrough will emerge when we witness the first Islamist state to develop good ties to Washington* (Turkey is the leading candidate). A hardcore authoritarian Arab nationalist bloc may be a permanent fixture for some time as in Iraq, Syria, and Libya. The nucleus of a more liberal and democratic grouping within the Muslim world may emerge that perceives its interests quite differently than do authoritarian states, breaks ranks with them, and moves in independent directions. This is an event surely waiting to happen. Ironically it is external pressure, such as from Israel or the West, exerted particularly upon the Arab world that has so far lent credence to the ideology of "Arab unity." Arab unity forged under dictatorships will quickly die in a more successful and relaxed region, giving way to a softer form of a cultural Arab union.

Finally, *borders in the Muslim world will not remain sacrosanct* any more than anywhere else. Longtime Arab longing for greater political unity might find prospects for fulfillment, especially under regional democratization, providing more open borders and more open information flows that would facilitate greater integration of the region economically. Some kind of regional federalism to overcome arbitrarily drawn colonial borders would not be surprising: Greater Syria, Greater Mesopotamia, an Arabian Peninsula Union, and a federated Maghreb, all under democratic rule, are at least among the possibilities. Islamists would strongly support such unions.

But Islamists are not the source for an automatic shift to pan-Islamism in the region either. Traditional regional geopolitics will not vanish under any ideology, nor should it. *If all the states of the Middle East tomorrow were to come under Islamist governance, once the initial shock wore off, the old geopolitical relationships among them might remain much the same with old rivalries perpetuated, with some states opting for ties with the West and others not.*

"GLOBAL" REJECTION OF GLOBALIZATION

If the globalization process starts producing dramatic new winners or clear-cut losers in the international arena, some states in the Muslim world already in economic trouble could be attracted to some kind of broader united front against "American global hegemony" with almost certain nationalist and Islamist support. The significance of such a front would hinge heavily on the degree of support found in energy-producing states.

THE EMERGENCE OF NEW GREAT STATE PLAYERS

Despite current American dominance, the next decade or so may well witness a shift away from a world dominated by a single hegemon, based primarily on dwindling U.S. willingness to engage in an activist and costly foreign policy, widespread hostility toward U.S. unilateralism and "neo-imperialism," the emergence of a European power bloc, continued Muslim anger at unqualified U.S. support for Israel, resurgent Asian power, a continual shift of energy consumption patterns from the West to Asia, and a possible ad hoc coalition of regional states to blunt U.S. unilateralism or domination of the global order. Major world states disaffected with the American-dominated global order could make common cause with like-minded Muslim states, including Islamist governments.

China might find it easy to move into security-for-energy swaps with key oil and gas producers in the Middle East and the Caspian region. China can supply inexpensive weapons, training, and a willingness to commit to certain kinds of security guarantees, especially to the numerous weak oil-states of the Gulf, free of the kind of baggage that U.S. security guarantees bring with them. And if U.S. policies in the Middle East continue to be unattractive to Muslim states, Washington could easily become a less attractive security partner compared to the Chinese. China's concern for unrest among its Uyghur Turkish Muslim population will cause Beijing to seek friendly Muslim states to help deflect Uyghur appeals for Muslim backing to their cause.

Russia might be another such rival state, especially if it should successfully begin to reestablish its industrial base. While Russia's economy is still weak, it nonetheless produces sophisticated weapons systems that could entice some regional states into security arrangements that bypass the United States. Russia, of course, is seriously concerned about the threat of Islamist movements among its own Muslim populations, and it will attempt to prevent the infiltration of "Wahhabism." But as long as Islamist states do not directly threaten Russia, it can easily do business with them. Russia has grown close to Tehran after the initial flush of revolutionary fervor in Iran and has no special problems with Saudi Arabia.

Finally, the *European Union* may become a competitor or an alternative to the United States rather than partners in these regions on all but the most threatening issues—such as serious threat to oil security. Over time EU states, too, could be making energy-for-security guarantees with many Muslim states. While the EU is clearly "Western," it carries far less baggage than does the United States and is itself uncomfortable with U.S. policies toward much of the Muslim world. If international terrorism should grow, however, even with the demise of al-Qa'ida, and particularly if it targets countries other than the United States, Europe will not be a rival with the United States for influence with Islamist states but will make common cause with the United States. Radical Islamists take note.

India must be included in discussions of new regional players in the Muslim world. India has the second largest population of Muslims in the world after Indonesia—at least 120 million. Kashmir, of course, is the one region of India where a strongly concentrated population of Muslims is located and where the dissatisfaction of the population and mismanagement by India has led to serious insurgency. But more importantly, India is high on the list of major new markets for energy in the coming decades, along with China. It will be a major importer and is vitally concerned not only with the source of supply, but with the sea-lanes of communication that provides the oil across the Arabian Sea and Bay of Bengal. India has long had a major presence in the Gulf represented by the hundreds of thousands of workers at all levels of the economy in the Gulf states, and Indian military relations with the Arab world go back several decades. India is geographically far closer to the Gulf than is China and culturally far better attuned to it.

Muslim state relations with Asia thus represent a key new analytical question for the future of Islamic politics: how will Confucian and Buddhist cultures, plus the geopolitical interests of the diverse states in this huge region, interact with Islamists? Will cultural competition dominate, or will they share an interest in preventing American domination of the global order? As long as the United States maintains a high-profile involvement in the Muslim world, particularly promoting unpopular policies, Islamists will probably look first to the geopolitical challenge over even domestic considerations. Islamists are likely to be responsive to alternative players in the region until such time as any new Asian players are themselves perceived as heavy-handed or hostile to Islam.

Finally we should note again that Islamism has no monopoly on anti-Westernism: Islamism serves as a vehicle for a great many diverse forces that are not necessarily a product of Islam itself. Anti-Western views have operated through nationalist and socialist vehicles in the past but are currently in desuetude enabling Islamism to serve as the reigning ideological vehicle of the moment. Even in the Middle East, Gamal Abdel Nasser, Hafiz al-Asad, Mu'ammar al-Qadhafi, and Saddam Hussein are just a few of the strong anti-Western leaders who have nothing to do with Islamism whatsoever. Anti-Americanism is hardly Islamism's only preoccupation, but the War Against Terrorism has raised it to new levels.

AN ANTI-ISLAMIST GLOBAL COALITION

Perhaps the grimmest outlook of all for the Muslim world is *not that Islamists will come to power widely across the region, but that a long-lasting coalition of anti-democratic repressive regimes is emerging across the region,* supported by the United States, and, in certain regions, by Russia and China. Muslim autocrats are united in nothing if not in cooperation against Islamist movements that threaten their rule; regular summits of the various national *mukhabarat* (intelligence and security) organs already represent the most cordial international get-togethers in the region. This scenario intensifies authoritarianism in the Muslim world—arguably already one of the main causes of bad governance, tension, regional instability, and further association of "Western values" with local repression.

The darkest outcome of the U.S. War Against Terrorism would involve just such an increase in violent anti-American reactions and terrorist acts across the world and even in the U.S. homeland. This ugly confrontation might be sparked by either worsening of the Israeli-Palestinian situation, an Israeli expulsion of the Palestinians from the West Bank, or widening popular hostility against all U.S. military presence in the Muslim world. Such a course of events inevitably stimulates confrontations between Muslim states and the United States, as once pro-American regimes find themselves forced to adopt greater anti-Americanism as the sole means to maintain their own power. If radical Islamist terrorists sought to include Western Europe in stepped up terrorism, we would find a genuine, self-fulfilling "war of civilizations" emerging that would be hard to untangle for a long time to come. This can easily lead to "war" at the popular level between broad segments of Muslims, secular as well as religious, and an ever more assertive Washington hunkered down in a security mode. This would be the darkest scenario of all.

1 0

THE FUTURE OF POLITICAL ISLAM

ITS DILEMMAS AND OPTIONS

FOR ALL THEIR nearly unrivaled influence in the Muslim world today, Islamists face one supreme question: will they be able to rise to the challenges that confront today's ineffective leaderships and any potential leaders of the future? Islamists are good at identifying and articulating the grievances, but to succeed they must move beyond their present roles if they wish to remain relevant to societies' needs.

ISLAMISM AS IDEOLOGY?

The analysis throughout this book argues that *political Islam cannot properly be viewed as an alternative to other ideologies such as democracy, fascism, socialism, liberalism, and communism.* It cannot be put anywhere clearly on an ideological spectrum. It is far more useful to see it as a cultural variant, an alternative vocabulary in which to dress any one of these ideological trends. It is hard to argue that Islamism is a distinct program in itself, even though we can identify certain predispositions such as a conservative social agenda, a call for political change, a defensive cultural/nationalist bent, and a rhetorical call for adoption of Islamic law that means many different things in practice. This is a political movement that makes Islam the centerpiece of its own political culture and then proceeds to improvise on what this means in the local political context. *Islamism is therefore not an ideology, but a religious-cultural-political framework for engagement on issues that most concern politically engaged Muslims.*

THE ISLAM THAT SAYS NO

Islamists must develop a clear, positive, specific, and constructive agenda for society and state. If the quest for "authenticity" in Islam—defined in opposition to the quasi-Westernized authoritarian status quo—becomes the dominant goal of Islamist parties, the chances are good they will remain trapped in a quixotic quest—one that condemns them to a permanent negative role as guardians of self-defined cultural gates lacking forward vision. The parties will come to represent only "the Islam that says no," a negative and joyless approach obsessively focused on what is forbidden and wrong. There is very little agenda, especially among the fundamentalists, for what is inspiring, joyful, constructive, or forward-looking. Yet one key function of all religion is to instill inspiration, joy, and meaning into one's vision of life. The "Islam that says no" fails entirely in this enterprise. This narrow and reactive approach is intensified by a concentration upon the threats to Islam from the outside world—a defensive posture based on rejection of the external world rather than focusing on the positive goal of improving governance and society in the Muslim world. In the end it is only through genuine strengthening and improvement of Muslim governance that Muslim societies can resist Western domination and adopt viable alternative approaches.

The fundamentalist Islamists have demonstrated a particular tendency to reduce Islam to the symbolism of Shari'a law and then sometimes even reduce Shari'a to family law and the code of penalties (*hudud*) as somehow representing Islam in its most "authentic" or quintessential form. Such a posture will reduce Islamists to little more than nuisance value in their societies. They thus abdicate responsibility for grappling with the really hard issues of making Islamic values relevant and applicable to today's complex social and economic issues. Olivier Roy suggests that the very inability of politically active Islamists to withstand the repressive power of the state has propelled numbers of them toward this more apolitical and fundamentalist view of increasing irrelevance.[1]

DEFENSE OF TRADITION, OR CHANGE?

Islamists often seem caught between two poles: guardians of tradition, or vanguard of change. Most of them recognize that change is essential across Muslim society But pursuit of a reformist role requires them to cooperate, or even compete with liberal secularists. In philosophical terms, reaching a compromise is manageable, but in the rougher world of practical politics, each party is competing for a slice of the electorate. Islamists cannot neglect courting the conservative constituency of society, but that may automatically condemn them to adopt highly conservative positions and even to support the social status quo. In Kuwait the Muslim Brotherhood has already split over whether to support women's voting rights. The debate has led to formation of at least two different movements among Islamists, one fundamentalist (*salafi*/Wahhabi), the other Brotherhood-based and more moderate.

How should the Islamists deal with the liberals? If they expend their ammunition on attacking the liberals, as they often do in Egypt and Kuwait on social and cultural issues, they are in reality supporting the state agenda—which is to weaken liberal reformers and block change. The Islamists are in effect weakening the forces of change that would benefit the Islamists themselves through increased political openness. Their risk in concentrating upon politics is that it inevitably leads to pursuit of tactical advantage at the expense of longer-range ideological or strategic influence. In times of hardship, any community or ideology tends to revert back to basics, to the purity of their ideals. Thus Islamists may be retreating back to hardcore interpretations of Islam, particularly on social issues: limiting the participation of women in society, calling for tighter dress codes, intensified calls to censoring literature and ban art, insisting on separate male and female education, and opposing liberalization of Family Law.

A CONSERVATIVE-LIBERAL SPLIT AMONG ISLAMISTS?

As Islamist movements continue to proliferate, liberal Islamists will eventually be led to break sharply with conservative and fundamentalist Islamists. Which group will fare better? It depends on the time, country, and local circumstances. In Pakistan, for example, we witness the disturbing spectacle of a strong policy-oriented mainstream Islamist organization, the Jama'at-i Islami, under severe pressure from the narrower and much more radical Islamist groups that assume more uncompromising lines on Kashmir, sectarianism, and social issues. The badly deteriorating situation in Pakistan contributes to the rise of more extreme Islamist groups there. But in Turkey, where there is (relative) prosperity and no sense of an imploding state and society, the mainstream Islamist party (Refah/Fazilet/AK) is strong, Islamist radicals are few, and the movement is rivaled on the social level only by the even more modernist and apolitical Nur Islamic movement of Fethullah Gülen.

But these fault lines may not readily lead to splits. Islamists have historically been reluctant to engage in public criticism of other Islamist movements, especially when they all feel themselves under the gun from local regimes as well as from hostile Western governments. But after 11 September, we are beginning to see sharper divisions emerging among fundamentalists and moderate Islamists. Such thoughtful public debates and critiques are in fact essential if the intellectual and ideological environment of the movement is to evolve and mature.

ISLAMISM MOVES TO THE LEFT?

A key contention of this book is the astonishing absence at this point of a "left" on the political spectrum in most of the Muslim world—leading to the question of whether Islamists will take advantage of this vacuum. Communists and socialists, who flourished during much of the Cold War period, have now lost importance and figure very little in Muslim politics. Yet "the left" cannot disappear; it is an integral part of the political spectrum anywhere that focuses upon burning social and economic causes and issues. How radical will Islamist movements ever seek to be—not in terms of violence or bloodshed, but in advancing a dynamic social and economic agenda directed particularly toward amelioration of mass grievances? The heavy Islamist emphasis on justice ('adl) would seem to lead naturally to a more radical position on social and economic issues. Yet to date, Islamist movements have demonstrated remarkable social and economic conservatism, especially in view of the pressing need for deeply rooted social and economic reform across the Muslim world. Their timidity so far raises a serious question again about just how "opportunist" Islamist parties really are.

In Pakistan and Egypt the Islamists have opposed serious land reform that is desperately needed. In Pakistan they have also opposed extension of the income tax where it is the rich who benefit most from its absence. In Kuwait most Islamists have opposed suffrage for women. While Islam is certainly not a radical religion, one of its principle goals—a more just political and social order—should in principle spur Islamists to adopt more radical policies of reform and economic and social justice. Perhaps the most ubiquitous feature of Islamism, the struggle against corruption, constitutes the most radical Islamist challenge to the status quo anywhere—a significant start. But the great questions of gross maldistribution of economic benefits, huge disparities in income, and feudal systems of landholding and human control remain largely outside the Islamist critique. Iran, in fact, is the only place where Islamists have taken up a more radical social and economic agenda. Will Islamists yield to the temptation to adopt more radical socioeconomic policies down the road, especially as social grievances reach higher levels, offering a rich mine for political gain? A columnist for *al-Hayat,* Joseph Samaha asks whether Islamists have by now gained enough legitimacy in the political order of so many Muslim countries that they are now content to abandon the quest for "the great change" and are everywhere willing simply to settle for a piece of the political game based on the status quo.[2]

THE DANGERS OF ISLAMIST REACTION-BASED POLICIES

Will useful Western political values be rejected simply because their provenance is perceived as tainted, and the Western political agenda suspicious? Islamists will need to determine what it is they are really rejecting, the ideas themselves or their source. The problem is not made easier when Western projection of its own political values into foreign policy has been frequently selective, uneven, self-serving, and characterized by double standards and convenience. The message is corrupted by the messenger.

Yet Islamists regularly fall into this trap of conflating the two. One example is attitudes toward Iraq. Most Muslims are well aware that Saddam Hussein has violated nearly all Islamic precepts of just rule and has harshly oppressed and killed Islamists and slaughtered hundreds of thousands of Muslims in neighboring Iran and Kuwait. Yet when Saddam is confronted by Western armies, large numbers of Islamists—indeed, most Muslims—perceive Western military intervention as an even greater threat. Saddam is a hero simply because he stands up to America. Similarly, the NATO war against Serbian ethnic cleansing in Kosovo in 1999 came in for heavy criticism by many Islamists and other Muslims who showed greater concern over NATO muscle-flexing in a new region than the fact that NATO was actually protecting Kosovar Muslims in Europe against the oppression of Serbian Christians.

When American Vice President Al Gore publicly criticized Malaysian Prime Minister Mahathir Mohammad for his 1999 slanders and show trial against Anwar Ibrahim, a popular and distinguished Islamist leader, large numbers of Malaysians took offense, not because they disagreed but because it appeared to represent unwarranted Western interference in offering criticism of the Malaysia. And in 2001, while acknowledging that the 11 September attack on the World Trade Center was a crime, nearly all Muslims strongly opposed the American military attack on Afghanistan and the overthrow of the Taleban government in the U.S. War Against Terrorism. Yet the Muslim world in previous years had nearly unanimously opposed the Taleban regime as representing a primitive and embarrassing form of Islam. In the end another American attack against a Muslim country was perceived as worse than either the regime or its fall. Such knee-jerk reactions indicate something is badly amiss on both sides.

In short, Islamists show greater obsession with attacking the perceived "enemies of Islam" than they are with developing their own independent values. Only when

Islamists can liberate themselves from this type of knee-jerk reaction will they be free to proclaim their own values, which may or may not coincide with Western values or interests.[3]

ISLAMISM AND SHARI'A (ISLAMIC LAW)

Is the Shari'a really the central theme or focus of Islamists, or do they have broader goals? Fundamentalist Islamists in particular single out the Shari'a as the essential element, the *sine qua non* for the creation of a genuine Islamic state and society. All of this overlooks the debate over the very issue of what "Shari'a" really is. Is it to be narrowly understood as no more than the Islamic legal code (*fiqh*) as constructed by *'ulama* over time? Islamist modernists reject this narrow and traditional view. Or is Shari'a a far broader concept of alternative "ways" to God in its original meaning?

Even full application of Shari'a law, in the eyes of many Islamists, is not enough in itself to constitute everything an Islamic state is meant to be. Shari'a law can be applied more or less fully and yet the state still prove incapable of wise and just governance on the grander political, economic, and societal issues. Something more is clearly needed, something that can be inspired by Islam or derived from Islam, but it will require human wisdom and legal sensibility. As most of Islam is concerned with moral principles, understandings of the world, and Man's relationship to God and society.

It is difficult, however, for the non-Muslim observer to question the centrality of the Shari'a, not only for the Islamic state but even as the chief agenda of Islamist parties. *Yet even to the outside observer there is no visible correlation between application of Shari'a law and the attainment of a better society and governance in today's Muslim world.* Few would deny the importance of the values of the Shari'a in theological and philosophical terms, but one can still *question its centrality in meeting the major dilemmas of Muslims today.* Are the leading states approximating full application of Shari'a today—Saudi Arabia, Pakistan, Iran, Afghanistan under the Taleban, or Sudan—demonstrating any greater success in governance? *The basic reality is that no Muslim state has made any significant progress toward creation of a more ideal society as it has come ever closer to full application of Shari'a law.* These regimes have not advanced toward a more ideal society in traditional "worldly" measures, shared by Islamists, such as economic improvement, educational policy, justice in society, social tranquility, equity of the economic order, better governance, cultural attainments, national power, or social support for the regime.

Of course the Shari'a is central to the Islamic concept of strengthening the moral understanding of individuals and society. But the Shari'a is largely operating in the moral sphere of human life and is not equipped—indeed, is not *intended* to deal with the practical political, social, and economic problems that plague all modern societies and states. These problems, while possessing a moral component for which the Shari'a can provide some very general guidelines, are usually of a more technical, administrative, institutional, or legal nature involving the evolution of political society within a contemporary political structure. Indeed, many modernist Islamists emphasize that the Shari'a is not some magic pill or a module that one simply plugs in with instant results. Islamists in the Indonesian Muhammadiya point out that they are concerned with "far more important issues than application of Shari'a": they seek to strengthen a Muslim nation's education, health, economy, and society—a task that represents the "greater Shari'a" or path of God.

The failings of contemporary state and society run deep, requiring reform and change in the direction of good governance. Islam's stress on the concept of just governance and a just society can serve as an inspiration for bold change even if it is not a blueprint. But because of the symbolic power and politicized nature of invoking Shari'a today, even modernist Islamists tread carefully to avoid seeming deevaluation of the role of Shari'a in contemporary life.

Every one of the societies mentioned above that have made major strides toward full application of Shari'a to one degree or another still suffers significantly from social injustice, economic inequity, major corruption, lack of answerability from the ruler, administrative incompetence, poor governance, and unwillingness to permit popular participation in the political process. Every one of them, starting with Iran, is still mired in the classic questions: whose Islam, or which kind of Islamism, are we talking about? Is the government answerable to the people? Do the people have a say in what they want? Who has the right to interpret Islam—or any other ideology? Has life significantly improved on either the material or moral level? Any examination of these societies reveals that the problem of corruption, brutality, exclusion, arbitrariness, bad policies, struggles for power, abused institutions—all still exist, despite serious efforts to create Islamic government and a serious role for the Shari'a. While no one can expect perfect governance, *in principle we should be able to expect some serious progress toward improvement in these areas as serious steps are made toward greater application of the Shari'a. In fact we see in most of these states policies and conditions that are at least as bad as states that give little or no weight to Shari'a.*

Now, let's be clear. This is not a failing of Islam itself. Few Islamists would claim that political Islam is the same thing as Islam. The problem is that Islam has not yet been interpreted freshly, boldly, and widely enough as it might apply to contemporary political and social conditions. Islamists have not made clear distinctions between what issues are related to Islam and what are "secular" political issues. The deeper values of Islam have not been made relevant or applied to what are nearly universal political problems in the political and social life of human beings. Islamic concepts as demonstrated in its *fiqh* (the body of Islamic jurisprudence) and political philosophy are largely linked to historic time, place, and circumstance, making them difficult to apply today without serious rethinking or *ijtihad*.

God did not, of course, hand down the Shari'a; he transmitted the Qur'an, which the Prophet sought to implement according to his best understanding—as seen in the Traditions of the Prophet—and human scholars created the Shari'a based on these two sources. Shari'a law is thus a man-made compilation over many centuries of various jurisprudents' understanding of how the Qur'an and the Traditions could be more concretely applied to what was premodern society. Interpretations and emphasis can and do differ over time in accordance with contemporary reality.

In fact, I find it far easier to accept the vague slogan that "Islam is the solution" than the more concrete thought that "the Shari'a is the solution." The first idea suggests that Islam offers a rich body of philosophical and moral thought that can offer general guidance, insight, and wisdom to troubled contemporary societies. The second idea suggests that *there already exists a concrete body of law that will automatically answer all needs if only fully applied.* The *hudud* (Islamic punishments) certainly offer no automatic remedy: whether a thief is jailed, or his hand amputated, will not greatly change the moral problem of theft. The real social issue of crime is whether harsher or less harsh punishment is more effective—a debate conducted in all societies.

Shari'a is actually deeply aware of differing social conditions that might produce theft and gives judges wide legal latitude in its interpretation and application. Adultery, too, can be made punishable by law, however harshly, if society desires, but the exact type of punishment is not central to the argument of morality. Is stoning (going back to the Old Testament) closer to God's will than lethal injection if society decides to apply the death penalty for adultery? *Fiqh* is bound in time to an Islamic past, many of whose features are long gone and rarely interpreted in a contemporary light today. Slavery, for example, has been a nearly universal human institution of all societies since the beginning of mankind; it is mentioned in the Old Testament, the New Testament, and the Qur'an as well, and legislation regarding the proper treatment of slaves was made in the Shari'a, but today hardly any Muslim suggests a return to those days.

Conservative social values have been maintained by every society in history in a manner relative to its time. But how realistic are those specific traditional conservative policies, designed for a premodern era, in the face of the social, economic, and technological realities of today? Today women are universally a part of the labor force, a birth-control pill exists, and widely diverse social mores are practiced; these are all appropriate subjects for debate from both a conservative or liberal position. Conservative social values are fine, but they have weight, impact, and acceptance only to the extent that they are relevant to contemporary realities and needs. *Islamic moral principles can be made permanently relevant through regular reinterpretation in accordance with existing realities and community consensus.*

INTEGRATING WESTERN AND ISLAMIC POLITICAL CULTURE

The irony for political Islam in the twenty-first century is that *only the integration of broad aspects of Western political thought and political experience will enable Islamism to survive as a meaningful political force*—particularly in the area of democratic institutions. But conversely, *the evolution of broader political thought in the Muslim world cannot decisively advance or flourish unless it specifically comes to incorporate and digest Islamic political thought and traditions as well.* Western political models for governance in the Muslim world will shrivel like transplanted trees unless they include the nourishment of Islamic culture from which political Islam emerges. This process is both inevitable and essential for the advancement of genuine and "authentic" political thought in the Muslim world.

After all, there is no "authentic" thought today; all of world thinking draws on earlier traditions from different civilizations at different times. Even ancient Greek thought, long thought to be the original root of Western culture, now is understood itself to have drawn heavily upon earlier Near Eastern civilizations. If Islamist thought draws upon "Western" thought today, it is drawing upon modern institutions that have their roots in the Near East.

It is only when Islamic political and social thought itself—long restricted or frozen—begins to evolve through interaction with external forces that real intellectual growth and institutional development will emerge. At the same time, efforts in the Muslim world to advance political and social thought *totally independent of the framework of Islamic culture* is doomed to be fractured, unintegrated, rootless, and alienated.

Thus the superficial "Westernization" we see at the elite level in the Muslim world provides a misleading measure of genuine political and intellectual progress within these societies, even if it commands superficial Western admiration. Westernization-by-fiat represents the imposition of a Western overlay on top of Islamic culture and practice, primarily benefiting the elites but failing to reach down into the roots of Muslim society and culture. It is not surprising that we see backlash on the part of the majorities of these populations who feel their traditional values ignored and themselves left behind in the modernization process of the elites. Indeed, "Westernization" and "secularism" have gotten a bad name when they are perceived locally as the reigning ideology of despotic and often corrupt rule that enjoys strong Western support.

Interestingly, the efforts by various Muslim regimes to assume protective Islamic coloration in hope of satisfying the masses and gaining greater Islamic legitimacy have been much less serious than the efforts by political Islam to grapple with Western concepts. Traditional Islamic culture has been compelled to integrate Western ideas selectively because it perceives their value in a future Islamic order. Islamism has no option but to come to terms selectively with Western political values as the reigning body of political thought at a global level. The result has been more positive than negative in engendering genuine political evolution in a context that does not lobotomize Islamic tradition.

Islamist movements, then, represent the first serious intellectual interaction between the two forces of Islamic and Western political thought in ways designed to bring about some kind of true integration rather than modernization through a walling off of tradition. Some Islamists (and most Westernizers) are happy with walls between the two cultures, but most people are not. They realize that the interplay of cultures and civilizations will not advance as long as one key element in the process is absent. Thus political Islam in the end becomes a primary vehicle for the confrontation, debate, inculcation, integration, and reconciliation of these grand cultural forces of Islamic and Western culture at the most essential level, bringing about gradual accommodation and rapprochement on both the intellectual and grass-roots level. Naturally there is no one "political Islam," and different groups will move toward acceptance and integration—or rejection—of selected Western political ideas and institutions at different rates. But the process is inevitable.

Turkey will be the first country to succeed in reaching a genuine reconciliation and integration of Islamist and Western liberal democratic tradition. I am referring not to Turkey's Kemalist secularist elite that essentially rejects the Islamic experience, but to the new synthesis emerging in Turkey through gradual admission of modernist Islamists into social and political institutions. This is happening because Turkey has advanced farther in establishing modern institutions of democratic governance than any other Muslim state, an evolution shared by its Islamists. So Turkey's task now is to open up fully its democratizing system and to reach back to integrate those social and ideological elements that were left behind or excluded during the forced Westernization project. Most of Turkey's elite is already on the way to recognizing this inevitability: they appreciate necessity of this integration in the interests of social harmony, and they recognize that the pressures from these excluded social elements can no longer be easily ignored in a democratic state that aspires to membership in the European Union.

ISLAM AND LEADERSHIP

Islamist movements are *potentially* capable of providing leadership in most of their chosen policy arenas, and many are already doing so. But even if Islamists find guidance in Islamic values for a broad range of contemporary questions, they must still demonstrate that the *specific inspiration* that they avow is relevant to the problems at hand. If it is not relevant, it is not the fault of Islam but of their own faulty understanding, interpretation, and lack of political imagination and talent. Different Islamists in different countries will come up with different ways to understand and apply Islamic guidance. No one can predict how successful they will be, but they represent at least one popular force bidding to open the political order inside presently largely unsuccessful authoritarian states. Islamist movements will remain on the political scene for a long time until eclipsed by those with better answers and better organization.

Is there anything new about Islamism's current broad range of political and social activity? Yes, Islamic movements in the past could mobilize the public on an *ad hoc* basis on specific issues—such as the Indian Mutiny against the British, or the anti-British movement over tobacco taxes in Iran early in the twentieth century, or the anti-colonial struggle in Algeria. But while individual Islamic leaders periodically employed Islamic rhetoric to mobilize the public on specific issues, the modern Islamist movement is no longer an ad hoc coalition. It consists of a standing organization with formal organizational rules, major funding, a staff, and involved in an ever-evolving political and social agenda. This does not mean that Islamism is a monolith. Islamists learned a lot by watching the mobilization techniques of the communists and Arab nationalists in the middle of the last century, the first such movements to aim for mass mobilization.

PRACTICAL SOCIOCONOMIC CHALLENGES

Politics matters a lot, but so do some hardcore socioeconomic factors. Political economist Alan Richards identifies nine key socioeconomic challenges that any Middle

Eastern government must face if these societies are to overcome their declining position in the world, regardless of politics. Governments must face "restoring economic growth, restraining population expansion, providing jobs, alleviating poverty, coping with urbanization, saving water, obtaining food, halting environmental destruction, and attracting money for investment from foreign and domestic savers."[4]

We might ask in which areas the Islamists have developed any new approaches. In the areas of coping with urbanization Islamists have made a signal contribution in many countries through their broad array of social services. Most of the other tasks are can be fulfilled only by a government, not by political movements, but in general we see few new ideas among Islamists as yet. As Islamists move into politics through parliament, they will be forced to deal with these tasks more closely, perhaps offering opportunity for contributions to policy thinking. Attracting money from foreign investors may be one of the harder tasks for the Islamists, judging by their record when in power and their anti-foreign suspicion when out of power.

Another pioneering study published by the UNDP in mid–2002 identified three major crisis areas for the Arab world that require urgent attention: lack of freedom of the political order, which prevents Arab states from utilizing the human potential of their citizens and from initiating needed reform; the woefully low level of education of its citizens, making them unfit to adapt to the conditions of the contemporary world; and the low social status of women, which damages the advancement of both the professional and social potential of Arab society.[5] In these three areas Islamists have focused only on the first requirement, the need for political liberalization and reform. In the areas of education and women's advancement, Islamists face a crucial choice. They can either opt to support the traditional, conservative, and ossified "Islamic" approaches of the past that have helped bring Arab society to its present low status in the world today, or they can take the lead in developing new and contemporary understandings of the spirit of Islam to spearhead change and genuine renaissance. Which way the Islamists go—and they are not a homogeneous group—will determine whether they will be a vital part of the future of the Muslim world or relegated to irrelevancy and obstructionism.

STRESSING THE UNIVERSAL IN ISLAM

Religions can see each other in two quite different ways: they can look either to their commonalities or the differences. Each choice carries immense implications. To emphasize commonality implies a quest for coexistence and understanding, an overcoming of cultural differences, and above all attaching major value to the *very act of coexistence* and tolerance as part of a religious outlook. To emphasize difference is to seek out difference, to value those differences and to treat religious orthodoxy and separateness as a high value.

Profound differences in psychology and sociology lie behind the choice. The psychology that emphasizes difference over commonality rests on insecurity of religious and social identity and on the vulnerability of the community; it stimulates focus upon difference—to identify, emphasize and protect what is uniquely mine that is threatened by what is yours. To stress commonality requires some degree of social and communal security and confidence in which one does not feel threatened by "the Other," however powerful.

Communities under stress will adopt a conservative strategy that gets back to basics, stresses the essentials, the hardcore traditions, the "gut" culture, the uncompromising message designed to protect oneself and one's culture from external power. These conditions largely characterize the Muslim world today as cultures under siege, pushing them toward embrace of the most uncompromising and purest form of religious expression. This is a key explanation for the rise of narrower and more intolerant views of Islam today, one that weakens the position of those Islamists who are interested in broadening and liberalizing interpretations and understanding of Islam. The present regional and international environment surrounding the Muslim world today is not conducive to promoting liberalism inside the community.

Yet Islamist movements face a huge challenge here in overcoming this mentality of insecurity to boldly face the changes required. Islamism cannot flourish over the longer run if the quest for authenticity is taken to mean a search for what is *exclusive to Islam* and what *separates* it from other beliefs. These differences may be relevant to maintenance of community tradition but not to the nature of a universal religion. Islamists will politically flourish over the long run only to the extent that they seek to find what they have *in common* with other beliefs. This is one meaning of pluralism, and it represents the first step toward creating a body of universal values that can be shared with other parties and groups, even if it is not enough to constitute a basis for political alliance.

Dr. Ali Mazru'i speaks of a Kenyan Islamist party whose membership is open to members of any religious beliefs as long as they subscribe, not to Islam but only to certain core Muslim *values* identified by the party as central to its role.[6] The Nur movement in Turkey seeks to identify common values with other faiths, almost deriving in these dialogues an "Islam without Islam"—that is, a religious belief stated in universal terms for people that don't use specifically Muslim cultural vehicles. A value-centered approach lends immense suppleness to the movement and makes it less threatening to outsiders than one based on ritual. Many Muslim communities and mosques in America today are similarly reaching out to non-Muslim members of the community to find common answers to common problems.

Today, many Westerners are themselves uncomfortable with some of the directions that Western society is taking that they view as unhealthy. Many wonder how Western society can weather the challenges of the postmodern era with its massive atomization of society, release of untrammeled individualism, lessening sense of community and social obligation, broadening diversification, if not chaos, among competing ideas, values, interests, and interrelationships, widening income gaps, and domination of the marketplace as the most powerful force upon society. Movements abound that search for correctives to glaring social afflictions. In this sense no one can be sure whether or not some kind of eventual convergence could eventually develop between the modern Western world and religious tradition, including Islam, over shared issues of concern for the moral foundations of a healthy society. I am not speaking about an alliance between Muslim and Christian fundamentalists but a broader shared vision of the common moral problems and dilemmas faced by all societies. Any such convergence might represent a retreat, among other things, from some of the more rampant features of Western individualism in the name of greater social cohesion, long an interest of innumerable social scientists, including the American communitarian movement.[7]

RELIGION AND THE POSTMODERN CHALLENGE

The striking feature of the our "postmodern" era is the continuing assault upon the concepts and verities of modernism. Modernism has essentially been a four hundred year project, a process of moving away from faith and belief (as well as simple superstition) as a basis for understanding the workings of the material world. Modernism entails an embrace of reason, rationalism, science, positivism, and empiricism. As a result, every religion has been compelled to rethink many of its deeply held positions on issues of the material world and to consider the nature, source, and extent of religious authority. All religions have been forced to recognize that modernist thought has been the reigning philosophical foundation of modern society. The Enlightenment established a new faith in the forces of education and rationalism, creating a new optimism whereby informed and rational humans would make wise and hence moral choices for the well being of themselves and society. Authority could now gain acceptance only by demonstrating provable skills and knowledge and not by insisting on respect for tradition and seniority. While empiricism replaced faith-based or mystical explanations of the material world, it did not—and can never—supplant religion on issues of spiritual and moral values. Science can never offer answers to philosophical questions as to why we are here on earth, what the purpose of individual life should be, and what the meaning of death is. Nor is it supposed to.

But lurking doubts about the universal benefits of rationalism and positivism existed from early on in various critiques of the Enlightenment project—even as positivism marched forward in our age of remarkable technological and scientific advancement. And the many critics of modernity indeed found vindication of their fears in the moral blight of the twentieth century; many tens of millions of people were killed by "rational" state processes and material ideologies in a fashion truly unsurpassed in the history of the world, casting serious doubt upon the values and even validity of the *moral* foundations of modernity. Modernity tore apart tradition—belief in an ordered firmament that relegated consecrated places to everything in a divine order—and replaced it with alleged (often morally blind) reason, a formalized amoral bureaucracy, and the non-human agencies of industrialization and market forces. But the materialist and despiritualized potential of rationalism and reason became ever more chilling as the consequences of twentieth century political life unfolded. Nietzsche had early on speculated upon the moral and social costs of the "death of God." Freud cast doubt upon even the very possibility of genuine rationalism in the human mind, which he revealed to be dominated by the demons of hidden drives, urges, and obsessions lurking in the byways of the subconscious, revealed only partially through the imperfect art of psychoanalysis.

The assault upon religion and divinely revealed wisdom went one step further with the gradual emergence of postmodernist thought. With postmodernism the very existence of "truth" itself became suspect, viewed as an utterly relative concept. The great postmodern vision was to enshrine multiplicity of outlook, relativism, the virtual non-compatibility of differing narratives of each of our distinct lives, and the declaration that power determines what is "truth." How can a white American male's understanding of historical and social "reality" not differ from that of a black female? Does a triumphalist American vision of the world bear any relevance to the weakened Muslim's vision of that same reality? The truth of one person's or one culture's narrative now differed sharply from another's. Recognition of this multiplicity of narrative and the role of relative perspective in assessing "truth" is undeniably profoundly liberating in terms of hallowing the individual, encouraging social and political equality, and reining in imposed subjective moral values that have masqueraded as absolute.

Thus religion comes in for hard times from both the modernist—who replaces faith with science and reason—and from the postmodernist—who denies the existence of any uniform rationality, any one truth or single valid perspective in a sea of relativism. Or, as stated eloquently by Muqtedar Khan, "The postmodern being, whose heart without faith is empty and mind without reason is immature, can destroy the fragile foundations of modernity, ridicule the memories of tradition but can neither comprehend nor deal with the postmodern resurgence of faith. . . . Those waging a losing battle for modernity against postmodernity reject the resurgence of faith as a return to backward premodernity."[8] But Muqtedar Khan also argues that "while the significance of nearly all religions has receded to the 'private domain' or even into vestigial customs and occasional rituals, Islam has experienced a major resurgence in the twentieth century." This is undoubtedly true in many respects, but we need to ask a few hard questions as to what this really betokens. Does it represent yet another cycle of the classic phenomenon of Islamic renewal that has appeared at various periods of crisis in Muslim history? Or this time does it represent something substantively different in providing new thinking about the role of Islam in governance and society under the unprecedented new conditions of Muslim life: overwhelming globalization and democratization of the state and society in a postmodern world?

If Islam is merely passing through another cycle of Islamic renewal in time of crisis, then the present Islamic resurgence, once it has fulfilled the political and social roles of forcing regeneration and change in the Muslim world, may then fade for the same reasons that we perceive a fading in the *public practice* of other religious faiths. To put it another way, if other major world religions have not found "adequate answers" to the major political and social crises of our era will Islam then fare any better? But the challenges of modernity and postmodernity may in fact not be answered by *any religion*—at least in terms of forging new institutions and law. The contribution of all religions, including Islam, may lie ultimately on the private level of conscience whereby the individual finds moral guidance to structure one's life when existing public structures fail to meet spiritual and moral needs of society. Indeed, for *da'wa*-oriented groups, it is precisely and only through individual reformation that the foundation for moral change at the societal and institutional level can ever take place.

Indeed, this process may characterize the future of all religions. We have entered an era of intensified individualism and relativity of values. The socially destructive features of modernity and postmodernity, as well as the atomizing concepts of democratization, pluralism, and tolerance, place immense new weight on the shoulders of the individual to determine how to live his or her life around a cultural and religious smorgasbord. This is already evident in the strikingly new do-it-yourself aspect of religious life in America today in which *the individual decides what is the most appropriate tailored body of belief for his own life.* And what is valid for American society today tends to be adopted tomorrow in Western Europe, not out of imitation of America but because America is the first country to reflect the features of increasing postmodernism. As other countries undergo the same objective economic and social change, they too will tend to follow in many of the American patterns that also developed out of objective conditions that are slowly but inexorably spreading.

I am suggesting there may be something of a universal trajectory for religion in its interchange with human culture, affected naturally by political, social, and cultural differences but ultimately tending in the same direction over the long run.

The growing forces of evangelical Protestantism today offer a parallel signal of change, particularly as witnessed in Latin America where it sharply challenges traditional Catholicism. Here Catholicism has long functioned as the received birth-faith of every individual in which the Church oversees all of life's passages from cradle to grave in a paternalistic fashion. Yet this tradition is challenged by evangelical Protestantism whereby we witness a specific individual, at a specific place and hour, declare a new, voluntarily made covenant with God—a specific act of will of the autonomous individual that differs sharply from the mere passive or often unconsidered acceptance of life within a received religious cultural cocoon of Catholicism established from birth. Indeed, the force of Protestantism in Western history heralded the emergence of the autonomous individual on the social and economic stage able to think for himself or herself in a new economic environment that spurred individual initiative. It is already evident in many Islamist movements that individuals acquire new responsibility to think for themselves on the meaning of the Qur'an and the Traditions of the Prophet rather than simply accept it blindly and imitatively. In the Reformation this self-empowered religious interpreter was capable of remarkable social development but was also able to drift off into radical and fringe religious and social belief and community. We see this identical process in Islam today. Education is the profoundly empowering process forcing all individuals to think for themselves. There is no longer a single model, there are multiple models for the moral life, the good life, in a mix-and-match marketplace.

Thus we may be truly entering the age of the individual, a pattern of life requiring ever greater individual responsibility for one's own life, increasingly isolated from the traditional supports and strictures of family- or clan-imposed restrictions, liberated from the strictures of a once traditional homogeneous and static society and from the strictures of the paternalistic and authoritarian state itself. Under these new conditions of life, the individual is compelled to answer for his or her self-development to a far greater degree than ever before in history. A pluralistic society and state will no longer be able to provide the vital framework or the moral crutches and support available in the traditional paternalistic pattern. Rather than rendering religion moot, it is *precisely under these conditions that the role of religion and values may become essential,* because the independent, atomized individual will require such guideposts more sorely than ever before. The power and significance of personal religious values independently arrived at are far greater than those simply uncritically inherited without much thought or analysis. Secular values can also be adopted, but they still have to be founded in something quite concrete and even able to be "celebrated" or ritualized in some sense to have full emotional and community weight. The modern individual's faith will represent an active choice designed to meet the individual's needs.

We have consistently noted in this book how a variety of *non-religious issues* have strengthened political Islam, enabling it to serve as a vehicle for grievances and aspirations. The following question then arises: might the gradual alleviation of these same grievances serve to remove them as sources of support to Islamism—apart from the spiritual message itself of Islam? Islam will always remain valid as a faith of course, but *it will probably come to assume a lower profile on the* political *horizon as other forces also serve to alleviate those same non-spiritual grievances. Alternative political parties, under greater political liberalization, will also pursue many of the same political, social, and economic agendas that Islamism pursues, thereby weakening Islamism's considerable monopoly of the political field at present.*

In other words, it is still unclear whether the resurgence of Islam today is primarily a *religious* phenomenon, or a phenomenon of the *sociology of religion* responding to definable challenges to Muslim society in the modern era. Many Muslims may be uncomfortable even with these very categories of thought.

Islamists need not fear obsolescence anytime soon, however, since democratic revolution and change in the Muslim world is still palpably weak in most countries. If Islamist movements fail to find within democratic structures the political success that they seek, they may become disillusioned with the process. At that point they face the crisis of deciding whether to accept permanent minority status within the parliamentary and political order—with the ability to influence but not decide the debate—or to withdraw from the system entirely. This is in effect a decision about *whether Islamists wish to rule or to influence.*

In the meantime, political Islam is enjoying a rare moment in history during which it is able to act relatively free of rivals, challenge the existing political order in the Muslim world, force change, and put Islam back on the cultural and intellectual map. We do not know how long this interval will last, but it has already had profound implications, and the West had better attend to dealing with it in all its diversity in a serious fashion, or the repercussions may be unpleasant for both sides.

A PROGNOSIS

I have offered a number of variables that will decisively impact upon the future course of political Islam and identified issues that must be dealt with positively if these movements are to survive. No one, of course, can predict which of these roads is the most likely, but I will nonetheless offer my best guess in the briefest of forms as to where we will actually see these movements go in the next twenty years or so. The rationale for these hypotheses is contained in earlier discussions on alternatives; I offer here only conclusions.

- The next two decades will place far greater demands and pressures upon Islamist movements as they actually gain some position within the political order across the Muslim world. While violent Islamist movements can and indeed should be constrained, non-violent ones should not. Movements will therefore no longer face the challenge of existence and survival but the need to deliver to the publics some productive and useful answers to problems.
- I anticipate a worsening of the relationship between international Islam and the United States, based on several factors: ultimately inconclusive results from the War Against Terrorism, its probable failure to end terrorism, and the greatly increased resentment across the Muslim world as an outcome. This process may well result in more extensive terrorism against Americans specifically, but not necessarily of a spectacular nature. Such a situation will place the United States in a deeply defensive position across the Muslim world.
- As increased small scale terrorism takes its toll against the United States, the tensions between *Muslims in the West* and Western populations will grow internally, creating an uglier domestic situation in which civil liberties are increasingly affected by a "bunker America" mentality. Islamist movements, the target of suspicion as the breeding ground for anti-Americanism, will feel the brunt of U.S. pressures overseas, probably accompanied by increased license by authoritarian states to crack down forcefully against them. This will push large numbers into greater violence in a choreography of self-fulfilling prophecy.
- Many Islamist movements will therefore be distracted away from the basic task that launched much of their activity: the strengthening of Muslim society in all senses: political, social, economic, military, and moral. They will instead

focus on defense and even revenge. They will have little opportunity to develop a more open and liberal agenda under these constraints and pressures.

- Not all movements will fall into this trap. In states with reasonably functioning democratic orders, Islamists may help keep the social fabric together rather than be victims or destroyers of the political order. Islamist movements in states such as Turkey, Malaysia, Kuwait, Jordan, Bahrain, Morocco, and Yemen will probably survive this confrontation. The situation of others is far less certain.

- Islamists will become more engaged in support of national liberation movements of Muslim minorities who are restive under their domination by harsh Russian, Chinese, Indian, or other rule; the movements will adopt greater Islamist aspects to bolster their nationalist impulses. Russia and Africa will be especially vulnerable to the use of religion as a vehicle in what are basically ethnic struggles.

- The fate of political Islam is integrally linked to the cause of reform more broadly. Islamism is not the only vehicle for reform and change by any means, but it will be the dominant one, especially in closed societies.

- The multiple social forces and grievances that drive political Islam today will continue to impel it as long as such grievances exist—and they are hardly about to go away. If political Islam does not effectively adopt these issues and seek to alleviate them, then other forces will emerge to adopt them. The leading alternative candidate here is leftism. Political Islam will either adopt the radical reform agendas of the left, or it will yield them to the left and lose prominence. When that happens we will probably see a resurgence of struggle between Islamism and the radical left, somewhat reminiscent of the 1970s.

- The above scenario is dark, reflecting the nature of many world problems that provoke dangerous responses, especially in the Muslim world. This environment has direct impact upon political Islam. A more optimistic reading of the next few decades would have to posit as preconditions:

    ◆ A more benign, less confrontational international order and the diminution of terrorism in general;

    ◆ The abandonment by Washington of relentlessly harsh, peremptory, and unilateralist policies toward the Muslim world in the context of the War Against Terrorism, and the adoption of more sympathetic cooperation and engagement with the Muslim world;

    ◆ The attainment of a just solution to the Palestinian problem;

- Significant reform and political change in the Muslim world, supported actively by the United States;
- Improved conditions in most of the developing world, and especially in the Muslim world, that ameliorate the current mood of impotence and anger and offer hope and sense of progress;
- High domestic incentives for populations in the Muslim world to reject any sympathies for potential terrorism against the United States as irresponsible, unproductive, and damaging to clearly more promising alternatives before them.

In short, Islamists have embarked on a notable odyssey—the effort to make their past civilization, based on a framework of Islamic culture, relevant as an element of future development. Many different forces have attempted to ride the vehicle of political Islam, some with damaging and vicious results, others with constructive, productive, and innovative ideas for bridging the Islamic past with the Islamic present. The combined pressures, however, of domestic and international forces and confrontations will hinder the more creative forms of Islamist liberalism from emerging as dominant for quite some time. Political Islam has within it the potential to play a positive or a harshly negative role in the future development of the Muslim world. We can only hope that liberal Islamists will persevere to work toward renewed understanding of Islam in the modern age and a universal form of Islamic values, find allies in the process, and more toward the changes and reforms so desperately needed. If Islamists cannot rise to this challenge, they will be soon supplanted by other political forces that do have something to offer.

NOTES

CHAPTER 1

1. Martin Kramer, "Islam's Sober Millennium" *Jerusalem Post,* 30 December 1999, http://msanews.mynet.net/Scholars/Kramer/.
2. Ali A. Mazrui, "Islam and the End of History," *Iranian Journal of International Relations,* vol. 7 #1, 1995, p. 3.
3. Jared Diamond, *Guns, Germs and Steel: The Fate of Nations,* (New York: Norton, 1997), pp. 409–411.
4. Jeffrey Sachs, "Islam's geopolitics as a morality tale," *The Financial Times,* 28 October 2001.
5. Martin Kramer, "The Muslim Middle East in the 21st Century," 25 November 1998, Dayan Middle East Center Website.

CHAPTER 2

1. Steven Bruce, "Fundamentalism, Ethnicity, and Enclave," in Martin E. Marty, and R. Scott Appleby, eds., *Fundamentalisms and the State: Remaking Polities, Economies, and Militance,* vol. 3 of series (Chicago: University of Chicago Press, 1993) p. 51.
2. For a good discussion of these issues, see Robert D. Lee, *Overcoming Tradition and Modernity: the Search for Islamic Authenticity* (Boulder, CO: Westview, 1997) pp. 1–7, 184.
3. I thank Professor Daniel Brumberg at Georgetown for this thought.
4. Dale F. Eickelman, and James Piscatori, *Muslim Politics* (Princeton: Princeton University Press, 1996) p. 136.
5. For a good brief summary of this potential shift in political culture in Malaysia, see Chandra Muzaffar, Ulama as Mentri: the Challenge of Transforming Malay Political Culture," 24 December 1999, International Movement for a Just World Website, http://www.jaring.my/just/.
6. Ibid.
7. For a definitive treatment of this topic, see Ann Elizabeth Myers, *Islam and Human Rights* (Boulder, CO: Westview Press) 1991.
8. Ahmad Mousalli, "Modern Islamist Fundamentalist Discourses on Civil Society, Pluralism and Democracy," in Jillian Schwedler, ed., *Toward Civil Society in the Middle East?* (Boulder, CO: Lynne Rienner Publishers, 1995) pp. 35–36.
9. Serif Mardin, "Civil Society and Islam," Summary of a paper published in *Civil Society,* ed., John A. Hall (New York: Polity Press, 1996).
10. George Joffe, "Maghribi Islam and Islam in the Maghrib," in David Westerlund and Eva Evers Rosander, *African Islam and Islam in Africa* (Athens: Ohio University Press, 1997) p. 77; Olivier Roy, "Pourquoi le 'post-islamisme,'" *Revue du Monde Musulman et de la Mediterranee,* #85–86, p. 9–10.

11. Nilüfer Göle, "Secularism and Islamism in Turkey: The Making of Elites and Counter-elites," *The Middle East Journal,* Winter 1997, p. 57.
12. See for example Anis Abd el Fattah, "Liberating Fatma: the centrality of the need to address the rights and roles of women in Muslim societies." Muslimedia.com is the Internet edition of *Crescent International,* Newsmagazine of the Islamic Movement, December 2001.

CHAPTER 3

1. John Voll, *Islam: Continuity and Change in the Modern World,* second edition (Syracuse: Syracuse University Press, 1994), pp. 21–23.
2. Voll, *Islam,* pp. 21–23.
3. Charles Kurzman, *Liberal Islam* (London: Oxford University Press, 1996), pp. 5–6.
4. I owe these insights to Laith Kubba, from an interview in April 1999 in Washington, DC.
5. Kurzman, *Liberal Islam.*
6. R. Hrair Dekmejian, *Islam in Revolution* (Syracuse: Syracuse University Press, 1995), pp. 94–95.
7. Dr. Mansoor al-Jamri, "Contemporary Currents in Islamist Political Thought," first published in the London-based *Al-Quds,* 22 January 1999, a summary of which is also available on Islam 21 Website: http://islam21.org.
8. For one incisive, yet controversial discussion of this issue see Carolyn Fluehr-Lobban, ed., *Against Islamic Extremism: The Writings of Muhammad Sa'id al-Ashmawy* (Gainesville: University Press of Florida, 1998).
9. Fluehr-Lobban, p. 91, in which 'Ashmawi refers to his own earlier work, *The Roots of Islamic Law.*
10. I borrow this turn of phrase from Professor Jon Anderson at Catholic University, Washington DC.
11. 'Abdullahi Ahmed An-Na'im, "Shari'a and Basic Human Rights Concerns," in Kurzman, *Liberal Islam,* op. cit. p. 236.
12. Qaradawi as quoted in John L. Esposito, and John O. Voll, *Islam and Democracy* (New York: Oxford University Press, 1996), p 45.
13. Farish A. Noor, "Interview with Syed Hiader Farooq Muslimaudoodi," taken from *New Straits Times* (nstp.com.my), 15 April 2001, posting from Noor (korawa@hotmail.com).
14. Farish A. Noor, "UMNO, PAS and the Ulama—Challenges and Obstacles to Reform," 12 May 2000, Deputy Director of International Movement for a Just World (JUST), Kuala Lumpur, (korawa@hotmail.com).
15. One good source of materials on that topic is Charles Kurzman's edited volume *Liberal Islam* (New York: Oxford University Press, 1998).
16. Fazlur Rahman, *Islam and Modernity* (Chicago: Chicago University Press, 1982), p. 23, italics mine.
17. Shaykh Rashid al-Ghanuchi, "Self-Criticism And Reconsideration," *Palestine Times,* Issue #94, 1999. http://www.ptimes.com.
18. Dr. Mohammed Shahroor, "A Proposed Charter for Muslim Activists," August 1999, http://islam21.org/charter.
19. Sadek J. Sulaiman, "Democracy and Rule of Law," in Charles Kurzman, ed., *Liberal Islam,* (New York: Oxford University Press, 1998), p. 98.
20. S. M. Zafar, "Accountability, Parliament, and Ijtihad," in Charles Kurzman, ed., *Liberal Islam* (New York: Oxford University Press, 1998), pp. 71–72.
21. Laith Kubba, "Short words on Islam and Democracy," http//:islam21.org.

22. Laith Kubba in a personal exchange with the author, July 1999.
23. Dr. Asghar Ali Engineer, "Reconstruction of Islamic Thought," Institute of Islamic Studies, India, http://Islam21.org.
24. Cited in Dale Eickelman and James Piscatori, *Muslim Politics* (Princeton: Princeton University Press, 1996), p. 34.
25. Fazlur Rahman, *Islam and Modernity* (Chicago: Chicago University Press, 1982), p. 23.

CHAPTER 4

1. For one discussion of this concept as it relates to the Muslim world, see S. M. Shamsul Alamm, "Islam, Ideology and the State in Bangladesh," *Journal of Asian and African Studies*, vol. XXVIII, 1–2 (1993), p. 94, although the details of his discussion are based primarily on the Bangladeshi model.
2. Mark Juergensmeyer, *The New Cold War: Religious Nationalism Confronts the Secular State* (Berkeley: University of California Press, 1993), pp. 1–8.
3. See Graham E. Fuller, "The Next Ideology," in *Foreign Policy*, Spring 1995.
4. David E. Sanger, "Shipwreck in Seattle," *New York Times*, 4 December 1999.
5. For an excellent discussion of the problems of globalization, see John Gray, *False Dawn: The Delusions of Global Capitalism* (New York: The New Press, 1998), pp.209–235.
6. Gray, p. 192.
7. Gray, p. 191.
8. Gray, p. 193.
9. Craig R. Whitney, "Keeping French Fears of US Dominance at Bay," *New York Times*, 1 December 1999.
10. Robert Kaplan, "The Coming Anarchy," *The Atlantic Monthly*, February 1994.
11. Kaplan, op. cit.
12. David Ownsby, "China's War Against Itself," *New York Times* 15 February 2001.
13. Peter L. Berger, "Four Faces of Global Culture," *The National Interest*, Fall 1997, pp. 27–28.

CHAPTER 5

1. I am grateful to Professor Augustus Richard Norton, Boston University for this definition.
2. For a provocative and thought-provoking discussion of terrorism, see Eqbal Ahmed, "Terrorism: Theirs and Ours," A Presentation at the University of Colorado, Boulder, October 12 1998 as reproduced in Turkistan Newsletter, 1 Oct 2001.
3. Khaled Abou El Fadl, " Terrorism Is at Odds With Islamic Tradition," *Los Angeles Times*, 22 August 2001; professor at the UCLA School of Law and author of "Rebellion and Political Violence in Islamic Law," Cambridge University Press, 2001.

CHAPTER 6

1. Timothy Carney and Mansoor Ijaz, "Intelligence Failure? Let's Go Back to Sudan," *The Washington Post*, 30 June 2002.
2. See Kalim Siddiqui, *Stages of Islamic Revolution* (London: The Open Press, 1996).
3. One of the best portrayals of failing Islamist ideology in daily life in Iran is available in Farhad Khosrokhavar, and Olivier Roy, *Comment Sortir d'une Revolution Religieuse* (Paris: Editions de Seuil, 1999).

4. Peter K. Bechtold, "More Turbulence in Sudan," in *Sudan: State and Society in Crisis,* ed., John Voll (Boulder: Westview, 1991), p. 1.
5. Martha Wenger, "Sudan Politics and Society," *Middle East Report,* September-October 1991, p. 3.
6. See Mohamed Elhachmi Hamdi, *The Making of an Islamic Political Leader: Conversations With Hasan Al-Turabi* (Boulder, CO: Westview, 1999).
7. Timothy Carney and Mansoor Ijaz, "Intelligence Failure? Let's Go Back to Sudan."
8. Williams, Brian, "The Continuing Decline of Afghan Statistics," Reuters, 3 August 1997.
9. Bailey, op. cit.
10. Kathy Gannon, "Afghanistan Exiles Fear Taleban," Associated Press, 17 February 1999.

CHAPTER 7

1. Seyyed Veli Reza Nasr, *The Vanguard of the Islamic Revolution* (Los Angeles: University of California Press, 1994), p. 15.
2. Mumtaz Ahmad, "The Tablighi-Jamaat," in Martin E. Marty and Scott Appleby, eds., *Fundamentalisms Considered* (Chicago: University of Chicago Press, 1992), pp. 510–524.
3. Zeki Saritoprak, "The Nur School of Turkey and Political Islam: A Comparative Discussion," in manuscript form, 1999.
4. "Vast extent of the 'Gülen Empire'," *Briefing* Ankara, 28 June 1999.
5. For further details, also see Hakan Yavuz, "Toward an Islamic Liberalism? The Nurcu Movement and Fethullah Gülen in Turkey," *The Middle East Journal,* Autumn, 1999; Bülent Aras, "Turkish Islam's Moderate Face," *Middle East Quarterly,* September 1998; and the definitive book on the founding of the movement, Serif Mardin, *Religion and Social Change in Modern Turkey: The Case of Bediüzzaman Said Nursi* (Albany: State University of New York Press, 1989).
6. See a fascinating discussion of this rivalry in London in Tayfun Atay, "Bir Naksibendi Söyleminde Vahhabilik" (Wahhabism in a Naqshbendi Discourse), in *Kimlik Tartismalari ve Etnik Mesele* (Identity Debates and the Ethnic Issue), *Türkiye Günlügü,* Ankara, April 1995.
7. S. V. R. Nasr, "The Rise of Sunni Militancy in Pakistan: The Changing Role of Islamism and the Ulama in Society and Politics," *Modern Asian Studies,* 34, 1 (2000), p. 149.
8. Seyyed Veli Reza Nasr, *The Vanguard of the Islamic Revolution,* p. 149.
9. Rashid Ghannushi, "Islamic Movements: Self-Criticism And Reconsideration," *Palestine Times,* No. 94 (April 1999).
10. Jillian Schwedler, "A Paradox of Democracy? Islamist Participation in Elections," *Middle East Report,* Winter 1998, p. 27.
11. Olivier Roy, *The Failure of Political Islam* (Cambridge: Harvard University Press, 1994), pp. 75–77.
12. Rashid Ghannushi, "Islamic Movements."

CHAPTER 8

1. Paul Johnson, *A History of Christianity* (New York: Simon and Schuster, 1976), pp. 92–93, 178–179.

2. Muslim Public Affairs Council, MPACnews, 19 November 2001, quoting Graham from remarks on "NBC Nightly News" on 16 November 2001, (broadcast@lists.mpac-news.org).

3. Maulana Muhammad Masoud Azhar, "Fundamentalism," no date, Taliban Website, (http://www.ummah.net/taliban/) downloaded 24 January 2000. The above passages are my own summary of the message.

4. For a less traditional discussion of this problem, see Graham E. Fuller and Ian O. Lesser, "Persian Gulf Myths," *Foreign Affairs*, May 1997.

5. For detailed treatment of this argument, see Graham E. Fuller, "Redrawing the World's Borders," in *The World Policy Journal*, Winter 1997.

CHAPTER 9

1. Ibrahim Karawan, "The Islamist Impasse," (London: International Institute of Strategic Studies, 1997).

2. For an excellent discussion of this phenomenon in Egypt, see Steven Barraclough, "Al-Azhar: Between the Government and the Islamists," *The Middle East Journal*, Spring 1998.

3. See Dale F. Eickelman and Jon W. Anderson, "Print, Islam, and the Prospects for Civic Pluralism: New Religious Writings and Their Audiences," *Journal of Islamic Studies* 8:1 (1997).

4. Eickelman, p. 125.

5. I am grateful to Iraqi Islamist Laith Kubba for this observation.

6. Nilüfer Göle, "Secularism and Islamism in Turkey: The Making of Elites and Counter-elites," *The Middle East Journal*, Winter 1997, p. 58.

7. See Khosrokhavar and Olivier Roy, *Iran: Comment Sortir d'une Revolution Religieuse*, especially chapter 5, "Individu, Jeunesse, et Espace Publique" (Paris: Editions de Seuil, 1999).

8. Isma'il al-Faruqi as quoted by John Voll in "Islamic Issues for Muslim in the United States," in Yvonne Yazbeck Haddad, ed., *The Muslims of America* (New York: Oxford University Press, 1991), p. 212.

CHAPTER 10

1. Roy in a personal exchange with the author.

2. Joseph Samaha, "Are the Islamists going mainstream?" *Mideast Mirror*, 9 June 1999.

3. Fahmi Howeidi, "Why Moslems should support NATO in its punishment of the Serb butchers," in *Mideast Mirror*, 6 April 1999, citing *al-Ahram;* and al-Effendi, Abdelwahhab, "Why Arab commentators should be cheering NATO," *Mideast Mirror*, 20 April 1999, citing *al-Quds al-'Arabi.*

4. Alan Richards, "The Political Economy of Economic Reform in the Middle East: The Challenge to Governance," from the executive summary in RAND DRR–2763053102 (manuscript), *The Political Economy of Economic Reform in the Middle East*, prepared for RAND Project, "The Future of Middle East Security" Santa Monica, forthcoming 2002.

5. "Self Doomed to Failure: A special report on Arab development," *The Economist*, 6 July 2002, p. 24.

6. Ali A. Mazru'i, "Islam and the End of History," *Iranian Journal of International Relations,* vol. 7 # 1, 1995, p. 22.
7. I make this argument in greater detail in my book *The Democracy Trap: Perils of the Post–Cold War World* (New York: Dutton, 1992).
8. M. A. Muqtedar Khan, "Postmodernity and the Crisis of "Truth," *A Return to Enlightenment,* Volume 2, No: 1 (Jan 21, 2000).

INDEX